This is an inspiring book about educational courage, about a law school for working-class people of all ages, that challenges the orthodoxy of the profession with its unique vision.

    —**Howard Zinn**, author of *A People's History of the United States*

This story of the building of the MSL demonstrates that a spirit which de Tocqueville noted in his visit to America in the 1830s still lives. "The right of association seems to me by nature almost as inalienable as individual liberty." And he observed that the better use of association was made in America than anywhere else in the world.

    —**Eugene McCarthy**, former U.S. Senator and presidential candidate

Copyright © 2004 by
The Massachusetts School of Law
4501 Forbes Boulevard
Suite 200
Lanham, Maryland 20706
UPA Acquisitions Department (301) 459-3366

PO Box 317
Oxford
OX2 9RU, UK

Library of Congress Control Number: 2003117120
ISBN 0-7618-2838-9 (paperback : alk. ppr.)

AGAINST THE TIDE

Debbie Hagan

Hamilton Books
an imprint of
University Press of America,® Inc.
Dallas · Lanham · Boulder · New York · Oxford

To my parents,

who filled my life with opportunities that they never had

Preface

Imagine the public uproar if the government dictated what professions our children could and could not pursue. For instance, what if the government decreed that children of upper-income families could become lawyers, congressmen, senators, judges, governors, and corporate CEOs? However, the children of less-privileged families could not.

Instantly we'd all cry out, "Un-American." Who of us does not believe that it is our God-given, unalienable right, as free Americans, to select our life's work? Most of us grew up believing that our future held a cornucopia of options. Also we believed that we could overcome poverty and oppression by sticking with our dreams and working hard. Certainly hundreds of thousands of Europeans believed this as they cast their eyes at America—the land of opportunity. They left behind families, possessions, and all the comforts they'd known to face uncertainties, in a wild, new nation.

In America, even an Illinois farm boy could rise above poverty and the lack of formal education to reach the lofty position of President of the United States. Abraham Lincoln studied law and moved up the social ladder all on his own. He achieved this through determination and hard work. In a sense, he paved the way for all Americans to excel by perseverence. One truly understands the magnitude of Lincoln, and his meaning to all people, in standing at the base of his 19-foot-tall memorial in Washington D.C., seeing his pensive gaze at the Washington Monument and the weight of a fractured nation on his shoulders. Encircling him are his profound, but succinct words: "All men are created equal."

It's this as much as Lincoln's iconic image that serves as our American ideal. It's the compass of inspiration that guides many people through life, particularly the poor, disadvantaged, and oppressed. Over the years, many people have followed Lincoln's footsteps. They've set out on roads to better jobs, education, and better lives through the study of law.

Legal education has opened doors for many people, including the disadvantaged, as Lincoln proved. Law gives access to power. Statistics bear this out. There are currently one million lawyers in the United States. While it's a big number, it's just four-tenths of one percent of the entire nation's population. Within this slender pocket of people rests the country's greatest power. Lawyers make up 53 percent of US senators, 46 percent of state governors, 37 percent of federal congressmen, and 17 percent of state legislators. All judges are lawyers, except for a few minor traffic court judges. Lawyers are active in real estate investments and in Fortune 500 corporations. They are often corporate vice presidents or heads of their companies. Lawyers are often university vice presidents, and many become presidents. Well-known figures in this latter group include Derek Bok of Harvard, Kingman Brewster of Yale, Gerhard Casper of Stanford, Edward Levi of Chicago (and earlier in the century, Robert Hutchins of Chicago), James Freedman of Dartmouth, Michael Sovern of Columbia, Michael Heyman of California Berkeley, Gordon Gee of Vanderbilt, Lee Bollinger of Michigan [now of Columbia], Robert O'Neil of Virginia, Robert Stevens of Haverford, Thomas Jackson of Rochester, and many others.

However, the question is, can anyone, from any socio-economic background, become a lawyer? Or are there glass walls that block certain segments of society from entering law schools? Does the legal profession actually hinder some segments of society from entering its ranks and, thus, prevent them from entering politics, finance, business, and university administration?

To answer these questions, it's important to look at the history of the American Bar Association. In 1878, lawyers who sought to return dignity and sophistication to their profession formed this association. In essence, they wanted to go back to a pre-Jacksonian era, in which lawyers and judges worked within a close-knit, aristocratic fraternity. This was the way Alexis de Tocqueville saw it when he visited the United States in the early 19th century. The ABA founders had no trouble finding lawyers who went along with this idea. Together, over the years, they drew up rules outlining how much college education a lawyer needed in order to practice and what kind of school a lawyer should attend. Further, they established prerequisites for those sitting for state bar exams, which had to be passed for a lawyer to practice the law he'd learned. The ABA decided that only those individuals who had graduated from an ABA-approved school would be able to sit for these exams. Those who had either studied on their own or who had graduated from non-ABA-approved schools were frozen out of the system.

Most state supreme courts enabled the ABA to carry out this plan. This eliminated any notion of following in Lincoln's footsteps by means of self study. It also meant eliminating many free-standing (non-university), independent law schools that predominantly served minorities, working class students, and those typically shut-out of legal education. To become a lawyer, one needed to attend an ABA-approved school—no matter how costly it might be or what courses it offered. In general, legal education rested entirely in the ABA's hands.

Over the years, the ABA has continuously upped the ante, requiring more years of schooling for lawyers, causing higher tuitions, and demanding passage of stringent entrance exams that favor white, upper-income students. This practice has effectively weeded out the poor, immigrants, minorities, and those of working class or disadvantaged backgrounds. This, for some ABA members, was the ultimate goal. Not all, of course, sought this. However, the practice has enabled the legal profession to evolve into one that is predominantly accessible only to those of higher-than-average socio-economic means.

Few law schools have been able to deviate from the ABA's stringent rules or break through its stranglehold over legal education. In the 1970s, Antioch College Law School, in Washington D.C., set out to offer a practical program that specialized in legal public service. The ABA withdrew the school's accreditation and shut it down. Laclede School of Law, in St. Louis, established a similar type of school—practical and economical. The ABA refused to approve it, so it too was forced to close.

Then came the Massachusetts School of Law—a school designed to be practical, affordable, and accessible to students who had been shut out of most opportunities in legal education. The school's founders aimed, in the school's mission, to give hard-working students a chance at legal studies. In admissions, they looked more at a student's experience, drive to learn and succeed, and aptitude for law. The school's founders devised their own innovative test to predict which prospects would have the aptitude for legal studies. Idealistically they built their school, oblivious to the obstacles the ABA would put in their way. They saw only the social good that could come of their plans. They knew that their school stood out from all others, but they thought innovation to be a good thing. Naively, they even believed their school would be held up as a role model for other law schools to follow. That did not happen.

The ABA had its own plans. That's when MSL's founders began to see the ugly reality of legal education—how a few powerful individuals controlled a profession that provides the entrée into some the nation's most powerful jobs. Because the courts and the government are made up of lawyers, MSL's faculty and staff learned that the profession operates as a fraternity with brethren looking out for one another. In this light, it's not surprising to find out that the courts have refused to change the system or compel the ABA to change it.

Thus, the government, through the courts, does limit the professional choices for tens of thousands of Americans. It endorses legal education for the more privileged sectors of American society, and it discourages minorities, second-career seekers, and the working class from practicing law.

In March 2000, curiosity led me inside the Massachusetts School of Law. I had read the newspaper accounts of the brave little law school that had thumbed its nose at the mighty American Bar Association. It was a classic David spitting in the eye of Goliath type of tale.

What intrigued me most was the school's resolve to maintain its unique identity. Not only had it challenged the ABA in one court but in many. It had stood before the leaders of this powerful association time and again, challenging its principles.

Repeatedly it condemned the Association's lack of diversity before the Department of Education. It accused the Association of antitrust violations and anti-competitive tactics before the Department of Justice. Thus, I entered this school wondering what kind of people would doggedly pursue such a case without relenting. That's when I met Dean Lawrence Velvel, whose mind worked like a spinning top and who spoke passionately about fairness, elitism, morality, and truth—causes he believed had to be fought and won.

In Nelson Mandela's autobiography, *A Long Walk to Freedom*, he describes in detail how prison guards tried to rob him and other political prisoners of their dignity to weaken their spirit and destroy their resolve. Similar tactics were used on MSL as it has tried every way possible to be recognized by the ABA and the legal profession.

"As a leader, one must sometimes take actions that are unpopular or whose results will not be known for years to come," wrote

Mandela. "There are victories whose glory lies only in the fact that they are known to those who win them . . . one must find consolation in being true to one's ideals, even if no one else knows about them."

This is Massachusetts School of Law—a school whose adversaries have ensured its permanence and strength.

This account of Dean Velvel and the Massachusetts School of Law is based on two years spent at the school, interviewing and observing the faculty, students, and alumni.

All the events and accounts in this book are true. The scenes are reconstructed based on newspaper accounts, trial transcripts, various letters and documents, and notes. In addition, the book is based on countless interviews with persons who attended Massachusetts School of Law or were familiar with the school and its founders. No names in this book have been changed.

Prologue

To take your chance in the thick of a rush with firing all about,
Is nothing so bad when you've cover to 'an, an' leave an' likin' to shout;
But to stand an'be still to the Birken'ead drill
  is a damn tough bullet to chew,
An' they done it, the Jollies—'Er Majesty's Jollies—
  soldier an' sailor too!
Their work was done when it 'ad n't begun; they was younger nor me an'
you;
Their choice it was plain between drownin' in 'eaps
  an bein' mopped by the screw,
So they stood an' was still to the Birken'ead drill, soldier an' sailor too!

From Rudyard Kipling's poem, *Soldier an' Sailor Too*

At daybreak, off the southern-most tip of Africa, at Cape Agulhas, the HMS Birkenhead foundered on an unmapped rock. The date was February 26, 1852, and the cry, "Women and children first!" meant that the ship was going down to those who didn't know it already. The ship had only three lifeboats for its 650 passengers. That meant 445 men would drown or be eaten by sharks.

The majority of passengers on board were British Army, Royal Marine, and Royal Navy troops, enroute to the Kaffir War on Africa's East Coast. They lined up on the deck of their wrecked ship, in military style, shoulder to shoulder, as wives and children drifted away. Erect, unflinching, powerless, they listened to the steady beat of the drums.

The ship splintered like a matchstick. The mast crashed to the deck. Still, the soldiers kept a stiff upper lip, as the British do.

Chins up, they remained in formation, listening to the drums beat, as they stared at the black sea rising up to claim them.

A century and a half later, in 1994, this vision came to Dean Lawrence Velvel as he sat in the well of the American Bar Association's House of Delegates. A sea of ABA opposition rose around him, and, at that moment, he stood powerless, facing the invincible, unjust force opposed to him.

Velvel, a short, stout man with a neatly-trimmed white beard and mustache, had just spoken to the crowd. He and his colleagues had tried to convince the 400 - 500 lawyers, deans, and law professors that the school he had founded, the Massachusetts School of Law, should be accredited by the American Bar Association even though it didn't meet all of the Association's accreditation standards. He believed an exception, which was called for in the ABA's written standards, should be made for the school. It was different.

"We seek to offer legal education of high quality and to offer socio- and economic mobility to minority people, to white ethnics, to working class people, and to people in mid-career," he said, speaking emphatically. "And we seek to inculcate ethics . . . and to provide education to people who are among the less privileged in American society at a reasonable tuition rate that remains the same year after year . . . ."

The school had tried to satisfy expensive ABA accreditation standards as best it could, he told them, but satisfying costly standards meant squandering the school's resources, which also meant increasing tuition and, thus, excluding the very people whom the school sought to serve. Seeing the unsympathetic faces before him, Velvel realized this did not matter to the members of the House of Delegates. As if the huge room had swallowed up his words, or as if he had never spoken them at all, he stood in this vast, uncaring vacuum.

Velvel often wondered what possessed him to enter such a stodgy profession full of self-anointed, spuriously high-minded individuals like these. He wasn't like them. Neither were his faculty nor his students at the school.

The lawyers before him, comfortable, well-fed, and dressed in their fine, expensive suits, knew nothing about financial hardships. They knew nothing about MSL's faculty and students. They knew nothing about the obstacles they had overcome and the sacrifices they had made. He doubted if any of them knew what it was like to grow up in a housing project and to yearn to live better and more comfortably but face obstacles at every turn. Students at MSL knew this. Many had been so determined to change their lives that they worked two or three part-time jobs to scrape up enough money to go back to school and study law.

Had any of these delegates done that? Had any of them ever struggled like this? Velvel didn't think so. He doubted if any of them knew what it was like to be the first in their families to enter college, to proceed alone without any mentors, or to wake up in their mid-30s to see time passing by and the dream of becoming a lawyer nearly gone. Such thoughts, most likely, never crossed their minds. Fate had dealt them a good hand and made them complacent. They didn't know enough to even be grateful.

That day, after Velvel had entered the room and sat down, Norman Redlich, dean emeritus of the New York University School of Law, told the House that MSL had a student/faculty ratio of over 100:1. "Could you, as parents, accept that type of ratio for your children?" he asked. He accused the school of retaining over 40 percent of the students' tuition, admitting students without valid testing, and inadequately preparing students—thus, having the lowest bar passage rate in Massachusetts.

Pauline Schneider, chairwoman of the ABA Accreditation Committee, stepped up to speak after Redlich. She accused the school of trivializing the ABA's standards and of not being genuinely interested in teaching minorities, as Velvel had said.

Velvel listened to the delegates make one false or distorted accusation after another, and he swelled with rage. They had made up their minds and aimed their comments to sink MSL.

As the school's position foundered in this room, Velvel threw back his shoulders in the realization that nothing more could be done here. He and the faculty of MSL, like the men on the HMS Birkenhead, would stand proud and face the consequences in silence. *To stand and be still to the Birken'ead drill is a damn tough bullet to chew.*

When ABA Chairman Phillip Anderson told him that he had the last five minutes, Velvel walked to the podium.

"I won't need that much time," he said. "It's a damn hard thing to sit here, and to get up here and . . . to refrain, as I shall, from any characterization of the things I have heard said, in laundry lists, about our law school. If those things were true, we have no business here . . . and frankly we should be taken out and put up against the wall."

He continued, "All I can say, in closing, ladies and gentleman, is that we are not HMS Birkenhead. All I can say is to reiterate the famous statement of Daniel Webster to the Supreme Court of the United States, 'It is, as I have said, a small school, sir, but there are those who love it.' And regardless of what happens in this body—where the opposition brought out the artillery, which we cannot hope to equal, presidents of the past, presidents future, chairs past, chairs future, people who know nothing about our school, who have never been there, who don't know our professors and don't know our students . . . it is a damn hard thing to stand and be still when the drummer boy beats the Birkenhead drill. There will be another day, regardless of what happens here."

Velvel sat down, and the House took a voice vote. Overwhelmingly, they voted to oppose the school. There was no need to take a physical hand count. Clearly Massachusetts School of Law had lost again.

Chapter 1

Merrimack Valley, Northern Massachusetts
Spring 1986

Sirens rang across Lake Mascuppie, rousing residents of the Tyngsborough bedroom community who might have slept late that Saturday, March 29, 1986, the day before Easter. At 6:50 a.m., firemen Tim Madden and Richard Blechman ran to the tanker and sped out of the firehouse. They spotted a gray cloud rising on the horizon.

As the tanker rolled into the driveway of the Tyngsborough Stable, firefighters watched 20-foot flames shoot up and over the two-and-a-half story barn. They leapt from the cab and wrestled a hose to the blaze. Fire Chief Richard Singleton waved his arms and ordered them to set up a water fog to save the house. Flames licked the porch and scaled the clapboard. Water shot out the hoses, casting a halo over the firefighters.

Assistance came from the nearby communities: Dracut, Chelmsford, and Westford. After several hours, firefighters extinguished the blaze. Nothing was left of the barn but wet, coalblack rubble. The house remained, though it was severely damaged.

Arson investigator Paul Larkham of the Tyngsborough Police Department pulled into the yard. Wearing heavy fire boots, he stared at the smoldering cinders. As if reading tea leaves in the bottom of a cup, he tried to figure out just how this fire started. In doing so, he discovered four horses dead in their stalls.

"Where's Boland?" Larkham shouted to the fire chief.

He shrugged and yelled, "Neighbors say he's on vacation." He raised his eyebrows, as if uncertain.

A few years earlier, Singleton had fought a fire at the same address. When that fire broke out, the home's owner, Michael A. Boland, had been away again—that time at a town finance committee meeting at City Hall. Because Tyngsborough didn't have an arson investigation team, no one investigated. So Boland rebuilt the house and life went on.

However, Singleton described the current fire, to a *Lowell Sun* reporter, as "suspicious. It is definitely under investigation." He wouldn't say anything more publicly. It was a hot fire—the kind in which one would expect to find some type of accelerant, such as gasoline, involved. Then again, most barns held some kind of gasoline, needed for power lawnmowers and other farm equipment. What struck Singleton and Larkham as strange was that this fire didn't begin in the spot where one would expect gas to be.

Larkham and Harold Waterhouse, of the Lowell police department, investigated. As Larkham searched, he came upon a five-gallon, plastic bucket—a common, white joint compound container with a handle and ring around the cap. It had red markings on the side, as if words had been handwritten with a red, felt-tipped marker.

This intrigued him. Larkham pulled out his camera and snapped a few pictures. He had had several dealings with Boland and found him to be smart, but cagey—the kind of individual who could talk his way out of just about anything. One thing Larkham had learned about arsons: the fire starter always left something behind. If Boland had set this fire, Larkham thought, he would find something in the ashes. He felt certain of that.

*****

As a businessman in northern Massachusetts, Boland exemplified the American go-getter with big dreams, business acumen, and irrepressible ambition. He had an MBA from Rivier College, in New Hampshire, and a variety of skills. He had worked as an accountant and had run several businesses. He had been an educator, teaching at Lowell High School, then at Chelmsford High School. At Boston University he had taught retail management, and at Newbury College he was a department chairman. He had done all this before even turning 38 years old.

Physically he was an ordinary-looking individual—short, slightly stocky, with brown hair and eyes, and a close-cropped beard. He had survived a tough childhood, born on September 16, 1948, in the mill town of Lowell in northern Massachusetts. His home, he would say, was a "housing project type of atmosphere."

In the 1950s, Lowell had fallen on hard times. No longer was it the illustrious "Spindle City" of the 1850s that led the country in cloth production. By the early 1960s, the looms had stopped, and the red brick mill buildings stood empty, ghostly reminders of its bustling early days. Lowell was noted for having the highest unemployment in the country, which fostered high crime and political machines.

Making personal connections with the right judges, politicians, lawyers, teachers, business people, and community officials was the standard mode of business operations in Lowell, and Boland was a quick learner. At a young age, he used his paradoxical charms—street smarts, boyish innocence, intelligence, and slick salesmanship—to edge into the right circles.

This enabled Boland to move out of Lowell and enjoy a better life in the suburbs of Tyngsborough. There he owned a nice home with a horse stable. But no matter how much he achieved, he wanted more. He wanted enough power, money, and prestige to ensure that he would never return to his poor roots. Namely, he wanted a law degree.

However, entering law school was difficult in the mid-1980s.

Approximately 12,000 individuals applied to Boston's six area schools, which had seats for only 3,700 or so students. Only a third of the applicants could get in, and law schools chose from what they considered the best and brightest—those who had the highest grade point averages and scores on the Law School Admission Test (LSAT). Applicants with top scores mostly came from white upper- or upper-middle class families. Those from poorer families who needed to work to pay for their tuition, who had less than a 3.0 grade point average in college, or who didn't seek legal education until mid-life were systematically rejected by Boston's traditional law schools.

Because Boland was well into his 30s when he entered law school, he ended up at the only school that would accept him: Southern Massachusetts-Rhode Island-Avins Law School (its name was later changed to Southern New England School of Law). This school accepted all who could pay their way. In fact, Dr. Alfred Avins, the school's founder, told state officials that only "lack of motivation" would disqualify a student. His goal was to give access to anyone who wished to study law. The program ran over the weekend and was strategically designed around students' work schedules. Classes were held Friday nights and all day Saturday. The school was situated 50 miles south of Boston in Fall River, Massachusetts (on the Rhode Island border)—90 miles south of Boland's home. Though far for Boland, many students traveled from New Hampshire and Maine. Avins designed the program so that they could spend Friday night in town and take classes on Saturday before returning home.

The school had one major drawback. It didn't have a license to issue law degrees. In 1984, three years into the program, Avins sought this license from the Massachusetts Board of Regents. The Board sent a team of legal educators to inspect the school.

Among the inspectors were Bob Bard, an honors graduate of Yale Law School and law professor at the University of Connecticut School of Law; Leo McAuliffe, a reference law librarian for the Social Law Library, a major law library in

Boston; Carl Singley, dean of the Temple University Law School; and Thomas M. Debevoise, former dean of Vermont Law School.

Nothing prepared them for what they found. The school was housed in a former beauty shop on Main Street. Students who wished to see Avins walked through a coin-operated laundry and up a rear set of stairs. A furniture store, also owned by Avins, doubled as a library. Blocks from the school, it was technically in Rhode Island. The library housed a collection of damaged and out-of-date books arranged by authors' last names. Open on Saturdays from 9:00 a.m. to 5:30 p.m., the library wasn't accessible to most students. They were in class from 9 a.m. to 4 p.m. In addition, the school didn't have a budget or financial records. There were no full-time professors. Only one instructor had any teaching experience.

Inspectors were so stunned by what they saw, they persuaded the state not to grant the school a license. Concerned that the state might be misleading students by even allowing such a school to be open, inspectors wrote, "It appears that Massachusetts law may permit an individual to proclaim that he is a law school and to collect tuition indefinitely without any investigation by the state. The state evidently can only investigate if and when the individual applies for degree-granting authority. We recommend that if this is the effect of current laws, they be examined with a view to possible change." However, no changes were ever made.

Acutely aware of the school's flaws, Boland thought that he could set up a better school, between his entrepreneurial skills and his teaching background. In a spirit similar to Francis Cabot Lowell—the industrial revolutionist for whom the town of Lowell was named—Boland took someone else's idea and improved upon it.

Lowell had traveled to Britain, in the early 19th century, to see the famous power textile looms. The British guarded their loom plans so carefully that customs officials routinely ransacked luggage looking for secreted plans. While inspectors may have looked through Lowell's luggage, they wouldn't have found loom

plans. They were locked in his head—Lowell had a photograph-
ic memory. When he returned to the Merrimack Valley, Lowell
knew not only how to replicate the power loom, but how to
improve upon it. He hired a machinist to build the looms, and he
added machines that would handle all stages of textile production
under one roof.

Similarly, Boland familiarized himself with Avins' operation
and set out to replicate it—but with his own improvements.
Boland felt that the Merrimack Valley, being northern
Massachusetts' fast-growing, high-tech region, was ripe with
opportunity. Boland, like Avins, would market to individuals who
sought a legal education as either a second career or a way to further an existing career.

Initially, Boland planned to offer classes on Thursday night
and all day Saturday, giving students a break in between.
Weekday classes and a full-time program would begin once he
had enough students.

Margaret Talkington, an Avins law school classmate, agreed
to help him. Peg, as Boland called her, was an athletic, five-and-
a-half-foot brunette. For 15 years, she had taught business courses at Veterans Memorial High School, in nearby Peabody. She
held a bachelor's degree in business education from Salem State
College and a master's degree in education from Suffolk
University in Boston.

To gauge public interest, Boland and Talkington surveyed
judges and lawyers in the Merrimack Valley. They asked them
what they thought of their law school plans. The response was
more enthusiastic than they had expected. In fact, a number of
judges and lawyers asked if they could teach. So on August 19,
1985, Boland incorporated Commonwealth School of Law, nam-
ing himself as president. Seventeen students put their money
down, and classes began in a rented classroom at Notre Dame
Academy High School in Tyngsborough.

Among the students was Judy Forgays, a striking girl, with a
heart-shaped face and icy-blue eyes. In her 20s, she had recently

graduated from the University of Lowell and was looking for something more to do. Upon seeing an ad for the school in the *Lowell Sun*, Forgays' father urged her to apply. He would even pay, he told her. "That carries a lot of weight when your dad tells you to do something," she reflected years later. Tuition was cheap—only $3,500 per year—and Boland told her that she didn't have to worry about interviews or LSATs. As far as Forgays was concerned, there was no reason why she shouldn't go.

By the second semester, Commonwealth School of Law moved to the Downes Professional Building at 1201 Westford Street in Lowell, which offered room to expand. Plus, the rent was cheaper. Boland planned to hire a dean, he told students. He did hire someone but fired him right away. Boland preferred managing the school himself.

In an article that appeared in the *National Law Journal*, Boland told journalist John C. Metaxas, "We're not a diploma mill. We are a traditional law school." He also told him that he and Peg had $150,000 invested in the school. Within six months, Boland bragged to another reporter that there were 1,000 applications on his desk, and he was buying a three-story building in Lowell.

Incoming students, like Forgays, didn't question what Boland or Talkington told them and the media. Some entered completely unaware that the school didn't have authority to grant law degrees or didn't understand that state approval hadn't been sought. Others knew it but didn't realize what a gamble they were taking. Many of the students were older—older than Forgays—in midlife, in their 30s and 40s, and knew that this was their only hope of earning a law degree.

*****

In the spring of 1987, Diane Sullivan went about her usual routine: working, attending college at night, and exercising in between. Employed by Commerce Bank and Trust Company, she had worked her way up from teller to bank vice president. Now she was about to graduate from Fitchburg State College. But Sullivan couldn't see how that would change anything.

Really she wanted to go to law school—a dream that she'd had as long as she could remember. She couldn't explain exactly why this idea had come to her. It wasn't as if any of her relatives were lawyers. In fact, none of them had even graduated from college. Still, Sullivan saw the legal profession as one that commanded respect. Lawyers had to be smart to understand the intricacies of case law. They took shattered lives and made them whole again. They spoke up for people hurt or mistreated. Sullivan loved learning, so she saw this as the right fit for her.

Upon leaving high school, Sullivan should have entered a pre-law program. However, her family didn't have money for college. She grew up in a blue-collar town where her father worked in a paper mill. The company helped him buy a house for a few thousand dollars. Sullivan's mother had been raised in an orphanage, which sent her out on the streets at age 16. She never finished high school. Sullivan's parents paid their bills and put food on the table, but there wasn't money for college.

Sullivan explained her financial needs to her high school counselor. Being the first in her family to consider college, she didn't know about scholarships, grants, or loans. The counselor didn't enlighten her either. He told her to get a job and save her money.

Sullivan did that. She became a teller at Fitchburg Savings Bank, where she earned $60 a week. She dropped change into a jar whenever she could. When the jar grew heavy, she poured the change out and made stacks around her like a king piling up riches. But these were just pennies, nickels, and quarters rather than gold. It took her two years to save up enough money for one course at Fitchburg State College. To reward herself for her hard work, she enrolled in the course that most interested her, business law.

The instructor, Elliott Zide, admonished her and her classmates, "I'm going to treat you like first-year law students." He intimidated most of the students, but Sullivan found him and the course exciting. She imagined being in law school.

Zide set the bar high and kept it there throughout the semester. He finished up with a tough exam on which Sullivan earned a 95. Across the top of her paper Zide wrote, "You should consider law school." The teacher couldn't have paid her a higher compliment. At that moment, she knew she had to do whatever it took to get to law school.

More determined than ever, Sullivan threw change into her jar. She saved until she had enough money for a second class. As Sullivan's income increased, she became a regular night student. She eventually earned enough to take several classes at a time. By 1986, Sullivan was within four courses of graduating.

As Sullivan worked on her undergraduate degree, admission into law schools grew more competitive and tuition costs increased faster than the rate of inflation. Harvard Law School's annual tuition grew from $4,580 in 1979 to $11,135 in 1986—an increase of 143 percent in only seven years.

In general, law school tuition escalated faster than all other tuitions, except for medical school. In 1974, the average law school student paid approximately $2,305 a year. Twelve years later, that same student paid $8,286 a year—an increase of 259 percent. This eliminated many working class applicants. With a national median income of $34,000, the average family would need to to spend a fourth of its annual gross wages just to send one child to law school. Parents could send a child by taking out a second mortgage or make the child incur the debt, leaving that child financially strapped for decades. Of course, the alternative was to forget law school, even though this might hinder one from becoming a governor, congressman, corporate CEO, financier, or even a university president later in life, as such positions are often filled by lawyers.

Though Sullivan had the grades and talent to attend any law school, including Harvard, she didn't have the money. There was a second stumbling block. She worked in Worcester, 40 miles from downtown Boston. Commuting back and forth at night, during rush hour, would be a logistical nightmare. She didn't believe that she could do it.

At home, in Sullivan's bedroom, she looked at a print on the wall, *The Winner*, by Norman Rockwell. It had always held special meaning to her. The image was of a 10- or 11-year-old girl with a black eye, who sat on a bench outside the principal's office. The girl with her white socks rolled down to her ankles and her braids askew, held her head up. She was the winner of the fight and proud of it. Sullivan liked that. Friends and family had looked at the print and remarked, "That's you, Diane." That's the way she saw herself, too. She had been a rough and tumble, freckled-faced girl, who played as hard as the boys did, determined to be the best that she could be.

That spring, in 1987, Sullivan stopped in the gym on her way to work. When the man on the weight machine before her finished up, he turned to her and asked, "How much do you want me to take off?" She shook her head as she stepped into the weights. "That's okay," she said. "I'm putting more on." She made a point of doing this without any assistance. The man shook his head and laughed. On the machines, as in life, she was determined not to let anything keep her down. She lifted, pushed, and pulled, making herself strong. It was the way to get ahead—be focused, and fit.

On her way out of the gym, she bought a *Worcester Telegram & Gazette*, and headed to her office at Commerce Bank & Trust Company. There she sat down and read the newspaper. On the third page, she spotted an ad for Commonwealth School of Law. She stared at it, as if she couldn't quite believe what she was seeing. It was a new law school in Lowell—just 35 miles from home and work. She skimmed the text: *Part- and full-time programs. Applications being accepted for fall 1986 semester.*

But she wouldn't be ready by fall. She had four more undergraduate courses to complete. The thought of this new school needled her brain all day, until she wondered, could she finish up her undergraduate classes during the summer? Then she would be ready for fall classes. She decided that after waiting so long, she just couldn't let this opportunity slide by. Before the day ended, Sullivan called Commonwealth and requested a catalog.

*****

In the town of Quincy, just south of Boston, a blue mist hung over the green sea. The early morning sun peeked over the horizon when Mike Mattson, a tall, lanky young man in his early 20s, drew a deep breath of sea air. With salt on his lips and cool sand between his toes, Mattson felt his senses come alive. He loved the beach.

Mattson spotted a gray lump on the seawall and jogged to it, kicking sand from the bottom of his feet. It was John Cascarano, Mattson's friend since elementary school. Cascarano was stretched out asleep across the top of the wall.

"You gonna sleep all day, Bookie?" Mattson shouted, giving his best friend a playful nudge. The two men couldn't have been more different. Cascarano was short—just five-feet, three-inches—and Mattson was tall, well over six feet. Cascarano was a bookworm, always reading. When he finished high school, he entered college. Mattson didn't care about school. He barely finished high school. In fact, he might not have graduated had his teachers not felt sorry for him—the kid from the projects, who grew up in a dysfunctional home with an alcoholic father. After high school, he got married and went straight to work.

Cascarano groaned and raised his head. His hair was as rumpled as his shirt. Black lines under his eyes showed that he'd barely slept.

Mattson leaned against the wall, "So, how'd it go this morning?" On weekends, Cascarano dug clams for a seafood company. It enabled him to make a few extra dollars. He sat up, rubbed the sleep from his eyes, and made a pained expression as he rocked his hand from side-to-side. "I really need the money," Cascarano said. "Tuition is coming up again." He had just entered Commonwealth School of Law and was struggling to come up with the money. Mattson couldn't believe how hard his friend worked and studied. Cascarano even wore a headset and re-viewed tapes of classroom lectures as he dug clams.

"Hey, thanks for waking me up," Cascarano said. "I gotta go."

"What's your hurry?"

"I've got to be at Fenway Park," he said, brushing the sand from his shorts. "The Sox are playing the Yanks." Cascarano had four part-time jobs: clam digging, bartending, cab driving, and selling hot dogs at Fenway Park.

"Hey, maybe you can get me in?"

"Get outta here. How am I going to get you in? Do you think I'm going to see any of the game? I'm working."

"At least you'll be there." They looked at each other. "Hey some of the guys and I are going to have a few beers tonight. You know, get together and have some fun."

"Yeah," John smiled. "So, swing by the bar." John's parents owned a place in Dorchester called JC's Café. It was in the his-toric Strand Theater area, known as Upham's Corner. The area had fallen on hard times and served a poor community. Cascarano worked there nights, when he wasn't driving a cab.

"Come on," Mattson urged. "Don't you ever take a break?"

"Look, one day you'll thank me for this when you're calling me from jail, begging me to get you out."

Mattson punched his friend. Cascarano let him have it back. For a few minutes, they rolled in the sand, just as they had done when they were in grade school. For those fleeting seconds, Cascarano forgot about his classes at Commonwealth.

*****

Commonwealth's catalog arrived at Sullivan's house in a small, ordinary-looking envelope. If she hadn't been looking for it, she might have mistaken it for junk mail. Pictured on the cover was a Gothic castle-like building made of stone, complete with spires, clock tower, and turrets. Instantly Sullivan thought of Harvard or even Oxford or Cambridge. She imagined toting heavy book bags up the marble steps, passing under granite porticoes, and sitting in old, high-ceilinged classrooms at heavy oak tables.

She checked to see how much it would cost: $5,100 for full time students and $3,800 for part-timers. For her, it was expensive, but she realized that it was less than other area schools. She would have to charge it to her credit card and pay it off over time, but she could do it. This thrilled her.

Sullivan flipped through the rest of the brochure, which contained pictures of a library filled with books and computers. Reading the text, she learned that the school still had to meet state standards before it could grant law degrees, but by the way the text was worded, that appeared to be a formality. The school appeared to be close to having its license. She wasn't concerned. Her mind raced; she was going to law school!

Having never been to Lowell before, Sullivan became lost on registration day. She drove slowly up and down the streets, looking for the castle-like building that she had seen on the cover of the school's catalog. One look at the cheap, low-rent neighborhood told her that she had made a wrong turn. Instead of ivy-covered brownstones and marble buildings, the street was littered with fast food restaurants, used car lots, discount retailers, and a garbage dump.

Perplexed, she drove slowly reading the street signs. She knew that if she didn't find it soon, she would be late.

Looking for help, Sullivan pulled into a gas station and approached the attendant, who stood in a coffin-sized booth behind a layer of bulletproof glass. She asked him where she could find the law school. The clerk pointed across the street. Sullivan shook her head, figuring that the dime-sized speaker must have distorted her words. She shouted that she was looking for Commonwealth School of Law at 1201 Westford Street. Then she pressed the catalog to the window, showing him the picture of the stone building.

"That's city hall," the attendant's mechanical-sounding voice replied. He pointed across the street to the drab, cheaply-made two-story concrete professional building. Brown metal pillars around the exterior made it look like a prison. "That's the law school," he said. Sullivan's heart sank.

She drove across the street, and as she entered a glass and metal door, she smelled rubbing alcohol and industrial cleaners. Everything about this place repulsed her. She noticed a board with white changeable letters, spelling the names of the building's occupants, which included various medical specialists, including Joseph Downes, a chiropractor. Listed at the bottom was Commonwealth School of Law.

Sullivan proceeded down a dark, narrow hallway with identical, evenly-spaced doors. Nothing could have been further from how she pictured law school. Just before she found the registration desk, she considered returning to her car and driving away. Then she reminded herself that she had come here to study law. She didn't have to like the building or the school. All she had to do was obtain her law degree.

Sullivan was shown the first-year books—contract books, tort books, and study aids—more books than even a fast reader could get through in a semester. "Are we expected to buy all of these?" Sullivan asked the man next to her.

Dressed in a business suit, he appeared in charge. He eyed her, smiled, and said, "I can't imagine getting through law school without them."

Sullivan bought them all. It took her three trips to pile them into her Mustang. After the last trip, she closed the hatch and watched the businessman from inside leave with a young girl, perhaps half his age. They didn't see her as they climbed into a blue Corvette on the other side of the parking lot. When the car pulled out, Sullivan read the bumper sticker: "My other car is an airplane." With squealing tires, the car shot off.

Sullivan tried to make a connection. Hadn't she seen this guy before? She remembered that she had brought the Commonwealth catalog with her. She flipped through the pages and found the picture. It was the same man, she decided. It was the school president, Michael A. Boland.

On her way back to Fitchburg, Sullivan moved through traffic oblivious to the sounds. The phrase "fly-by-night" kept running through her head, reminding her of phrases such as "take the money-and-run" and "sleight-of-hand"—phrases that evoke images of deception. Had she really been deceived, she wondered. Certainly the school's catalog had been misleading. If she had known the school was in a dingy professional building, she never would have enrolled. Now, she worried, what else was the school not telling her? She had a very bad feeling about this.

The thought of all of the books in the back of her car increased her anxiety. She couldn't read them all in four months. Sullivan gripped the steering wheel, trying to hold on and not break down.

At home, as Sullivan stepped from her car, her legs felt limp and her hands shook. Her mother came out to greet her. After one look, she asked, "Di, are you okay?"

"I don't know, Mom," Sullivan said, her voice breaking up. "I don't know if I can do this—there are so many books. Look at them all. And the school . . . ."

Her mother laughed. "Just quit," she said. That's what her mother wanted. She wasn't thrilled that her daughter had decided to go back to school. She had hoped that her daughter would take a break, relax, and have some fun—maybe meet a nice guy, settle down, and have some kids.

"I've paid my money," Sullivan said, surprised at how resigned she sounded. This was her one chance to become a lawyer. Quitting meant giving up and ending the dream.

*****

Once classes started, Sullivan realized that she was not alone in her worries. Students at Commonwealth questioned the professors about the school's degree-granting authority. Students often turned to Steven H. Kropp, a short, thin man in his early 40s. During the fall Contracts class, Kropp answered students' questions about the school's status in obtaining a state license. He explained that the Massachusetts Board of Regents licensed law schools, giving them authority to confer law degrees.

From the back of the room, someone called out, "Doesn't the school need to be accredited by the American Bar Association?"

Kropp replied, "No." In Massachusetts, a law school needed only to be state-licensed. Massachusetts was one of a few states where any graduate of a state-licensed school (ABA-approved or not) could sit for the state bar exam.

"Why didn't the school obtain its license before it opened?" someone asked.

Al Zappala, a 37-year-old student, took interest in this conversation. Though his classmates sounded concerned, he had already talked about these issues with Boland. The school president had told him that the Board of Regents had already approved the school. The issuing of the license was merely a formality.

Kropp explained that it was possible for an established university or college with adequate physical and financial resources to start up a law school that would have a license from its inception. However, a new, freestanding school, such as Commonwealth, had to convince the Board of Regents that it would run a quality program. The school had the challenge of establishing a library, faculty, and law school building all on the funds received from school tuition. But once the school was established, the Board of Regents could send out a group of independent legal experts to inspect the school. If the school met with inspectors' approval, it could be licensed.

Could be? Zappala thought about this. It wasn't exactly what Boland had said. This surprised him.

"What happens if the school isn't licensed?" a student asked

Professor Kropp.

The professor weighed the question and then said that they had nothing to worry about. The inspection committee was scheduled to visit the school in December, and it would be impressed with Commonwealth's progress in just one year. If not, the school would fix whatever problems existed and invite the inspectors back. He reminded students that no one would be graduating for three years.

"Doesn't the school have preliminary approval?" Zappala asked, his voice louder and more intense than he had intended.

Kropp looked curiously at him. He started to reply but stopped. "Any further questions should be taken up with the administration," he said, looking down at his notes. "Let's get back to Contracts."

Zappala watched the instructor. He thought back to a conversation he had had a few months earlier with Boland. The school president had told him that Commonwealth's license would be automatically issued after one full year. There would be an inspection, he said, but it was merely a "rubber stamp." That's the way he put it.

Now Zappala realized that Boland had misrepresented the situation. He didn't know why this surprised him, really. Nothing at Commonwealth turned out to be the way it had been explained or presented in the catalog. The library, which closed at 3 p.m. most days, was supposed to have 15,000 books. In reality, it contained no more than 8,000. The school's much-touted computer research capabilities consisted of a single computer. Moot court, specialized seminars, and a law journal, which were listed in the school's newsletter, were nonexistent as far as he could tell.

It occurred to Zappala that he and his classmates were so desperate to become lawyers, they would accept whatever conditions the school offered and believe whatever story Boland fed them. They had all their hopes of becoming lawyers pinned on this school. That made them more vulnerable and gullible.

When Zappala first heard about Commonwealth, in the spring

of 1986, he met with Boland. "Tell me why I should go to Commonwealth over Suffolk," he asked the school's founder. When Zappala was 24 years old, he had briefly attended Suffolk University School of Law. He became overwhelmed relatively quickly—a wife, kids, and a business—and his life was too full for law school. He entered and withdrew from Suffolk twice. Ultimately, he decided to keep his Salisbury manufacturing business and forget about law school. But now that he was getting divorced, he had more time to himself. He could go back to school, he decided, as long as it was close to home.

Zappala liked Boland, who appeared to be a bright, friendly guy. The school president mentioned knowing James Campbell, Lowell's city manager, and U.S. Senator Paul Tsongas, also from Lowell. Boland said that both men supported the school, and Zappala knew a school with such political connections would be a success.

When he asked Boland for an application, the school president shook his head and said, "If you're good enough for Suffolk, you're good enough for Commonwealth." He waived the application fee as well. Zappala liked that. Getting into Suffolk had been tough, particularly taking the Law School Admission Test, filling out endless forms, and submitting transcripts. Here all he had to do was chat with the president, and he was in. He had walked out of that initial meeting at Commonwealth feeling optimistic and confident. He was certain that he would get his law degree this time around.

Months later, now in Kropp's classroom, Zappala realized what a mistake he had made. Boland had deceived him. Worse, he had fallen for it. He had run several businesses and could spot a snow-job pretty quickly. But Boland was smooth, and, in an odd sort of way, Zappala admired how clever he could be. Not just anyone could pull the wool over his eyes.

In his own defense, Zappala decided that he could be smooth, too. He lived by the philosophy: "Keep your friends close, keep your enemies closer." He decided that's what he would do. He would get close to Boland and see for himself what was going on.

*****

On Thursday, December 4, 1987, four legal experts pulled into Commonwealth's parking lot: Robert Bard, professor at the University of Connecticut School of Law; Howard Glickstein, dean of Touro College of Law in New York; Edward Bellefontaine, librarian for the Massachusetts Social Law Library; and Frank Gomes, treasurer of Post College in Waterbury, Connecticut.

Carrying leather briefcases and dressed in business suits, the team came in looking very serious. They moved up and down Commonwealth's dark halls, asking questions. After a short while, Boland took them to lunch, and they didn't return for three hours.

Back at the school, students watched the clock, wondering why the inspectors were gone for so long. Zappala, who waited with another student, Juan Ortiz, told him this was a bad sign. He knew that they should be looking at the classrooms and at the library or interviewing students and faculty or going through the school's financial records. Could it be that they were so unimpressed, they didn't need to look any further?

After the inspection team returned and finished up at Commonwealth, Boland indicated quite the opposite. He walked into a class of day students and said, "It looks like you will be graduating in 1989."

There were cheers, but Boland quickly cautioned them that nothing was official. The team had said that the school was headed in the right direction, and it had the makings of a great institution, he told them.

In students' minds, the school was approved. Based on his assurances, they put their money down on another semester. They brushed matters of state licensing, degree-granting authority, and ABA approval aside. They had plenty of other issues preoccupying them: work, family, classes, and final exams.

*****

After four months of waiting to hear the results of the Board of Regents' report, a rumor circulated, in May 1987, that the report had come in. Students expected Boland to make an announcement, but days passed without him sharing a word with the students. Finally Boland entered the Civil Procedure class and told part-time students that the report was in and that it was good. He said that inspectors were impressed with the library and thought very highly of the school. Boland admitted that the school needed to make a few changes but added, "We're in much better shape than Southern New England School of Law." That was Avins' school.

Comparing Commonwealth to such a terrible school concerned students. In fact, student John Lakin sensed that the school president was nervous and said, "I want to take a look at that report."

Boland told them that Professor Kropp was synopsizing it and that all students would eventually receive a copy.

"I want to see the full report," Lakin insisted. Cascarano and Zappala echoed the same sentiment.

Boland insisted that the report contained confidential material. They would all receive summaries that would tell them everything they needed to know. He asked students for their trust and support, assuring them that everything would turn out fine.

After class, Lakin met up with another student, Dick Ahern, a short, burly Irishman. Older than most of the students, in his 40s with grown children, he was a father figure and voice of experience for many students. Lakin told him that the Board of Regents' report was in and repeated what Boland had said about synopsizing it.

"I smell a rat," Ahern said. His square face turned a light shade of crimson. He muttered a few curse words and then said that he thought it was a public document.

"I'll get a copy of that report, even if I have to drive down to the Board of Regents office myself," he told Lakin. Born to a working class family, Ahern had learned to be enterprising, to think on his feet, and to stretch a dollar. He had been a businessman, working in sales for Quick Roll Leaf, a New York company. At another job, he had repaired elevators. Like Lakin, he expected his studies at Commonwealth to lead him to a better life. So far, however, he had seen nothing but toil and aggravation.

The next day, when Zappala returned to Commonwealth, Ahern was in the administrative office. His face as red as a stop sign, Ahern motioned for Zappala to come over. Ahern asked the school's secretary, Pam Pelosi, to find Boland. He needed to speak with him immediately. Pelosi dialed Boland's home number, but he didn't answer.

The students sat face-to-face in the library. Ahern pulled out a bundle of papers that he had highlighted with a yellow marker. He adjusted his glasses and read: "Typically, a licensing or accreditation inspection of the school involves an evaluation of the structure the school has built on its foundation. Commonwealth has not yet established a foundation. It has not created the base on which it can build and which is required before the school can hold itself out as a school for the training of professionals. Until that base is established, it is difficult to assess properly any other aspect of the school's operation."

Commonwealth has not yet established a foundation. Ahern's voice shook. He told Zappala that the inspectors had found the school so deficient that they couldn't comment on its program. Contrary to what Boland had said, Commonwealth had not only failed the inspection, but the inspectors found so many deficiencies that they didn't do a full inspection but limited their comments to three key areas: financial resources, legal structure, and education.

Ahern read again, "The visiting team deems the current

legal/administrative structure severely deficient and the availability of the necessary financial and professional resources to start up a law school inadequate."

Even the library, which Boland claimed that inspectors had praised, was described as "sorely deficient" and "crowded," and they found critical research materials missing. Boland had planned to expand the library, but the inspectors told him that his space was not large enough to hold all of the books and publications he needed.

Ahern read again: "All authority at Commonwealth is vested in two non-lawyers who are also the school's most highly-paid employees." The school had a two-person board of directors—Boland and Talkington. No board meeting minutes existed, which state and federal regulations required of nonprofit organizations, such as Commonwealth.

Flipping through the pages, Ahern looked for one paragraph that was the key to the entire report. When he found it, he pounded it with his finger and read: "A law school requires that ultimate authority be vested in a board which includes lawyers and legal educators and whose members have no financial interest in the school. The founders of Commonwealth seriously erred in attempting to organize the law school without any assistance from professional legal educators experienced in part-time legal education. Until the weakness is remedied, it is impossible to evaluate the program . . . ."

In other words, the inspectors said that the school needed a dean, a legal professional who could guide and direct the school, set policies, and develop educational curricula. However, Boland had dismissed this. He believed that he was fully capable of running the school and didn't want to share the school's management with someone else. He said that based on his experience, he believed that hiring a dean, for such a small school, would be a waste of money.

Students pressured him, and Boland finally conceded and hired a dean: Lawrence R. Velvel, a legal educator, constitutional law scholar, litigator, and antitrust specialist.

Zappala, Ahern, and another student, Steven Moses, met with Velvel as soon as he was hired. He looked like a dean with his thinning hair, neatly-trimmed beard, and large, owlish glasses. He listened thoughtfully as they spoke and had a sweet, paternal smile that put them at ease. Velvel told them that he had a solo law practice in Washington, D.C., but he intended to scale it back. By the end of August, he hoped to be settled in New England.

Zappala considered him to be self assured—a nice guy overall. At times, he seemed almost patronizing of Boland's remarks, which Zappala felt was a good sign. The school needed someone strong-willed, independent, and principled to handle Boland.

Subsequent to the formalities, Ahern asked, "Do you know what we call this place?"

Velvel shook his head.

"Comedy School of Law," Ahern said, adding that none of them would graduate unless he could change the school and bring it up to state standards.

Velvel curled up his index finger and placed it over his upper lip, furrowing his brow.

"Boland's a snake. You can't trust him," Ahern continued. Zappala nodded in agreement. Ahern told Velvel that Boland had misrepresented the Board of Regents' report and then tried to hide it. He said that Boland was a megalomaniac—a man who wouldn't turn over power to anyone—not even to a dean.

Velvel said that he thought they were wrong. He had signed a contract that gave him decision-making power. Then, as if to offer some reassurance, he said that he had developed a strategic plan for bringing the school up to state standards, and he and Boland had both signed it.

Ahern was surprised. So was Zappala. Neither of them believed that Boland would do that. They asked if they could see the plan. Velvel shrugged. He didn't mind.

Zappala thought Velvel to be nice, but naïve. He knew how convincing and manipulative Boland could be. After all, he had been fooled by him, and he wasn't the type of guy who could be easily deceived. Thus, part of Zappala feared that Velvel would be eaten alive.

"You'd better watch out," Ahern said.

"I'll be fine," Velvel replied.

Zappala and Ahern exchanged glances. They weren't so sure.

Chapter 2

The Dean

Draft card burnings, anti-war protests, feminist marches, racial riots, and political assassinations punctuated the year 1968. Lawrence R. Velvel, a 28-year-old law professor at the University of Kansas Law School, wanted to do his part in opposing the Vietnam War. He abhorred the pointless killing of 300 to 400 American men and boys each week.

Velvel sought to prove in the courts that a president couldn't fight a war lawfully without a Congressional declaration of war. He had dug through legal cases and found constitutional proof that supported his position.

On July 11, 1968, Velvel entered the U.S. courthouse in Topeka. In a bold, unorthodox move, he had sued Lyndon Baines Johnson. At that time, cases that challenged executive actions were brought against a named cabinet member, rather than the President, who was considered immune from such action.

"The Constitution states in clear and unequivocal language that the Congress shall have the power to declare war," Velvel had written in his brief. He was prepared to argue that point before the judge.

Before Velvel had filed the lawsuit, a friend of Velvel's, another University of Kansas law professor, visited Velvel in the small, split-level house that he shared with his wife and two children. Velvel's friend urged him not to proceed with the lawsuit, warning him that it would reflect badly on the faculty and the school. It would ruin his career. The two professors talked for hours. Velvel listened but felt morally obligated to file the lawsuit against the President anyway. Young and idealistic, he believed justice would prevail in the end. He intended to prove to the court that this war was illegal.

If Velvel's high confidence faltered, it was in entering the large, dimly-lit courtroom. It was one thing to think intellectually about the war in the privacy of his office. It was quite different to stand up before a group of lawyers who were 10 to 30 years older than himself and far more conservative. They supported the President and the war effort. Intimidated, Velvel felt like a stranger in a strange land.

"Velvel versus Johnson," the clerk announced. Laughter rippled through the courtroom.

Velvel realized that they were laughing at him, a young, no-name law professor with the foolish idea of suing the President of the United States. Still, he was shocked. He had never experienced such an open display of emotion, particularly by professionals, in a courtroom.

When Velvel approached Judge George Templar, he could see that he wasn't amused. Velvel explained that an everyday citizen, like himself, had the right to sue. The war had restricted American citizens' civil liberties. Their tax dollars were being spent on a cause that they didn't support. In addition, the war had hurt the nation's economy, diverted money away from important social programs, such as welfare and education, and had inflated prices.

Pausing for a moment, Velvel noticed the judge's eyes fluttering, as if he were falling asleep. Velvel continued. He urged the judge to declare the war unconstitutional. Congress had never declared war. With the judge fighting to remain awake, Velvel realized his point was moot. He couldn't win.

As expected, Templar dismissed Velvel's case, three weeks later, saying that its scope went beyond his court's jurisdiction. Still, he complimented Velvel on his brief, describing it as "copious and persuasive." Later, describing the case to another lawyer, Velvel wrote, "I would rather be insulted and win, than to have the usual train of events, which is to be complimented and lose."

Velvel took the case to the Court of Appeals in Denver. In this court, Velvel could only challenge the District Court's claim that it didn't have jurisdiction over the case, because the court hadn't addressed the war's legality.

In Denver, on August 11, 1969, Velvel appeared before three judges. This time, Velvel figured that if he spoke bluntly, he would make the judges sit up and pay attention. Perhaps he might even shock them into looking more analytically at the case and their own prejudices.

Velvel told the judges, "I think the courts are biased on this issue."

Judge Tuttle appeared startled.

"What do you mean that the court is biased?" asked the judge, a southerner and civil rights supporter. "Is this an intellectual or an emotional bias?"

Intimidated by the question, Velvel backed down. "I think it's an intellectual problem, a doctrinal problem." In reality, he knew it was bigger than that.

Realizing what he had done, Velvel wished that he could start over. He had been right in saying that the courts were prejudiced. Seeing that he lacked the courage to back up his statement, he chastised himself. Throughout his life, he never forgot that lesson. The appellate judges ruled against him.

Velvel took the case to the U.S. Supreme Court. This was one of thousands of petitions received by the high court every year. In order for the nine justices to hear a case (referred to as granting certiorari), four of them had to agree to hear it. Only a few cases are granted certiorari each year.

When Velvel's petition came before the justices in early 1970,

they voted eight to one against hearing it. The dissenter was
William O. Douglas, who had believed for some time that those
"being marched off to jail for maintaining that a declaration of
war is essential for conscription" deserved an answer from the
American government to that important, undecided constitutional question.

Others on the Supreme Court preferred to avert the issue.
Several were friends of Lyndon Johnson's and were biased in
their support of the President. Although Supreme Court Justice
Hugo Black believed the Vietnam War to be unconstitutional
(which wasn't publicly revealed until after his death), he continued to vote against hearing Velvel's case and others like it. He did
so out of loyalty to the President, his close, personal friend.

About Black's duplicitous action, Douglas later wrote:

> America's young men did not get an answer from
> Warren's Court. Indeed, it never even heard a case
> involving a challenge to the legality of the Vietnam
> War. The reason was the Court's persistent refusal to
> grant a writ of certiorari in any proceeding that might
> have required it to confront this issue. Ten times
> between the spring of 1967 and Warren's retirement at
> the end of the 1968-1969 term, litigants seeking a rul-
> ing that the Vietnam War was unlawful asked the
> Court to hear their cases. In every single instance it
> refused to grant review. In June of 1969, as Warren
> was concluding his service as chief justice, a mother,
> whose only son had been drafted, wrote to Black,
> complaining that her boy was being required to par-
> ticipate in a war that was not only "unjustified" but
> also "not recognized by the Congress of the United
> States." "I implore you," she begged. "Get my son and
> all other sons out of Vietnam." Although addressed to
> a justice who was himself strongly opposed to the
> war, her plea was futile.

While Black's private view of Vietnam was inconsistent with

his actions, just the opposite was true of Abe Fortas. A long-time friend of Johnson's, Fortas acted as a hawkish war adviser after he was appointed to the Supreme Court, and he urged the president to continue with the war effort.

Nineteen cases challenging the war's constitutionality were ultimately brought before the Supreme Court; none were granted review. During this period, Velvel continued his legal battle to prove that Congress had to declare war in order for military action in Vietnam to constitutionally continue. Otherwise, it had to stop. Velvel became associated with more Vietnam War constitutional law cases than anyone. He even participated in the nationally-publicized Shea Bill in Massachusetts, intended to prevent Massachusetts residents from being required to serve in undeclared wars.

In their book, *The Judiciary and Vietnam*, authors Anthony A. D'Amato, law professor at Northwestern University, and Robert M. O'Neil, who was then law professor at the University of California and later head of the University of Wisconsin and the University of Virginia, described Velvel as an "indefatigable proponent of legal tests of the Vietnam war . . . sustaining the momentum and spirit of a diffuse campaign."

It was an apt description, because Velvel looked at every possible angle in fighting the Vietnam War case. That's how he handled matters that he truly believed in. He fought hard, with a resolve not to turn back. Though he never succeeded in having courts rule that there had to be a Congressional declaration of war for the president to engage troops in a long, sustained battle, he never gave up. He remained determined, because he knew that he was right.

*****

Lawrence Velvel was born on September 7, 1939, to Anna and Herman Velvel, Russian immigrants who had come to the United States in the early 1920s. The Velvels were Labor Zionists. Like those who had built Israel, they committed themselves to social justice and inculcated those same beliefs in their son.

The Velvels lived in Austin, a west-side Chicago neighborhood. Later they moved to the north side. Alienated from a largely Christian American society with different customs, they associated with like-minded eastern European friends and relatives that clung to Old World customs as they and other immigrants of their generation did. They ran a successful photo engraving business in downtown Chicago, enabling Herman Velvel to bring home $20,000 by 1955. In those days, it was a substantial income for an immigrant who had only a high school education. He flaunted his achievement by driving an impressive black Buick Roadmaster.

Herman and Anna's son, Larry, was rebellious, even at a young age. He insisted on speaking in English even though his parents conversed in Yiddish or Russian. Obstinate, opinionated, and precocious, Larry, by age seven, read the *Chicago Sun-Times* from cover to cover and remembered most of what he read. Intelligent, he skipped a year in school.

When Larry was 10, his six-year-old brother, Eugene, died from a brain tumor. During the months that followed his death, Larry's mother locked herself in the bathroom and screamed. Larry listened in horror. When he slept, he dreamed of his brother, who seemed to return as if still alive. Even after the screaming and the dreaming stopped, life at home was not good. He was not what his parents wanted him to be.

Larry wanted to be like other American boys. But for years he had been forced to spend every afternoon in Hebrew school. He looked forward to turning 13 and having his bar mitzvah. That meant that he could play baseball, football, and basketball with the other boys after school. That's not what Larry's father wanted. He counted on his son continuing with Hebrew school. When Larry refused, he watched his father take a butcher knife and slice up his football and basketball. To Larry's further dismay, his father told him that he could not return to summer camp if he quit

Hebrew school.

Larry quit Hebrew school and played ball anyway. Being short and small-boned, he never developed into a top-flight athlete. Despite his father's threats, Larry attended Camp Interlaken in northern Wisconsin. There he excelled in softball under the coaching of Marv Levy, who later became a Hall of Fame football coach with the Buffalo Bills. Years later a fellow camper referred to him as having had a "rocket arm."

Entering high school, just a few days after he turned 13, Larry was frustrated with the public high school he attended in Chicago, Senn High School. He wanted more of a challenge. At age 14, he asked his parents to send him to Evanston Township High School, a suburban school just north of Chicago, where they would have to pay tuition. Evanston was then one of the finest public high schools in the country, stressing high academic achievement. The Velvels valued education and had the money, so they agreed to send him.

Velvel had a thirst for reading and wanted to read faster so that he could read more books and magazines. So when a speed-reading class was offered during his senior year at Evanston, Velvel took it. In it, students were taught to read words in clusters, and the instructor drove students to read increasingly faster. Being the best in the class at speed-reading, Velvel became obsessed with reading faster. He started off reading 200 to 250 words per minute, but increased to 350 to 400 words per minute, and sometimes he could go as fast as 500 to 600 or even 700 words per minute. Still, he tried to read faster. Every time he sat down to read, he tried to race to higher speeds. Later in life, he heard Woody Allen joke about speed-reading: "I read *War and Peace* in 20 minutes. It's about Russia."

Velvel found Allen's joke painfully true. Reading became a race in which he perpetually tried to top his previous time. Ironically, he had taken the speed reading course to read more books and magazines. As it turned out, the reading became so stressful that he stopped.

Attending the University of Michigan after high school, Velvel studied little because he didn't want to read and face the pressure of reading faster. He studied so little that one semester his grade point average dropped to 0.4—on a scale reaching 4.0.

At Michigan, the only area in which Velvel excelled was economics. In spite of the reading stress, Velvel forced himself to read and memorize the 800-page textbook. He received As in Professor Shorey Peterson's two introductory economics courses. In the second of the two courses, he did not attend any of the small group sessions that augmented the large lectures given to hundreds of students. He cut the small group sessions because they were taught by a foreign teaching assistant who barely spoke English and who read the textbook to the class. (This was a problem that, in later decades, became a widespread scandal in the academic world.) Velvel figured that he could do just as well on his tests if he read the book on his own. He did this and got As on the tests, which should have meant that he would get an A in the course.

However, Peterson was known around Michigan's campus as a crusty old WASP, even among the faculty. The teacher prided himself on being one of the toughest and most challenging professors on campus—never an easy A. He was so dedicated to his work that he saved all of his class grade books and stored them in his library at home.

Thus, Peterson was dumbfounded when he learned that Velvel had never shown up for the small section meetings and had earned an A on his own. Any student who could do this, he knew, had to be extraordinary. Yet he feared Velvel was wasting his talents. Peterson was the kind of teacher who liked to impart a love for learning in such students and help them realize their own gifts. Peterson wanted to meet Velvel in person.

The teacher told Velvel that in order to receive an A, he would need to write a paper over the summer. Peterson's concern impressed the student. By fall, Velvel had finished the paper and enrolled in one of Peterson's elective courses—this one taught entirely by Peterson. Velvel didn't skip classes. Instead he came early and watched the professor carefully outline the day's lecture on the chalkboard. Velvel watched Peterson organize his ideas, and he copied the professor's notes. Velvel learned that each idea had a specific place and purpose.

This detailed, organized thinking was one of two great intellectual revelations Velvel took away from Michigan. The other came from English professor, James Gindin, who told Velvel that he thought well enough, except he would come to a point and stop. Gindin told his student that he would accept something as dispositive, not question it, and stop pursuing the line of inquiry. Gindin urged him never to stop the questioning or the pursuit, to accept nothing on faith, but continue to investigate the reasons why each point in the inquiry might be true or partly true, or false or partly false. These two revelations became the fountainhead from which Velvel would build his law career, teach law, and build a law school.

In 1960, Velvel graduated from Michigan with a bachelor's degree in economics. That fall, just after turning 21, he entered the Michigan Law School. To get through the many required law school casebooks, Velvel knew he had to stop speed-reading. It had become too stressful. Thus, Velvel disciplined himself to slow down and read just 25 to 30 words a minute. With pen in hand, he made check marks next to key words and phrases. Researchers would discover 30 years later what Velvel already knew, speed-reading took the pleasure out of reading and lowered comprehension of literature and complex material.

During his first semester in law school, Velvel worked hard, and when he received a final grade of C+ in a two-hour course about legal procedures during the late Middle Ages, he was disappointed. However, because he had gotten As in mid-year exams in two other courses, setting the curve in one of them, he was determined to excel and tried even harder. He read his casebooks early and prepared months ahead for his exams.

The year-end exams were for final grades in 28 out of 30 total first-year credit hours. On one of the tests, he received a B in a five-hour Torts class taught by Professor Luke Cooperrider, who had given a two-part test—approximately 40 percent objective and the rest essay.

When Cooperrider sent students their grades, he asked Velvel to see him. He explained that, even though Velvel had set the curve on the objective part, his essays were so long that he didn't read them. Cooperrider explained that this was why he had given him a C on the essay part of the test. Velvel was astonished—the professor hadn't even read his essays, which made up 60 percent of his test grade and final grade. Thus, he ended up with a B in both.

Cooperrider was prepared to offer Velvel advice on how to take essay tests—the predominate type of test in law schools. He asked Velvel how he had done on the rest of his exams. Velvel replied, "They were all As." On one he had set the curve. Obviously, Velvel didn't need Cooperrider's help.

The difference between an A or B on one law school test might seem small, if not insignificant, to most people. But to a law student, such as Velvel, there was a major consequence. The professor's refusal to read his essays in Torts had cost him the extraordinary accomplishment at the Michigan Law School of getting a perfect 4.0 average on the end-of-year final examinations, as well as costing him a 3.93 overall first year average and the status of being ranked first or second in his class. Despite this, Velvel said nothing. In the early 1960s, students didn't challenge their professors. Velvel's overall first year grade average was 3.7—excellent, especially in light of his undergraduate years. (In later decades, when students became accustomed to challenging their professors, Velvel considered Cooperrider's action as a form of cheating. The professor had assigned a grade to essays that he had not read.)

At the end of law school, Velvel graduated ninth in a class of 339 and was named to the law school academic honorary society, the Order of the Coif. Before his last year in school, he married Louise Rose, a pretty, dark-haired daughter of a traveling salesman. They dated for five years, got married, and after Velvel graduated from Michigan, they moved to Washington, D.C. Approximately 20 of their classmates moved there, too.

At the time, the nation's capital teemed with young, ambitious lawyers. Velvel worked two years in the U.S. Department of Justice honors program. He handled tax law cases and then moved to the Antitrust Division. After working for the Department of Justice, he worked for seven months as a legislative staff member for Senator William Proxmire.

In 1966, ready to move on, Velvel accepted a position teaching Constitutional Law at the University of Kansas School of Law, located in Lawrence. It was a small, academic town about 40 miles west of Kansas City. He was excited about the move because it gave him a chance to teach a subject that had become of enormous interest to the country since *Brown v. Board of Education* in 1954. The Velvels also thought that by moving to a college town, like Lawrence, they would, in a sense, be reliving their college days in Ann Arbor. They picked out an apartment that happened to be just two blocks from KU's football stadium.

But Lawrence wasn't Ann Arbor. Abolitionist free-staters had founded Lawrence in 1854. Shortly before the Civil War, William C. Quantrill, along with Jesse James and other Confederate guerillas, burned and pillaged the town, destroying 75 homes and killing 150 people—mostly adult men. In an effort to revive the town, Abraham Lincoln ordered the Union Pacific railroad to be constructed through the community. As a result, the town's population grew rapidly to 5,000.

By the mid-20th century, Lawrence had lost sight of its roots. In 1955, a 7'1" basketball player, Wilt Chamberlain, was recruited to play for KU's Jayhawks. He would be the first African-American on the team. Chamberlain wasn't thrilled about making waves and being the one to integrate a formerly all-white team, but he wanted to work with famous Jayhawk Coach Phog Allen.

Upon arriving in the Kansas City area, Chamberlain immediately faced the harsh reality of local segregation. The diner, where he stopped for a snack, demanded that he eat in the kitchen. Nearly all of the restaurants and movie theaters in Lawrence operated that way. Having grown up in the fully integrated city of Philadelphia, Chamberlain despised such treatment and told Allen that he was going home. Allen urged the young basketball player to stay and make a statement for his race. Chamberlain did that and led black students in public sit-ins. During his three years in Lawrence, Chamberlain battled discrimination, but by 1958, he had had enough. He joined the Harlem Globetrotters, who lured him away with an annual salary of $65,000—impressive for the time. Chamberlain left without looking back.

Despite countless invitations, Chamberlain didn't go back to KU until 1998, some 40 years later. That year, KU honored Chamberlain and retired his number 13 Jayhawk jersey. The next year, the basketball star died of congestive heart failure. He was just 63 years old. Though Chamberlain never elaborated on his estrangement from KU, many people speculated that he had a hard time forgetting the harsh bigotry he had experienced in Lawrence.

That bigotry still existed when the Velvels arrived in 1966, though it was less obvious. Anyone who wasn't white, Anglo-Saxon, and Protestant, be they Jews, African-Americans, or Hispanics, was likely to feel estranged from the small community, which had 50,000 residents. Approximately five percent of the population was black, living mainly in "East Bottoms," a section of town located adjacent to the polluted Kaw River. Rundown schools and broken, rusted playgrounds in that section of town contrasted sorely with the town's better-kept white sections.

By 1966, tension between whites and blacks had reached nearly a snapping point. Blacks objected to what would later be called racial profiling. Police routinely stopped African-Americans on the street simply to harass them. In the Lawrence high schools, black students had fewer opportunities than did their white counterparts. Students at KU vocalized their opposition. Beyond racial tensions, some KU students had become strident in their protest of the Vietnam War. Their counter-culture, drug-embracing lifestyle bucked the ultra-conservative mainstream.

Such was the atmosphere at KU when the Velvels arrived. Just 27 years old, Velvel was only a few years older than many of his students. They related to him and found him to be tolerant and empathetic. On one occasion, he wrote a final exam that he thought would take students three hours to finish. By noon, Velvel was surprised to see scores of students hours away from finishing. Concerned that they were hungry, he and Louise made sandwiches for everyone.

Velvel cared about his students, and they knew that. His passionate opposition to the Vietnam War earned their respect. Melvin Jenkins was one of five black law students at KU then and found Velvel exceptionally interested in minority students. He said that Velvel never talked about his Vietnam War cases in class, but students knew that he was "the man" on campus in terms of fighting the war. Students admired his courage for challenging the war's constitutionality and speaking out, even though it ran against the grain of the conservative, pro-war Kansas community.

Steve Pickard, a law student who had been a basketball player at Kansas State University, in Manhattan, Kansas, didn't know anything about Velvel when he saw him for the first time in 1968. Pickard recalled him being a curious individual on the court—short with an Ace bandage wrapped around his knee and thick-lensed glasses strapped to his head. He didn't dribble very well either. Pickard asked his friend, "Who's that?"

His friend laughed, "It's that crazy Con-Law professor."

Eventually Pickard and Velvel became friends. He learned that what Velvel lacked in basketball skill, he made up for in tenacity. He played with a do-or-die spirit, which was the way he did most things. He was hell-bent on succeeding. He never did anything halfway. It was either all or nothing for him.

*****

On February 17, 1970, after contempt of court sentences had been handed down by Judge Julius Hoffman in the trial of the Chicago Seven, students dressed in light jean jackets and short-sleeved shirts gathered around the Chi Omega fountain on the KU campus. It was unseasonably warm as students chanted, "Two, four, six, eight, stamp out the state." Each time the chant came around, profanities were added and the shouts escalated.

A year and a half earlier at the 1968 Democratic National Convention, seven anti-war individuals, including Abbie Hoffman, Jerry Rubin, and Tom Hayden, had been arrested for conspiracy to incite a riot. During the trial of the Chicago Seven, defendants mocked the judicial system in the courtroom, blowing kisses to the jury and marching in Nazi lock-step. Judge Hoffman found the seven, and the two defense attorneys, William Kunstler and Leonard Weinglass, guilty of contempt of court and sentenced them to prison terms up to five years.

On February 17, 500 KU students moved en masse down Jayhawk Boulevard, the main thoroughfare on campus, in protest of the war and Judge Hoffman's rulings. The crowd brought traffic to a halt. In front of the law school building, Green Hall, Velvel waited on the steps next to the larger-than-life bronze statue of former law school Dean Jimmy Green. When the crowd reached him, he spoke, "[Judge] Hoffman is posing a real threat to our society." The problem was more than just the judge, he said. The entire judiciary system had become a corrupt tool of the establishment. He referred to his own thwarted attempts to stop the war.

In his speech, Velvel told students that Judge Hoffman had cleverly skirted the maximum six-month contempt of court sentence that a judge could impose without a jury, by sentencing the defendants and their lawyers to numerous six-month sentences on a variety of contempt of court issues.

"It's part of a grand governmental conspiracy to break lawyers of representing radicals," he said, finishing his speech. KU's poet-in-residence W. S. Merwin read anti-war poetry, and after that, the crowd moved on to the Douglas County Courthouse.

Velvel stayed behind. He had spoken his mind and told the truth, and that was the end of that as far as he was concerned. However, to his amazement, his speech appeared the next morning as the lead story in the town's two newspapers, the *Lawrence Journal-World* and the *University Daily Kansan*.

What Velvel didn't realize was that while he was speaking, a 19-year-old student had climbed to the top of the Jimmy Green statue and painted it blue and red. The same student did more spray painting at the courthouse, where a window was also broken. Three people were arrested for petty larceny and vandalism. Ironically, like Abbie Hoffman and Jerry Rubin, Velvel too was accused of inciting a riot. Kansas State Senator Reynolds Shultz expressed outrage, saying an employee of the state should be squelching protests, not participating in them. Shultz, with State Senator Lester Arvin, asked KU Chancellor E. Laurence Chalmers, Jr. to dismiss Velvel.

Chalmers had worked hard at keeping the peace at KU, and he believed that it was within Velvel's right to speak his mind. After all, it was written in the faculty handbook that "a faculty member is free to express publicly, in speaking or writing, his own considered view . . . ." Beyond being unfair, Chalmers was concerned that Velvel's dismissal would fuel students' anger and start a riot.

When Chalmers refused to act, the senators took the issue before the Board of Regents. Velvel's name was one of 113 faculty members up for promotion.

Tom Ashton, a second year law student, convinced 190 students—approximately 80 percent of the law school student body—to sign a petition upholding the professor's first amendment rights. Five KU professors circulated a petition, as well, saying that the Board of Regents threatened academic freedom by punishing Velvel. In addition, Vernon Yoho, a Constitutional Law student, wrote a letter to Shultz saying that even though Velvel had his own strong views, he made sure that everyone in class had an opportunity to say what he or she thought. Yoho, a deeply conservative student, knew that Velvel wasn't as radical as the senators had characterized him.

When the Board of Regents met on March 30, Henry Bubb and Paul Wunsch, both of whom were regents, continued to oppose Velvel's promotion, which would move him up from associate to full professor. They also questioned promoting professor Frederic Litto, who had made a controversial play, "Kaleidoscope of the American Dream," a classic drama that depicted a change in U.S. attitudes from optimism to deep pessimism. Following the play's tour of Kansas, the U.S. State Department took the play to Eastern Europe, where it was part of a cultural exchange program. As a way of compromising between the professors and the Board of Regents, Chalmers offered to further investigate the issues being challenged and report back.

Outraged students declared April 8 to be Strike Day. Instead of going to class, 4,000 students congregated in front of Strong Hall, the school's administration building. There David Awbrey, student body president, demanded that the Board of Regents confirm the professors' promotions. Believing that the professors were being punished for exercising their first amendment rights, Awbrey said that he intended to take the matter to the American Association of University Professors (AAUP), which could censure the school.

After gathering on campus, students moved to Potter Lake for a "nude-in." Reports indicate that no one disrobed, and the crowd played, threw Frisbees, listened to rock bands, and drank beer—typical of college students on a spring day. Festivities concluded with a speech by Abbie Hoffman, who drew a crowd of 7,000 students at Allen Fieldhouse. Students listened while Hoffman shouted remarks that sounded strange to conservative Kansans:

"The dinosaurs running the country are going to be exterminated. Youth are going to make the revolution and are going to keep it. Destroy the institutions—destroy the university, and you learn how to make love."

When Hoffman concluded, there was no applause. "Lawrence is a drag," Hoffman sniffed, telling the crowd that he was going on to Dallas. With that, he pulled out a handkerchief resembling an American flag and blew his nose on it. The incident made national headlines. For the reporters who had missed it, Hoffman repeated it the next day at a news conference.

*****

Locals would have been surprised to learn that Velvel neither introduced Hoffman that night nor attended his speech. The media never made it clear that Velvel's controversial speech, given two months earlier, was not in support of Abbie Hoffman and the Chicago Seven, but against Judge Julius Hoffman and his harsh treatment of antiwar protesters and their lawyers. Ideologically there was a gulf of difference between the two positions. Yet many Kansans weren't able to discern between the two. To them, anyone speaking out against the government was a radical or an anarchist.

Most of the community would have been surprised to learn that the first and only time that Abbie Hoffman and Velvel met was on the KU campus, just before Hoffman's speech at KU. Velvel shunned flamboyance and detested Hoffman's theatrics. They stood in the way of the public accepting the truth about the war, the government, and the judiciary, he thought.

However, Velvel's honesty about such subjects "irritated the hell out of some people," Ralph Gage said years later. A reporter for the *Lawrence Journal-World*, Gage trailed Velvel much of that year. In conservative Kansas, where the public was less disillusioned with the government than elsewhere, Velvel was considered a radical.

In the spring of 1970, with the Vietnam War escalating and youth and racial unrest growing, reporters sought out Velvel to comment on the news. He provided interesting, provocative comments—a striking contrast to the general conservative Kansan point of view. Many of the locals didn't like that. In fact, some people told Louise that her husband should just "keep his mouth shut." That was the general philosophy in Lawrence: Shut up. Don't make waves. Look the other way. Take the road most traveled. If you buck the system, you'll pay the price.

This should have prepared them for what was to come—but it didn't. One night, an anonymous caller warned Velvel that there would be trouble that night. He'd better leave his house. Alarmed, the Velvels packed overnight bags and went to a friend's house. As predicted, there was a riot with firebombs, gunfire, and vandalism. Trucks with gun racks prowled the streets. Police watched the Velvel home, which remained untouched. But someone set fire to the Kansas Union that night, causing $1 million in damage. A savings and loan institution, two schools, and a judge's house were also set on fire.

At home the next night, Louise watched the evening news on television. That's when she heard the NBC anchor report wrongly that during the prior evening, students at the University of Kansas had set fire to the Student Union because two popular professors didn't receive promotions.

Louise was stunned. The fire supposedly set by students had nothing to do with Velvel's promotion but was in protest of racial profiling. Still Velvel had been linked once again to local violence. Alf Landon, an 83-year-old former governor and a popular conservative political spokesman, who lost the 1936 presidential election to Franklin Roosevelt by the biggest margin in history, referred to Velvel as an enemy of the state and said that if he were dean of the law school, he would fire him.

Lawrence Blades, dean of the law school, knew Velvel wasn't the way that he was being portrayed. He tried to assuage public opinion by inviting Velvel to alumni meetings. The gesture was a way of saying, "Look, he's really a regular guy."

As well, Louise became recognized around campus and town as the wife of the radical law professor. When she bought a new screen door at Wicks Lumber, the man behind the counter looked closely at her check, then looked at her from the corner of his eye.

"You wouldn't be any relation to that Velvel guy up on 'The Hill,' now would you?"

Louise stiffly replied, "He's my husband." With that, she shoved her checkbook into her purse and prepared to leave.

"Well, I heard him speak the other night," the clerk said. "Do you know, he's not as crazy as people say?" This incident made her realize that there was another side to public opinion.

When the Board of Regents met again, they promoted Velvel to full professor, showing that KU professors could speak their minds without fear of retribution. Velvel was pleased to have become a full professor at age 30, but the controversy and public condemnation had tainted his opinion of this Kansas community. As he told reporters, "I'm really happy. Some damage has already been done, but I hope we don't have to worry about future threats [to academic freedom]."

Within a week, a new threat rocked Lawrence and the nation. On May 4, Kent State University students protested Nixon's sending troops to Cambodia. Nervous National Guardsmen killed four unarmed students. The action stung a nation already emotionally raw. Anger exploded on college campuses everywhere. Violence prompted more than 500 colleges to close. At KU, students marched through campus with a coffin, halted ROTC review ceremonies, stoned the military science building, and went on strike.

Governor Robert Docking ordered the school to remain open. He warned that if students didn't go back to classes, he would send in the National Guard. In an effort to avoid a repeat of Kent State, Chancellor Chalmers offered an alternative. On May 8, before a crowd of 15,000 students in Memorial Stadium, Chalmers asked students to come back and finish out the year.

They didn't have to attend classes or take finals, but the university had to stay open. Those who wanted to go to class could go. Those who didn't could finish out the year by attending anti-war discussions and workshops.

Velvel presented the different point of view. He told students that if the university stayed open, it would mute their anger. "Strike," he told them. It was just the type of action that he had written about in his yet-to-be-published book, *Undeclared War and Civil Disobedience: The American System in Crisis*. He believed that in a democracy, ordinary rules and laws had to be peacefully disobeyed sometimes in order to sharpen opposition to intolerance, oppression, and discrimination.

If democracy didn't exist, stronger measures might be needed, he wrote. In particular, he thought about World War II Jews who had followed orders and were led unresistingly to their deaths. Why didn't they disobey, in their case violently so? Why didn't they fight? What had they achieved by being led like sheep? Those questions bothered Velvel.

"Let a mad government know you are not going to go along with usual things to allow them to go on with the craziness in Asia. If you refuse to go about business as usual, Nixon will get the message," he continued. "Legal, non-criminal, non-violent alternatives" will show the government that you will not participate in the system.

After that, Chalmers put the decision to a vote. Overwhelmingly students chose to keep the university open. That day, Governor Docking claimed victory, hailing the students' decision as "prudent." He referred to those who disagreed, such as Velvel, as part of "a sick society . . . that has degenerated America into a morally bankrupt nation."

Docking, a hack politician in Velvel's mind, outraged him. The governor considered those opposed to the Vietnam War as promoters of degeneracy and moral bankruptcy. Velvel encouraged students to send letters to their hometown newspapers saying that they vehemently opposed the war in Indo-China, and they were "remaining on campus not only for classes, but to work toward an end of the war."

It's uncertain how many students followed his advice; that summer, students and professors went their separate ways. Even Louise and the kids headed off to Chicago. Velvel remained behind, working feverishly on his book, reading galley proofs and making last minute changes. Once he had finished, he drove from Lawrence to Chicago—a nine-hour trip. He didn't stop to eat or look back. He was glad to get away and leave behind the small-minded, conservative town.

As he drove, he reflected on how things had been different on his recent trip to Boston. He had flown there to testify in favor of the Shea bill, in which a group of concerned citizens staged their own opposition to the war and challenged its constitutionality. While in Boston, Velvel spoke on radio shows and talk shows, and people listened with open minds and were generally receptive to his views.

The hearings on the bill drew such a large audience, of people of all ages, that they had to be moved to an auditorium. "It was really overwhelming to see the number of people in the audience who responded wholeheartedly and spontaneously. The way the testimony was handled in the Massachusetts legislature was one of the finest contributions to democracy I had ever seen," Velvel wrote later about that experience.

In his car, on the way to Chicago from Kansas, Velvel thought about the people he had met in Boston: Steve Worth, John Wells, Jim Shea, Bob Condlin, and the many political activists who thought like him, shared his views, and were dedicated to doing the right thing. It contrasted greatly with what he had experienced in Lawrence. It occurred to him that it was time to leave Kansas.

That fall, Velvel applied for the dean's position at DePaul University College of Law, in Chicago. He interviewed for it, presenting his ideas for school improvement. Months passed, and he heard nothing. He assumed someone else was hired.

In the meantime, Velvel accepted a position as professor of

law at Catholic University in Washington. It came with a 23 percent salary increase. He earned $22,000 a year, which seemed
like a lot at the time. He and Louise were thrilled to be back in
the U.S. capital, away from Kansas. There, they'd make a fresh
start once again.

*****

A few weeks into the fall semester, Velvel tossed and turned
at night, wrestling with the decision he had to make. He had just
returned from a second visit to DePaul, where he was unexpectedly offered the position of dean of the College of Law.

Though Velvel never drank in the morning, he got up early
that morning and poured himself a scotch. He had a tough decision to make, perhaps the toughest career decision in his life.
Louise and the children loved their new home in Rockville,
Maryland, but finances had proven tighter than they had expected. Their new house had cost two and one-half times what they
had paid for their home in Kansas, and Velvel's pay, spread out
over 12 months rather than nine, gave them $700 less a month.
Essentially they were broke. They couldn't even go to
McDonald's for dinner.

For the position of dean, DePaul offered Velvel a 60 percent
increase in salary—$36,000. It was a staggering amount. The
highest-paid law school dean in the county made only a few thousand dollars more than that. It was an incredible opportunity to
someone only 32 years old.

Velvel saw this as a rare, plum position. He had ideas for
rebuilding and improving the school. In terms of his career,
Velvel knew that he should take it. Yet his family had just moved
to Washington—the nation's political nerve center. Neither he nor
Louise wanted to live in Chicago, near his parents. Thus, they
chose to remain in the nation's capital. He explained this to the
officials at DePaul that morning.

This soon proved to be a serious mistake. Making ends meet

in Washington was so tough that when Louise gave birth to their third child, Sandra, she asked her doctor to send her home right away. The insurance company paid only $100 of the medical bill. She didn't know how they would pay the rest.

Velvel applied to the law firm Kirkwood, Kaplan, Russin & Vecchi (KKRV) for part-time work. The partners realized that one of their acquaintances, Bob Bard, had attended the University of Michigan around the same time as Velvel. Bard, who graduated from Yale Law School, described Velvel as smart to the law partners and said that they had met through an economics professor, Shorey Peterson. The KKRV law partners liked this. They liked to surround themselves with smart people—individuals who had graduated from major law schools near the top of their class. Thus, they hired Velvel. He did antitrust work there for two years, and then he moved to a bigger firm for a much higher part-time salary.

As Velvel soon discovered, the entire Washington legal scene mirrored the attitudes of the KKRV partners. Thousands of lawyers in the nation's capital were obsessed with being the best and the brightest, which Velvel began to see as a kind of Washington sickness. The lawyers all around him considered themselves the anointed of the earth. This elitist philosophy ran against the fiber of Velvel's own thinking—certainly contrary to what his parents had taught him about being socially conscious.

*****

As in Kansas, Velvel was a well-liked, respected professor at Catholic University. Among his admirers was Charlene Barshefsky, who took three classes from him.

"He was far and away the best teacher at Catholic," reflected the slight woman, who in her 40s became President Clinton's cabinet level U.S. Trade Representative, negotiating China's entry into the World Trade Organization. "He was alive and challenging," she said. As well, he could be intimidating.

As an international trade negotiator, Barshefsky earned the reputation of being a dragon lady. Though not a shrinking violet, even in law school, Barshefsky found Velvel to be an imposing figure: deeply serious, intense, and well-read. In her first class with him, Constitutional Law, she could see that the professor expected more than mediocrity. He expected students to be prepared and bring insightful comments to class.

A couple of months passed before Barshefsky felt that she had something to say. When she did, she raised her hand and made her comment.

"Umhmm, Miss Barshefsky, wasn't that rather obvious?" Velvel replied.

Deflated, Barshefsky knew she had to come up with something more enlightening before raising her hand again. Considerable time passed before she mustered the courage to make another comment. When she finally raised her hand, Velvel acknowledged it by saying, "So Miss Barshefsky, I see that you've rejoined us."

Rather than being put off, Barshefsky made her point.

"That was a wonderful argument," Velvel responded.

With confidence soaring, Barshefsky continued her argument. Right then, Velvel stopped her. "Miss Barshefsky, I'm going to teach you the most important lesson in your life," he said. "Once you've won your argument, curb your urge."

That struck Barshefsky. Curb your urge. She never forgot it, and she carried that lesson with her through her life and career.

Others at Catholic recognized Velvel's talents as a professor. In 1975, when Clinton Bamberger, Jr. did not seek reappointment as dean, Velvel became one of four candidates to succeed him. Before the law school's faculty and the university's search committee, Velvel presented his ideas for increasing the school's revenue and increasing the professors' salaries.

Classrooms at Catholic held no more than 60 students, and the rooms were often only one-third or one-half full. To Velvel's way of thinking, not all classes needed to be that small. There could be more classes of 50 to 60 students, which would increase the student body and incoming tuition revenues. The school could still have many small classes.

After two prominent Catholic scholars were offered the job and rejected it, the search committee and faculty accepted Velvel's ideas and voted to make him the next dean. But the job wasn't his until President Clarence C. Walton approved it. Velvel presented his ideas to Walton. When he called Velvel back for a second meeting, Velvel and his colleagues were certain that he had the job. To Velvel's surprise, the president told him that he had decided to appoint a conservative non-candidate, John Garvey, as acting dean. Velvel was shocked.

Walton and the school's vice president told Velvel that the Catholic University search committee was going to restart its search for a permanent dean. They didn't explain why, but Velvel and his colleagues figured it out. In fact, it was quite obvious. Velvel was Jewish, and this was Catholic University. Clearly, the president wanted a Catholic dean. While Velvel understood this, he also thought it unconscionable that the administration had previously pretended that religion—and liberal views—were irrelevant to holding this position.

Word spread among students and faculty. They circulated a petition protesting the decision. Half of the 700 law school students signed it. They formed a picket line around the law school, shutting it down. Still the president wouldn't change his mind.

Velvel realized that he had risen as high as he could at Catholic University. He would remain a professor there, earning a miserably low salary that would never support his family the way that he would have liked to. By turning down the position at DePaul, he had made the worst decision of his life.

For a while, Velvel began practicing law and teaching simultaneously. This dual role taught him that law school had nothing to do with law practice. After three years of school, students graduated but did not understand how to practice law. They didn't know how to make opening statements and closing arguments, examine and cross-examine witnesses, make evidentiary objections, and write jury instructions. They didn't know how to draft contracts, negotiate with prosecutors, handle everyday business matters, or set up their own practices. Law professors themselves had little or no experience practicing law, and students left school with a dearth of necessary skills.

Velvel believed practical skills could be incorporated into legal education, and he outlined his ideas in an article, "Suggested Improvements in Legal Education," published in 1978 in the *Journal of Legal Education.*

"A professor who currently practices in his fields of expertise will bring far more knowledge to the classroom than one whose teaching depends on information obtained solely from books or from a practice that ended years ago," Velvel wrote, emphasizing the need for professors who had in-the-trenches experience. "The current practitioner has an enhanced sense of the practical and of the way things are actually done, and he may have first-hand experience with some new problems in his field." Also, he believed that students, while in school, should help professors work on real cases.

"One does not become a law professor in order to get rich, but one should not have to be poor either," he added. Obviously, this comment came from being so poorly paid at Catholic. "If law professors cannot make a reasonable living, either through their basic salary or through their salary supplemented by practice, then I suggest that many persons who are willing to work hard may ultimately shy away from teaching in favor of far more lucrative full-time practice, where their efforts will be decently rewarded."

Velvel took his own advice, left Catholic University, and became a partner in a big law firm. There, in 1979, he met Robert H. Bork, who had been hired to assist the firm in some major antitrust litigation. A professor at Yale Law School, former U.S. Solicitor General, and former acting U.S. Attorney General, Bork worked mainly from his New Haven home. His wife was bed-ridden with cancer. For nearly two years, the two lawyers worked on and off together, sometimes at Bork's home, preparing court briefs, oral arguments, and petitions for certiorari asking the Supreme Court to hear cases.

Though Velvel disagreed with many of Bork's legal and political views, he got along famously with Bork and considered him to be a truly brilliant lawyer. Conversely, Bork saw talent, tenacity, and a tireless drive in Velvel. In recommending Velvel for a subsequent legal position, Bork wrote that Velvel's "work was well up to the quality of the work in the Solicitor General's office. He has a scholar's grasp of legal issues and a practitioner's ability to focus his learning precisely and powerfully on the issues in the case before him. . . . He rewrites a brief until every lurking ambiguity and unclear thought is eliminated. Several times, when I thought we were done late at night, I found Larry rewriting once more. Finally, he has excellent tactical judgment and shapes an argument to give it maximum appeal."

After the antitrust litigation ended in the early 1980s, the Washington-area legal arena had changed. Competition increased and business declined. Velvel moved on and became the founding chief counsel of the State and Local Legal Center, where he wrote Supreme Court briefs in support of state, city, and county governments. Then he became a partner in a large firm whose headquarters were in Los Angeles. When that firm began a downward slide toward bankruptcy due to insufficient business, he set up a solo practice.

With each change, Velvel grew more disgruntled with Washington. He had searched for a stable, long-term position where he could teach or practice law, support his family, and save for his children's education, but it seemed as if nothing worked out in Washington. A decade of experience had taught him that honest lawyers who thought independently, who would do the right thing, and who would speak their minds in the face of opposition, were undesirable. Also it was clear to him that firms did not want honest and independent thinkers. They wanted highly-

trained performers who would act unquestioningly as commanded. He couldn't operate that way.

Velvel decided to return to academics and called Bob Bard,
who taught at the University of Connecticut School of Law.
Velvel asked him if he knew of any teaching positions. Bard
laughed because he had just inspected, for the Massachusetts
Board of Regents, a northern Massachusetts school that needed a
dean. The school, Commonwealth School of Law, had failed its
inspection. Though it had been in operation for a year and a half
and some of its students expected to graduate and sit for the bar
in 1989, that wasn't going to happen without big changes, Bard
said.

The school's founder, Michael Boland, was a businessman
and not an attorney. Bard explained that the school needed a
dean, a legal expert who could develop academic policies and set
up a legally knowledgeable and independent Board of Trustees.

Velvel called Boland, and they agreed to meet at the school,
which was in Lowell, Massachusetts. Velvel found the law school
president to be affable, confident, quick on his feet, and boyishly
enthused about his school. He bragged about the school's rapid
growth and how it satisfied a need for affordable legal education
just north of Boston. The school attracted older students, who
sought to better their lives by becoming lawyers. He pulled out a
drawing of a proposed law center in downtown Lowell. He mentioned that he knew Paul Tsongas, the City Manager, and various-
politicians.

Boland introduced Velvel to his partner, Margaret Talkington,
and Velvel presented his plans for upgrading the school. Many of
his ideas came from the law journal article that he'd written
almost a decade earlier. Boland seemed satisfied, and he said that
he thought that they could work together. Boland explained that
the school's problems rested with the Board of Regents, who
insisted, as Bard had said, that the school needed a dean with a
background in legal education and an independent Board of
Trustees.

Boland implied that he wasn't enthusiastic about co-managing the school with a dean. The school president's face clouded over as he explained that he had lent the school a lot of money— nearly $300,000, he said. In fact, he had sold his plane to do so. Boland told Velvel that he had put every nickel into Commonwealth, and he feared someone might come along, take what he'd built, and throw him out.

When he heard this, Velvel thought Boland was paranoid for no legitimate reason. He figured Boland to be a wealthy man, with considerable power, who was trying to do something good for the community. Velvel couldn't understand why he would feel so threatened. In a law school, there was room for both a president and a dean, Velvel told him. Other schools had operated this way. Still Boland seemed uneasy.

Boland explained that he had seen founders ousted at other schools. For instance, the founders of Hampshire College had been thrown out, he said. It could happen at Commonwealth too. As best as Velvel could tell, Boland feared him.

Velvel didn't know what to say. On the one hand, he was excited to have the opportunity to return to academics, and Commonwealth was a small, young school where he could work on innovative ideas in legal education and contribute something worthwhile. On the other hand, Velvel sensed that Boland didn't want a dean who would use his power.

*****

Later that month, the Velvels visited Joe and Julia Fishelson in Wooster, Ohio. Joe was more than just an older cousin to Velvel. He was 25 years older than Velvel, a hero in his eyes. Fishelson had been a decorated World War II paratrooper and a brilliant man who had earned substantial wealth in business. When Fishelson was in his mid to late 40s, he completed the courses needed for a doctorate at Harvard Business School—an almost unheard of accomplishment for a middle-aged man in

those days. He then became a professor at two American universities before becoming associate dean of the Kaplan School of
Economics of the Hebrew University of Jerusalem. Later he
founded Red Head Brass Corp., which became America's leading
fire hose coupling manufacturer.

Velvel told Fishelson about becoming dean of Commonwealth School of Law. Fishelson made clear that he didn't like the
idea of Larry going back to academics at a no-name school.
Velvel explained that this was an opportunity to do something
good and try out some new ideas in legal education. In his gruff,
no-nonsense manner, Fishelson wanted to know what he really
knew about Boland. He stabbed at the heart of the matter,
because Velvel knew nothing about the law school president, just
the bits Boland had shared. Yet, he was selling his home, moving
his children, and resettling in a place where his family knew no
one. Despite Fishelson's misgivings, Velvel believed the time had
come to make a change. Washington had brought him nothing but
professional unhappiness. Thus, Velvel decided it would be best
to ignore Fishelson's concerns, make the change, and move on.

Chapter 3

Black Saturday

In the spring of 1987, a rumor circulated at Commonwealth that Michael Boland was in legal trouble. The buzz began when the sheriff delivered legal papers at the school. Students speculated that a disgruntled student had filed a lawsuit, which was pure conjecture.

Paula Dickinson, a Commonwealth adjunct professor, avoided such student gossip. But she empathized with students, having a background much like theirs. She grew up in the Greek ghetto of Lowell, as the daughter of Greek immigrants.

Dickinson taught legal writing, in addition to managing a law practice and caring for two active school-aged children. As soon as she finished teaching at Commonwealth, she headed home. She didn't hang around for idle gossip.

However, by August 1987, she suspected that all was not right at Commonwealth. Boland had done nothing to improve the school except hire Dean Lawrence Velvel, who was still settling in. There were no new course electives. The library was still inadequate, and there still wasn't an independent Board of Trustees. The function of such a board is to oversee the school's policies, academics, and finances and provide a healthy balance between the needs of the school, faculty, students, and community. However, at Commonwealth, the Board of Trustees consisted of the school's co-owners, Boland and Talkington.

Dickinson began to think something was awry when she unexpectedly spotted Boland at the Middlesex Probate Court in 1987. She walked over to him and joked, "What brings you here?"

"I'm here with my girl," he replied.

Puzzled, Dickinson didn't know what he meant. She looked around, but she didn't see a girl. Boland appeared to be with two adults. He looked nervous, and Dickinson felt uncomfortable, as if he were brushing her off. Boland didn't have any children, as far as she knew. So she didn't understand what he meant.

Boland introduced the couple next to him as his brother and sister-in-law. He explained that they were seeking guardianship of the girl. This puzzled Dickinson even more. Boland acted relieved when Dickinson said she had to go.

As strange as the incident was, she forgot about it until summer came. When Dickinson dropped her son off at the high school, she noticed Boland's Corvette parked there. His car was distinctive—royal blue with a white top. Over the next few weeks, she watched the car, and eventually she saw a young girl, no older than 16, getting out of it. Dickinson wondered, could this be the girl Boland mentioned? The thought made her uneasy.

Dickinson told Karen J. Edwards, the librarian at the law school, about it. Edwards had concerns, too. Several of her paychecks had bounced, and some of the school's book vendors called about overdue debts. Going into fall, both Dickinson and Edwards felt Commonwealth's future was uncertain. However, they trusted that the new dean would straighten out whatever problems the school and its owners had.

*****

During the hot summer of 1987, Velvel prepared for his move to New England. At his home in Maryland, he received a few letters from disgruntled Commonwealth faculty and students. He

answered each one as carefully and honestly as he could, reminding them that his duties at Commonwealth didn't begin until
August. Until then, they would need to talk with Boland.

One matter disturbed him more than the others. In July, a
group of students told him they were angry because Boland
refused to renew Shoshanna Ehrlich's contract. She was one of
two full-time professors at the school, known particularly for
being outspoken, independent, and at odds with the other full-
time professor, Steven Kropp. As Ehrlich explained it, she and
Kropp had "different teaching styles," and if she disagreed with
Boland, it was because he had "no appreciation of law school
teaching."

Protesting Boland's refusal to rehire a teacher whom they considered not only highly qualified but personally interested in
them, students circulated a petition declaring that the school president had acted unfairly. This struck an obvious chord with
Velvel. On two different occasions, students had protested the
way university administrations or others had treated him.

Thus, Velvel questioned Boland about it. Boland replied that
he didn't like Ehrlich's attitude. Velvel explained that traditional
academic institutions didn't hire or fire faculty based on professors' personalities. If they did so, many universities would lose
their best talent. Velvel explained that academic appointments
should be based on quality. To ensure this, he suggested that faculty appointments be voted upon by the dean and faculty. In the
end, Velvel persuaded Boland to rehire Ehrlich for the next year.

In early August, shortly before moving to New England, the
new dean read an article in the *National Law Journal*, touting
Commonwealth as "a different sort of law school," uniting "most
of the education innovations of the last 10 years." Boland was
quoted as saying that he "bet $3 million of my own money" on
the school's success. Within 10 years, he expected it to be "one of
the 30 best law schools in the nation." Further boasting, Boland
claimed to already have 22,000 books in the library.

Velvel knew none of this was true. According to what Boland

had told him, he had only $300,000 in the school, and the library had 12,000 volumes—just over half the amount cited in the article. He chalked it up to typically inaccurate reporting and thought nothing more about it.

On September 2, the movers packed his things and were scheduled to arrive, in a few days, at his new townhouse in Nashua, New Hampshire, just 12 miles north of Lowell. Before Larry and Louise arrived in Nashua, Velvel received a call from the school. The moving van driver had stopped there and demanded a certified check, but the school refused to pay. Velvel and his wife were stunned. Back in July, they had talked with Boland about their moving expenses. At first, Boland offered them only $2,000, but after Louise strongly objected, the law school president agreed to pay all of the Velvels' moving costs. This was written into Velvel's employment contract.

When Velvel called and reminded Boland of this, he claimed that he had forgotten. He paid the bill, and Velvel brushed it aside as an innocent mistake. However, Louise couldn't forget Fishelson's concerns—what did they really know about Boland?

*****

The arrival of the new dean improved morale among Commonwealth's students. Al Zappala, for one, felt encouraged watching the energetic dean bustle around the school. He also realized that increased funding from the jump in enrollment— 183 students from 71 the year before—would subsidize many of the school's needed improvements.

"There was a feeling that CSL had turned the corner and was at last on the right track toward [obtaining law] degree-granting authority," Zappala would reflect years later. He attributed that feeling to the 48-year-old dean, who had a quiet, contemplative gaze. Zappala liked the fact that he was open and upfront, more like himself than Boland. Velvel's plans for the school were innovative, yet practical, and, as a legal scholar, his knowledge and credentials offered Commonwealth much-needed stability and credibility. "He's just what the doctor ordered," Zappala thought.

More than that, the dean expressed genuine concern for students. Without pretense, he listened to and valued what they said. He urged Zappala to make improvements in the Student Bar Association—to call area law schools to see what services their SBAs offered. This would give Commonwealth's students ideas for tailoring their own SBA programs, he told him.

The dean apprised students of the changes he planned to make. He gave them school updates through bi-weekly memos. "Sunlight is said to be the best disinfectant," Supreme Court Justice Louis Brandeis had written, and Velvel believed in that. The dean set out to eliminate secrecy and behind-the-scenes maneuvering. He wanted to bring the school's successes and failures out in the open, so that they could be discussed and so that students, faculty, and administration could work in unified fashion to come up with fair, reasonable solutions.

When Velvel told students that the next state inspection would not take place until February 1988—not the fall of 1987 as Boland had promised—Zappala and the other students appreciated the dean's candor. Though disappointed, they sensed that the school was not ready for another inspection. They knew that it would be better to wait than to fail again. It was important that the class of 1989 graduate on time, and a winter inspection would enable them to do that.

*****

One of Velvel's main objectives, in the fall of 1987, was to broaden the decision-making power at Commonwealth. Since the school had opened, two years earlier, Boland and Talkington had made all of the school's decisions. Because they had financial interests in the school, they obviously held personal biases. The Massachusetts Board of Regents insisted that, before the school could be granted degree-granting authority, Boland and Talkington's power had to be shared among others—a qualified dean, faculty, and a team of legal experts. The team of experts would make up a Board of Trustees—a governing body of seven to 10 unbiased experts who would oversee the school's operations and policies. The school also needed a legal structure, which would set down clear-cut rules about the handling of faculty and staff contracts.

That fall, Velvel sat down with Dr. John Weston, of the Massachusetts Board of Regents, to find out what needed to be done. Weston, the Board's official in charge of inspecting schools, said that no law school had been started in Massachusetts and received Board of Regents' approval since 1943. However, he believed there was a need for another law school. He said that he received as many as three to four calls daily from prospective students who wanted to know when Commonwealth would receive state approval to grant law degrees. An increasing number of professionals, Weston said, sought legal education to either advance their careers or to escape dead-end jobs. There were six law schools in Boston, but only two had night programs, and the city's traffic and parking problems made them undesirable to many suburbanites. Thus, he thought, a new law school north of Boston and close to the I-495 beltway could draw students from as far away as New Hampshire and Maine. Hearing this, Velvel saw the school's potential. It could attract 500 students or more.

One thing concerned Weston about Commonwealth. It was becoming known as "the school of last resort." Accepting all those who apply was not good, Weston said. Poorer quality students would pull down Commonwealth's academic curve, resulting in lower expectations and performance. Then students might not be prepared to take the bar exam. That would be a disservice to students. At that point, Weston asked him what were the school's admission standards. Were the courses rigorous enough? Were students being prepared to take and pass the bar? Using adjunct professors was fine, he said, as long as experienced full-time professionals mentored those with less experience.

Velvel reacted to Weston's concerns by taking a hard look at Commonweath's classes. He sat in on every class and wrote down his observations on a yellow pad: *pointed questions, good questioning, gets the class involved, explains well, needs less talking and more questioning.* In general, he found the teachers effective and teaching in a Socratic way, by asking questions and evoking responses. Larry Beeferman was a full-time professor and graduate of Harvard Law School. He and Ehrlich were experienced. In Velvel's estimation, the others needed just a few pointers to bring them up to par. With Ehrlich's help, the dean developed a training manual, and soon they saw teaching quality improve.

That fall, Velvel wanted to hire two new full-time professors. At the academic job market in Chicago, run by the Association of American Law Schools, Velvel and his colleagues interviewed 40 people. They narrowed their teaching prospects to five candidates and invited them to visit Commonwealth. All were top-level graduates from some of the nation's most elite law schools. Velvel was surprised and gratified to see people of this caliber so interested in the school. In fact, the majority remained enthusiastic even after they saw the school's terrible physical facilities.

Marc Fajer, a Seattle lawyer, who was third in his class at Stanford Law School, was among the top candidates. Fajer stated up front that he was homosexual, just in case the school had a problem with it. Velvel assured him it wouldn't be a problem. Student Bar Association President Richard Ahern, who had also interviewed Fajer, wrote Velvel a memo that said, "I found Marc Fajer to be the most refreshing of all the candidates. Although there are some at [Commonwealth] who are homophobic, the vast majority want the best, brightest and most highly dedicated teachers available. Marc Fajer falls into this category. He should be offered one of the full time teaching positions. If he is not, then the administration and faculty's stated goal of academic excellence is highly suspect."

Boland didn't like Fajer and openly said so. He wrote to the dean, "I am deeply concerned about his background. At this time, I could not approve a faculty appointment for this gentleman." When Velvel asked him why, Boland replied that he did want to hire gays. The dean was shocked. He disagreed, but Boland said that he had made up his mind. He added that he didn't like having the SBA president, Dick Ahern, involved in the interview process.

Boland also added that he wanted Velvel to stop sending memos to students—bulletins that updated them on what he was doing at the school. Boland accused him of manipulating students—riling them up. Velvel said that he thought this to be unfair. Many of the students were bitter and suspicious of the school's administration and faculty, following what had happened in the spring. Thus, the dean thought that being up front and honest about the school's progress would ease this tension. Boland vehemently disagreed. If the school had weaknesses, he told Velvel, they were to keep them quiet.

The dean remembered Boland's paranoia from his initial interview. He also believed Boland to resent the fact that so many students liked him. After this encounter, Boland informed the dean that his office was being moved to the basement. He needed the room for more classes, he said. Yet, it seemed clear to Velvel that Boland wanted to remove him from the main flow of traffic in the school.

Though unhappy about being buried in the basement, Velvel continued working on a long list of projects. He increased the library's hours and developed a long-term plan to expand the school's size and number of books and periodicals. He instituted a blind grading system, and he made plans to hire both a placement and a recruitment officer. As well, he asked numerous legal experts around the country to sit on the Board of Trustees. Three agreed, contingent on being protected by liability insurance, which Boland agreed to provide. The installation of trustees was set for January 20—two weeks prior to the school's scheduled inspection by the Board of Regents.

Velvel drew up a new legal structure for the school—rules that governed academic appointments, tenure, salaries, and other matters. He used a common model that divided the power of hiring and firing faculty and staff among the president, dean, full-time faculty, and the Board of Trustees.

Boland objected to the new rules because the faculty could override his decisions. The faculty could veto any decision he made about faculty by a two-thirds majority vote. Also, the Board of Trustees voted on the president's position and set his salary. Boland opposed this, too. He feared the Board would fire him. Thus, he told Velvel that he would have Hale & Dorr, a major law firm in Boston, draw up new rules.

Weeks passed, and Velvel waited while Boland claimed that a new legal structure was being drawn up. Boland kept brushing the issue aside until December 29, when Boland finally told Velvel that he was unhappy with what Hale & Dorr had sent. He would come up with his own rules so he would remain in charge.

At this same meeting, Boland told Velvel that Commonwealth would probably need to hire a hotshot dean as soon as the school sought ABA accreditation. That wouldn't happen for another three to five years, Boland told him. Boland must have seen the anger that rose on the dean's face, because he then assured him that he was a "hell of a guy."

Velvel couldn't believe what he was hearing. All of the events over the last six months became clear to him—the dire warnings from Ahern and Zappala, Boland's own paranoia and evasiveness, and even the attempt not to pay for his moving expenses. Boland planned to use Velvel's credentials simply to gain state approval. Then he would get rid of him.

Velvel was angry and told Boland as much. He said that he never would have moved his family here if he thought this was a temporary position.

Boland replied that the school needed a real powerhouse, someone politically connected to win ABA approval. The dean knew that he was referring to William B. Lawless, the former dean of Notre Dame Law School and president of Western State University College of Law, in California, the largest private law school in California and the third largest private law school in the nation. It had 2,200 students. Shortly before Velvel was hired, Boland told the students that he had hired Lawless as a consultant on legal education, telling them that Lawless would "oversee all legal issues related to Commonwealth's attainment of accreditation by the Massachusetts Board of Regents and eventual approval by the American Bar Association."

Naturally, Velvel assumed, based on his conversations with Bard and then Boland, that once he was hired, he would assume full academic stewardship of the school. He had never met Lawless, and, as far as he knew, Lawless had never even been to the school. Still Boland claimed to be consulting with the California dean on a regular basis. Having previously caught the school president being dishonest (e.g., claiming to have forgotten his agreement to pay Velvel's moving expenses), Velvel wondered how often Boland talked with Lawless. In fact, he began wondering if Lawless' name was merely a threat that he hauled out and used whenever he needed to settle a debate in his own favor. (Later Lawless denied ever being Boland's consultant.)

Once Boland left, Velvel pulled out a yellow pad of paper and began writing. He wrote down every word of their conversation, just as he remembered it. Over the years, he had learned to do that—to take copious notes, which might protect him if there would be a dispute later. It also enabled him to channel his feelings, to express what he felt, even if he couldn't say it out loud. As he finished up the fourth page, he wrote clearly, as if reaching a new revelation, "I don't think he [Boland] is to be trusted. He's paranoid about being shoved out and about losing power, and I think he will change horses or deans if it suits his purpose. I damn well better watch out." Things had turned out exactly as Ahern had predicted.

*****

When Velvel returned to the school after the holidays, on Monday, January 4, 1988, he found the janitor busy with tools and a ladder. He was installing a television monitoring system on the ceiling outside of Velvel's office.

Curious, Velvel asked the janitor, "They record just motion, don't they?"

"No, sound too," he replied.

Later that day, Velvel asked Boland for more information about the cameras. The school president claimed that there had been a theft at the school over the weekend. Boland said he had been working late, and at around 1 a.m. he heard noises. He left his office to see what was going on, and he saw that a computer terminal and typewriter had been stolen. He decided then that he should install cameras that record movement in the building.

Velvel informed him that secret recordings of sound were an invasion of privacy and that most states had laws restricting their use. At minimum, they would have to tell students about it, Velvel said. No, Boland replied. They wouldn't.

All day, Velvel thought about the cameras. He realized how ludicrous the whole camera idea was. The halls of the school were dark at night. The cameras would record only shadows, even if a thief entered the building. For a security device to be effective, it needed to be connected to an alarm system or, better yet, to police dispatch. Boland wasn't going to do that.

The legality of the recordings also troubled Velvel. He called several lawyers and judges who confirmed that secret recordings of private conversations violated state wiretap laws. Violators could be sent to jail for up to five years. When the dean explained this to Boland, he said that he would turn the sound off.

"That's not enough," Velvel said. "Anyone can turn the sound back on." It didn't matter. Boland wasn't going to budge.

Later that day, the janitor returned to Velvel's office to speak with him. "Mike really chewed me out for telling you that the cameras pick up sound," he said. "I thought it was OK to tell you. I mean, you're the dean, after all."

In the basement, Velvel thought about this. He realized some time ago that Boland had no respect for his students. Recently he learned that he had no respect for him as a dean, either. But now he realized something new: Boland had no respect for the law—the very subject his school taught. What a strange irony, Velvel thought. Would the state license a law school that deliberately violated the law?

*****

By spring of 1988, Richard Ahern had spent approximately $5,000 on tuition at Commonwealth. What concerned him more than the money was the time he had invested. He couldn't even count the nights of sleep he'd given up for reading, working on papers, and preparing for classes. He had done all that in hopes of achieving a better life as a lawyer, moving up a notch in the world.

However, once Boland had hidden the Board of Regents' report, back in May 1987, he and the other students knew that continuing at Commonwealth would be a gamble. Even though Boland had promised to fix the school and claimed to have hired an educational consultant and to be searching for a qualified dean, Ahern lost faith in the school president.

Ahern liked the dean. He considered him to be a bit naïve in dealing with Boland, but he had a contract and a signed agreement to improve the school. Velvel had shown it to him. He respected Velvel for his legal credentials, and he believed that if anyone could bring the school up to state standards, Velvel could.

With that in mind, Ahern enrolled in the fall semester at Commonwealth. He became president of the Student Bar Association so he could stay on top of the school's progress in obtaining a state license. When he saw oversights and inadequacies, he told students. He decided to keep the students riled up to ensure that progress would continue.

Ahern figured that under his close scrutiny, Boland couldn't weasel out of improving the school. However, as 1988 started, and the spring semester was about to begin, with the Board of Regents' inspection only three weeks away, Ahern saw the school was still not ready. He knew that the dean had been working hard, but so much of what he had tried to do failed because Boland either refused to implement his suggestions or didn't follow through with plans. As far as Ahern could see, the school faced the same problems as with its last inspection. Simply put, Boland made all the decisions and controlled the school.

In mid-January, Ahern caught Boland in the hall and asked him several questions: When is the Board of Trustees going to be installed? What is the status of the liability insurance for board members? What improvements are being made to the library? Are new books and periodicals going to be added before state inspection? Are chairs and tables going to be added in the library? Annoyed, Boland told him to put his questions in writing. Ahern did that and sent the president a two-page memo listing his apprehensions about the upcoming inspection.

In concluding his memo, he reiterated a phrase Boland had often used, "When compared to Southern New England's [Board of Regents' inspection] report, we look like Harvard Law School." "But," Ahern added, "the real question is going to be, when compared to Harvard, do we look like Southern New England? Have we progressed far enough?" Ahern didn't think so. He knew that other students didn't think so either.

When a response didn't come right away, Ahern thought about Boland. What made him so secretive and evasive? He had claimed to be a successful teacher and businessman, but no one ever checked to be sure. Did he possibly have a criminal past? That would be devastating to the school. The Board of Regents would never license it. Ahern now knew what he had to do. He would run a background check on Boland.

*****

Boland's cameras were up and rolling on Saturday, January 16, 1988—registration day at Commonwealth. The cameras were mounted on the ceiling, but most students didn't look up that far. They were talking with one another, registering for classes, buying books, and writing checks. Even the most observant students didn't think twice about the cameras. They looked like any other security system installed in a mall or bank.

That day, Boland made sure everything ran smoothly as students put their money down on the next semester. Tuition was Commonwealth's only source of revenue, and the school needed the money to pay salaries and bills. Velvel suspected that the school had a cash flow problem, even though he had never seen the school's financial records. His paychecks were always late, and he figured Boland needed to hold onto the money as long as possible.

Later that day, when Velvel met with Boland and Talkington, the dean found them uncharacteristically generous. They agreed to raise professors' salaries—up to $45,000. As well, they agreed to spend money on a student recruitment program. Just before the meeting ended, Boland mentioned in an off-handed way that he would be adding local businessmen and attorneys to the Board of Trustees.

Velvel was surprised. Boland hadn't secured liability insurance for the trustees that they had already invited to the Board.

"How many?" he asked.

"Three."

Velvel paused. His employment contract specifically stated that they would select Board members together. However, Boland made it clear over the last few months that he would renege on that. That's why Boland had waited until the last minute to spring this news on him.

The next day, Velvel found a memo from Boland in his mailbox. It was dated January 16, the day before. He read, "Please be advised that I have secured commitments from nine local businessmen, attorneys, and individuals dedicated to quality legal education in this area. With the individuals you have recommended, this will bring the membership up to 15 members." Boland's total included the three trustees whom Velvel had already invited, as well as Boland, Talkington, and Velvel.

The dean couldn't believe what he was reading. Boland had just said that he had selected three trustees; yet, the real number was nine. Clearly, Boland would take control over the Board. Velvel wasn't going to accept that.

He confronted Boland and told him that he would reject his appointments, as he had the right to do under his employment agreement. Boland replied that he didn't care. He didn't intend to turn his future and that of the school over to a Board.

Velvel suggested that he sign a long-term contract with the school.

Boland replied that a contract could be easily broken. It sounded cavalier, Velvel thought, coming from the head of a law school. Despite their differences, Velvel wanted to compromise. He suggested that Boland name three or four trustees, including himself and Talkington. In turn, Velvel would name an equal number, including himself and a couple of others. Then they would mutually decide on one tie-breaking trustee. In the dean's mind, this was a huge compromise. He realized that the Board wouldn't be the fully independent, unbiased board that they had agreed to have, but a compromise would resolve the problem—at least for the moment—enabling them to move on so that they could install the Board and be ready for inspection.

When Boland didn't say anything, Velvel asked if he could at least meet and speak with Boland's nominees. And Velvel would do the same: Boland could speak with Velvel's candidates. It sounded reasonable, so Boland agreed to that.

However, Boland never shared his list of candidates with Velvel. Thus, the dean drafted a memo to the school president: "At the present time, I think it is essential for the future of the school and the students who have invested extensive time and money that we find some way to reach a compromise on the

Board of Trustees. I would welcome receipt of a list of proposed
Board members from you . . . . I do think it is crucial that the
Board be fairly comprised . . . ."

Later that day, Velvel found an envelope addressed to him in
his mailbox. He opened it up and found his memo torn to shreds.
What kind of person would do this? he wondered. It was
insulting and childish. Velvel returned to his office and found
Dick Ahern, looking as somber as a pallbearer, standing in his
doorway. He motioned for the dean to close the door.

He told Velvel that he had been researching Boland's background. According to police records, Boland had been charged, in
1979, with indecent assault and battery of a child under age 14.
Though the charges were dismissed, he was presently dating a
high school girl—someone who was listed as a runaway with the
Department of Social Services. In addition, in 1986, there had
been a fire in his barn that had killed four horses. Investigators
found it suspicious. When he placed an insurance claim for
$140,000 worth of law books, carpets, and other items, the insur-
ance company refused to pay. They claimed none of those items
were there.

If Boland were the moral character role model for the school,
they were in trouble, Ahern suggested. Lawyers, who are considered to be officers of the court, are required to be of good moral
character even to sit for the bar.

How would the Board of Regents look upon a person with
such a background leading a law school? They stared at each
other, in the the cool, silent basement, and realized that the school
would never make it as long as Boland was in charge.

*****

As Diane Sullivan, now a second-year student at Commonwealth, left Worcester and drove down the slush-covered high-
way into Lowell, the needle on the car's speedometer moved
steadily up. When friends remarked on the amount of driving she

did, Sullivan would laugh and say, "Fortunately, I'm a fast driver." To her, fast driving was a talent, like walking fast, talking fast, or writing fast. Moving quickly enabled her to accomplish more in a day. As she headed into Lowell, she kept mulling over the call she had received the night before from her friend Al Zappala.

"The dean is going to be fired," he told her.

"That's crazy," she replied. Boland couldn't fire the dean. The school had to have a dean for the state inspection, which was only two weeks away.

"He's going to be fired," Zappala repeated. In recent months, he had become friendly with Boland, believing this would give him valuable insights into the workings of the school. When he heard that the dean and Boland had fought over board appointees, he tried to persuade Boland to share his list of appointees with the dean. The school president replied that it was unnecessary. He was firing him.

"This will look bad to the Board of Regents," Zappala told him. "I think that you should compromise. Let me help you work it out with him."

Boland refused. He had already contacted Judy Jackson, who had been a finalist for the deanship in the spring.

As Zappala relayed this story, Sullivan couldn't believe what he told her. Without a dean, the school would never receive a license. It looked as if Boland purposely waited until students had invested money in the spring semester before making his move. Boland didn't give refunds, either.

Devastated, Sullivan told Zappala, "I don't want to be a failure." While Commonwealth's problems weren't her fault, she chose to attend a second-rate law school because it was affordable and accessible. She had made a poor choice.

As Sullivan pulled into Commonwealth's parking lot, she felt better seeing Zappala's car. She hoped he had better news.

In the library, she found Zappala. "So, what's the latest?" she asked.

"Shhh," Zappala hissed, pointing overhead. "The place is bugged."

Sullivan looked over her shoulder. To her amazement, she found a camera pointed at her.

"It records sound," he whispered.

Though she had always detested this building, now it felt bone-chillingly cold. They were being monitored. *Why?* she wondered. *Why was Boland so paranoid? Normal people didn't act this way,* she thought. *Was he involved in something perverted or illegal?*

"Do the police know about this?" she whispered.

Zappala shrugged. "Doubt it."

"Let's get out of here," she said with a shiver, looking tentatively over her shoulder.

As they headed to class and mingled with professors and students, Zappala whispered one last thing, "There's going to be a meeting on Saturday. Dick Ahern has put it together so students can talk with the Dean. Whatever you do, don't miss it."

Sullivan nodded. She would be there.

*****

As bleak as everything appeared, Zappala kept thinking there had to be a way to salvage this. The dean was going to be fired, and once that happened, the school would lose all respect with state inspectors and be denied its license once again. The only way he and the other students would be able to get their law degrees would be to try to enter another school and start over.

What school would take them—older, working students who needed to attend school at nights and on weekends? Not one law school in the area would allow them to transfer credits from Commonwealth. None. They would have to start all over, from scratch. Zappala didn't want to do that. This was his third attempt to obtain a law degree.

That's when it hit him. He could start his own law school. It was a business like all the other businesses. He knew that he could do it. The more he thought about it, the more intoxicating the idea seemed. He just needed to convince the dean and the other students to join him.

Zappala found the dean in his office. He entered and closed the door. "Larry, you're going to get canned," he said, speaking bluntly, as he often did.

Velvel looked up. He was surprised but then shook his head. "No, I don't think so."

Zappala sat down in a chair facing him. With his arms folded over his chest and his legs stretching out before him, he eyed the dean. "Boland's been bad-mouthing you from the day you started here. It's all been planned from the start. He told me so. You're going to get canned, mark my words."

The dean stared at him.

"I think we should form our own school," Zappala said.

As if the student had told a joke, the dean responded with a short laugh.

"No, I'm serious," Zappala said, not wanting to be dismissed. "We can do this. We can run a law school—certainly better than Boland."

Velvel twisted his face into a half-smile. "Okay, I'll keep that in mind."

Zappala knew that the dean wasn't taking him seriously, but this wasn't a joke. Soon the dean would find out. In the meantime, Zappala made a list of what he had to do. He would look for a building to rent, make lists of supplies and materials, and look for financial resources. Not only that, he would begin passing the word around about the new school.

*****

On Thursday, Velvel was in Texas working on a case that he'd started back in Washington. In his hotel room that evening, the telephone rang. Louise was on the other end, her voice frantic,

"Larry Beeferman just called. He says that you've been fired."

The dean immediately called Beeferman, who told him that Boland had held a faculty meeting that day. He announced that he would be firing the dean and listed various reasons: the dean was never there; he hadn't prepared a faculty manual or a discipline code; the legal guidelines for the school were no good; and he had discussed private school matters with students. Boland told them that he would tell the dean on Saturday and give him a chance to resign.

"This will be catastrophic to the school," Beeferman had told Boland at the meeting. "How will you explain it to state inspectors? Won't they look at the dean's performance and question why you fired him?" After all, one of the Board of Regents' inspectors, Bob Bard, referred Velvel to this school.

That didn't concern Boland. He said that he'd get rid of Bard—he'd ask for a different inspector.

As he listened to Beeferman's story, Velvel was quiet, though he raged inside. Damn Boland, he thought. Hadn't he tried getting along with him? Hadn't he accepted Boland's paranoia and tried to work around it? He had given in and compromised. He had worked tirelessly at trying to bring respectability to this slip-shod school, but Boland fought him every step of the way, put obstacles in front of him, and now Boland blamed him for everything. Damn him.

Then the dean looked at a pattern of confrontations he had had with his superiors. Perhaps, he thought, the confrontations were his fault. Perhaps they revealed a character flaw. Perhaps they were the reason why his honest efforts had been thwarted. Perhaps he couldn't get along with anyone. Then, as if by epiphany and contrary to the guilt and self-blame that had been drilled into him since childhood, he considered a different truth, one closer to reality. Others had pushed him down, stabbed him in the back. This had started in his last years in Kansas and continued after he returned to Washington. People thought him to be a powerless, nice-guy pushover.

All he had ever wanted to do was make a decent living and do the right thing. All of his efforts to do that had been stymied. Now, in the silence of a hotel room in Texas, 1,500 miles from home, he finally understood that there was no place in the world for nice guys. As Leo Durocher had put it, "Nice guys finish last."

That depressed him. His parents had so drilled into him the necessity of being a nice and modest person that he acted instinctively this way. When he experienced setbacks, he usually chastised himself and pointed to personal character flaws that led to the disaster. Now he wondered how his life might have been different if his parents hadn't been idealistic Labor Zionists who believed in social justice and taught him to think well of all people. If he had been born to different parents, he might have been raised with characteristics necessary to survive and succeed in America—ruthlessness, self-promotion, and a suspicious nature. Then again, perhaps his parents had had nothing to do with it, and he himself was just a headstrong jerk too concerned about trying to do what he thought was the right thing. Perhaps he just was unable to get along with people, although in his heart he didn't really believe that to be true.

Whatever the truth, over the years Velvel had learned that the only way out of these problems was to develop a battle plan. He wasn't sure what he would do about Boland and the job at Commonwealth, but he decided that he would no longer be a nice guy. He would stop that. Now he was going to be like every other no-good son-of-a-bitch in the world. He would be the meanest bastard on the block, and he'd let people know that up front, before they got started with him. If he came across like a drill sergeant having a bad day, then so be it.

If he was going to be fired, then so be that, too. He would fly home and pack up his office, and confront Boland on Saturday, but he wouldn't resign. No way. Boland would have to force him out. Not only that, he decided that he would go before the entire student body on Saturday and tell them the truth about what he had tried to do for Commonwealth and what Boland had done.

He would have his say, and he would forewarn students not to believe Boland.

He couldn't sleep and thus began writing what he would say.

*****

January 23, 1988, was a cold, dreary Saturday, and approximately 150 students jammed into the school's largest classroom. Like the game "Telephone," each student had previously heard something from others about the dean and the school. Everyone knew something important was about to happen.

Diane Sullivan entered the room feeling confused. Students stood shoulder-to-shoulder, beads of sweat rising on their brows, and fists clenched. The room was chaotic, a cacophony of sounds. Some students were shouting, shaking their fingers at one another, fiercely debating. Some were shouting that the dean didn't know what he was doing. He was trying to shove Boland out. Other students said no, the dean had tried to improve the school, but Boland held him back and had deceived him.

Dizzy, as if the world had suddenly spun in reverse, Sullivan looked around and saw chaos. John Cascarano, the student who dug clams to earn his tuition money, announced that he was quitting. Zappala talked of forming his own school, which sounded crazy. It was pure bedlam. Everyone spoke irrationally.

At last, Ahern came in. His face was red, as if he had run five miles. He addressed the students, shouting that he didn't trust Boland last spring and that he didn't trust him now. He was quitting, he said, and he suggested that other students do the same. There were shouts and cries around the room. Then he told the crowd that the dean wanted to speak.

Velvel, quiet and composed, stood before them, papers in hand. Scattered applause could be heard. He told the crowd that he had been fired. He recounted events leading up to his dismissal—what he had done and Boland's response or lack of response. He outlined how he had improved the school over the past five months and what he would have done had he stayed or had Boland not hindered him. Once he had finished, he, Ahern, and Zappala left the room.

Outside the building, Velvel said to them, "Okay, I'm ready to start that new school. What do we need to do?" He looked at the two of them.

Though Zappala had been the first to approach Velvel with the idea, Ahern wasn't far behind him. When he realized that the dean was going to be fired, he had said to him, "If you promise not to move away and take another job, I know that we can start our own school."

Velvel turned to the two businessmen and with a sense of urgency asked, "So when can we begin starting a school? Tomorrow?"

Zappala and Ahern looked at each other and were struck for the first time at what a crazy idea this really was. After all, setting up a law school would cost thousands of dollars, maybe millions. (The ABA said it cost $10 million to $50 million to start such a school.) Who knew how much it would cost? They didn't have millions or even tens of thousands of dollars. All they had was a dream—and confidence that they could run a law school— certainly, they thought they could do it better than Boland did.

*****

Hours after the dean's speech at Commonwealth, Ahern and Zappala called Sullivan at home and urged her to call Velvel. She didn't want to do it. "What am I going say?" she asked. She hardly knew the dean, and she wasn't even sure that she wanted to commit herself to such a far-fetched idea. As vice president at Commerce Bank, which financed businesses, she knew how expensive and risky a new venture could be. She couldn't imagine how the four of them would pull it off.

Yet Sullivan felt she could not refuse her friends. She called the Dean and explained that she planned to continue with her classes at Commonwealth. She had paid for the semester. Even so, she would help him start a new school.

Velvel asked if they could meet at her bank in Worcester. She agreed. OK, he said. They would be there tomorrow.

*****

As Zappala and Velvel drove on Route 290 to Worcester, Zappala was certain they had to be crazy to be out on such a treacherous night. Sleet flew horizontally, freezing as it hit the windshield, coating the wiper blades until they barely moved.

No, Zappala thought, they weren't mad. They were desperate. They couldn't let a blizzard stop them that night from meeting Sullivan, a group of Commonwealth students, and Karen Edwards, the Commonwealth librarian. They had to work fast to get this new school off the ground.

As Zappala saw it, he and the dean made a great team. The dean provided academic smarts, intellectual guidance, curriculum knowledge, legal expertise, and connections for forming a Board of Trustees. They needed all of these things. He provided the nuts and bolts business knowledge and would set up the physical plant.

At the bank, Velvel divided up tasks between the students. He jotted notes on a legal-sized tablet. Sullivan, John Lakin, and Zappala agreed to look for financing. To incorporate the school, Lakin said he would find an attorney. In addition, he offered to recruit students. Velvel said he would draw up a legal structure, talk to Bard and Weston, and work on a catalog.

Velvel assigned tasks to everyone, even to people not there. His wife Louise was given the job of designing application forms. Dick Ahern was to look for a meeting place. After an hour, Velvel closed his legal pad, which contained their "to do" list.

More snow had drifted over the cars in the parking lot, and the roads were ice covered. The two men headed back down Route 290 and talked about timing and the logistics of opening the new school. It had to be ready by fall—less than seven months away. Law students would either lose interest or apply to other schools if they didn't act immediately. Zappala and Velvel decided that they needed a building immediately.

Just then a car ahead of them spun out of control. It turned completely around, crossed three lanes of traffic and came straight towards them.

"Oh my God," Zappala said, realizing that there was little he could do. To either slam on the brakes or turn the wheel sharply meant throwing the car into a spin, which would inevitably make the situation worse.

"Nice and easy," Velvel said quietly.

Easy? They were about to die, Zappala thought. Still there was something reassuring about his words. Velvel repeated, "Nice and easy."

Both cars stopped, practically bumper-to-bumper. Less than six inches separated them. It struck them as a miracle. Had the crash occurred, Zappala thought, their plans would have ended. Being given this chance to continue with their plans struck Zappala as prophetic. He believed this law school was meant to be.

Chapter 4

Birth of a Law School

The mood at Commonwealth was somber following Black Saturday. In describing it to Velvel, Professor Shoshanna Ehrlich described a general pall over students, as if "a death had occurred." Students were confused. They didn't know whether to quit or stay.

John Cascarano took a leave of absence, claiming financial hardship. "I have been financing my tuition from day one," Cascarano wrote in a note to Boland. "Now I am broke." He figured any more money spent at Commonwealth would be wasted. He didn't believe the Board of Regents would ever approve the school.

When Daniel R. Perkins, a first-year student, told Boland that he was withdrawing, he was told that the school didn't have a withdrawal policy for first-year students. Thus, he would receive all Fs. Despite the threat, he withdrew and demanded a refund.

At the same time, Professor Larry Beeferman wrote a letter to Boland, echoing the sentiments of many of the students as well as the professors: "Recent events merely crystallized what had been my developing perception that the school would not be a hospitable place for me to pursue an academic career." He informed Boland that he would finish the semester but no more.

Karen Edwards, Shoshanna Ehrlich, Michael Coyne, and Paula Dickinson did the same thing. They felt obligated to finish courses underway, but they wouldn't return. A week after Black Saturday, 25 students had resigned from Commonwealth, and almost all of the faculty informed Boland that they would be leaving.

*****

Al Zappala warned students at Commonwealth that they were likely to end up as "orphans," a term used to describe individuals who had attended an unapproved law school that failed to obtain a license or had closed. Such students ended up either without a degree or with a degree that still didn't enable them to sit for the bar and practice law. They could start over at another school, but in all likelihood, they would face the same obstacles that had prevented them from entering those schools in the first place: cost, distance, admissions tests, or poor undergraduate grades. Further complicating the problem, most established schools would not transfer credits from unaccredited schools. The ABA wouldn't allow it.

Students at Laclede School of Law found themselves in a similar predicament in 1985. Laclede began on the Webster College campus in St. Louis County in 1978 and was Missouri's only night law school. Though a number of students had completed their course work, they couldn't sit for the state bar because the school wasn't ABA accredited, a requirement to sit for the bar exam in Missouri, as in most states.

Dean Noah Weinstein, a retired circuit court judge, never applied for ABA accreditation. To meet the ABA's standards, the school needed anywhere from $10 million to $50 million to pay for a large full-time faculty and a comprehensive library. Laclede didn't have that kind of money. Instead, students had access to two major law libraries, and the school employed 18 part-time practicing lawyers and judges as teachers.

Taking a different tack, Weinstein asked the Missouri Supreme Court to waive the state's requirement of ABA accreditation so that Laclede students could sit for the bar. The Supreme Court agreed to look into it, and, in June 1984 an investigating board found that the Laclede School of Law adequately prepared students to practice law. The board recommended that Laclede be granted a two-year provisional waiver, so that those who had already graduated could sit for the bar exam. The Missouri Bar and the ABA vehemently objected, and the Missouri Supreme Court ultimately turned down the waiver request.

Searching for yet another way around the problem, in February 1986, Weinstein initiated state legislation that gave the state Board of Education the power to accredit state law schools. Thus, four years after some students had graduated from Laclede, they were able to take the bar exam. They were lucky. Their law degrees could have forever remained worthless, leaving them unable to ever sit for the bar and practice law.

That is what Zappala told students could happen to them at Commonwealth. He announced that he was quitting in order to launch a new law school. He hoped that his classmates would join him. At 4 o'clock on Wednesday, January 27, Zappala entered Commonwealth's administrative office where Boland, Talkington, Kropp, and Judy Jackson (who had been named dean the day before) were sitting. He informed them that he was leaving Commonwealth.

"I'm going to start a competitive school right here in Lowell, and I'm going to tell the whole student body about it," said Zappala, who watched the color drain from Boland's face. The school president now faced his worst fear—students, professors, and staff were leaving en masse to a competing school.

Boland tried his best to appear unconcerned and asked, "Will you be accepting credits from Commonwealth?"

Zappala nodded, but he couldn't say how many.

Talkington told him that he would fail.

Jackson looked at him blankly and said nothing.

In a surprise move, Boland extended his hand. "Good luck," he said, sounding sincere. It struck Zappala as a genuine expression of friendship, which, under the circumstances, surprised him.

Zappala shook his hand and headed out the door. *Damn*, he thought, leaving the building. This was the third time that he had quit law school. To get his law degree now, he would have to build a law school. He shook his head, laughing at himself. What a strange turn of events this had been.

*****

Students at Commonwealth posed the question that Boland had asked: *Would the new school accept Commonwealth credits?* Some students had looked into going to Suffolk University Law School, Franklin Pierce Law Center, or Western New England School of Law. Some had offers, but the reality remained: none of their Commonwealth credits were transferable. All the money they had spent and all their hard work would be lost. This was a particularly bitter thought for students like John Cascarano, who had worked four part-time jobs to scrape together tuition money.

Velvel realized that receiving credits from a school like Commonwealth wasn't a great way to begin a law school. He wasn't even sure that the Board of Regents would approve of this, but he had to help these students salvage their legal education.

"You dance with the girl that brung you" was an old saying that ran through his mind. It fit Commonwealth's students, who were different from most law students he had met. They were older, in their 30s and 40s, and planned to begin a second career in the legal profession. Most of them had not taken the LSAT and would not have performed well on it if they had. They knew that. They had not attended fancy private schools or "elite" public colleges that might have prepared them for such a test. To them, college prepared them for better jobs, which they hoped would lead them out of their hardscrabble, hand-to-mouth existence.

Many of the students were like Sullivan, saving what little money they could in order to pay bills and their tuition. Wasting time and money was a luxury they couldn't afford. That philosophy applied to seeking legal education too. They couldn't conceive of squandering time and money on courses like "Law and Literature," which was offered by many law schools serving upper-middle and upper-class law students.

Students coming from Commonwealth wanted practical courses, which taught them everyday law skills, such as Drafting Contracts, Drafting Wills and Trusts, and Interviewing and Counseling. They wanted courses that taught them how to compose legal documents, including drafting complaints, answers, discovery requests, motions to dismiss, jury instructions, and motions for summary judgment. They wanted to know how, from beginning to end, to handle a case, how to meet with clients, to investigate, to gather information, to pick a jury, to deliver instructions, to argue before a judge, and to present closing arguments.

They needed to know it all because, in all likelihood, they would be working for themselves. They couldn't and didn't plan to enter major law firms and spend the next seven to 10 years being coached. They planned to hit the ground running. From day one, they needed to be able to arbitrate, mediate, debate, interview, and counsel. They needed to do all that, plus run their own law businesses.

Velvel was developing a curriculum that would cover that and more. He aimed for the school's courses to be both practical and intellectual. At the University of Michigan, Professors Peterson and Gindin had taught him the importance of training the mind. At the new school, professors would teach by the Socratic method—asking questions rather than lecturing. Students would be forced to participate extensively in class. Velvel wanted them to learn to think, to probe deeply, to organize their thoughts, and to be able to think and speak on their feet.

Having worked with Commonwealth students for five

months, Velvel began to understand how different they were from law students at Michigan, Kansas, or Catholic University. These differences had to be addressed in the school's admission policies (among other things, the school couldn't subject them to the LSAT) and in its curriculum. Certainly he was in favor of making legal education more practical and less esoteric.

One thing he knew for certain: tuition at the new school would need to be low, as it had been at Commonwealth. The school would charge only $8,000 a year for full-time students—half of what many other schools charged. To offer legal education at that price, Velvel and the founding students knew they had to keep costs low and operate efficiently. Initially the school would hire only four full-time faculty members, and it would rely heavily on adjunct professors—practicing lawyers and judges who earned most of their livings outside of academia. Faculty salaries would have to start off low, but they would go up as students enrolled and tuition monies came in.

The ABA claimed that it was impossible to offer both a high-quality and low-tuition legal education. But Velvel was certain he could do both. He believed students could receive an equally good education sitting in a $10 chair as in a $350 chair, the type used by many ABA schools. He believed the same information found in $50, $75, or $100 books could be retrieved electronically at a fraction of the price. There were logical ways of reducing spending that didn't shortchange students. However, the ABA and its schools deliberately chose the high-cost, high-tuition way of operating.

In addition, Velvel sought to inculcate ethics in law students. He considered legal ethics so important that he wanted it addressed in every course. Most ABA schools addressed it only once in one course. Morals, which sometimes led to different results than did ethics, ultimately would be discussed in every course too. Velvel also wanted law students to have the opportunity to specialize, as they could in other types of post-graduate schools.

Traditional in some ways, innovative in others is how Velvel envisioned the school. He would put into action some of the ideas expressed in the journal article that he had written in 1978. Ultimately, Velvel wanted a much-better-than-average law school. In fact, he wanted a school that served as a model for other law schools, that wanted to serve the less privileged, to emulate.

*****

Each week, Velvel sat in the Lowell Press Club surrounded by students and faculty members, with a yellow legal pad in front of him. On it were specific jobs with students' names and dates next to them. He kept everyone accountable for the tasks that they had agreed to do. The dates indicated when the students or faculty members were expected, or had promised, to complete the task. To Velvel's thinking, keeping a list of tasks was the best way to keep the momentum going and keep everyone on track. With four months left to open the school, everyone had to move quickly.

In students and faculty, Velvel infused a rallying spirit. Each person realized the responsibility of holding up this fragile structure; if one didn't hold up his weight, the whole thing could topple. No one wanted to risk disappointing Velvel, Zappala, Ahern, Sullivan, Dickinson, Beeferman, and all his or her classmates.

Velvel went down the list. "Contacting students. That's John Lakin, isn't it?"

Lakin told the crowd that he had been calling students at Commonwealth and recruiting them.

"Building . . . Dick?"

Finding a building had become a two-person task, involving both Dick Ahern and Al Zappala. A building would show that their idea was far more than a half-cocked dream. Plus, it would give them a place to meet and stage fund-raisers. Ahern wanted to keep the school either in Lowell or near it. He proposed calling it the Lowell School of Law, thinking that local politicians and developers would support it if it were named after the city. The name Lowell School of Law resonated with many people, so newsletters, napkins, and buttons were so printed, even though the group hadn't found the right space yet.

In the 1980s, U.S. Senator Paul Tsongas initiated a crusade to revitalize Lowell. He had convinced Congress to spend $40 million in building the Lowell National Historical State Park. Plans included converting several of Lowell's mills into museums and refurbishing the old canal system. Another $350 million in public and private funds were added to the pot, and, by 1984, the Spindle City was put back on its feet. Unemployment dropped to four percent—half the national average. Tsongas had performed a miracle, locals thought.

As part of the renewal of Lowell, a number of Lowell's mills were being renovated in 1988. They included Appleton Mills, a 19th-century textile mill, which was expected to be ready by August—a tight time frame to properly set up the school. Of greater concern to Zappala was the cost of finishing the space, which would require money they didn't have.

Shortly after looking at Appleton Mills, Zappala found the perfect building, but in Andover—15 minutes from Lowell but just 30 minutes from Boston. A bank was about to foreclose on a newly-renovated mill building owned by Jordan Burgess, who desperately needed another tenant to avoid the foreclosure.

Zappala looked at Burgess' long, red brick building in Dundee Park, a former mill complex. It sat only 200 yards from a commuter train line that went to and from Boston. It offered nearly 20,000 square feet of space, spread out over two floors. Large windows filled the rooms with natural sunlight. The space was clean and open, with exposed brick and beautiful oak wood around the offices. Heating, air conditioning, and carpeting existed. It was in move-in condition. The law school needed only to construct a few more walls for classrooms.

Burgess agreed to make some needed changes with a slight adjustment in rent. Also, he agreed to let the new law school, at no charge, use the space throughout the summer to recruit and set up the library and classrooms.

Dick Ahern wasn't happy about not being in Lowell. He anticipated negative political repercussions. But they had no other choice, as far as Zappala could tell. They were running out of time and needed to settle on a place quickly. Being in Andover, not Lowell, the school needed a new name, and John Lakin suggested that they call it the Massachusetts School of Law.

*****

Because tuition payments were not due until August, the school's founders had no operating cash. Nor did the students or professors any personal money to dip into. An accountant itemized line by line what they would need. He projected that the school would need $813,000 its first year. Salaries, library books, and rent topped the list of expenses. To raise money, the students hosted a couple of social events, charging $25 a person. That raised a few thousand dollars, which paid for some photocopying and postage. They had no idea how they would pay for major expenses. Sullivan arranged for Zappala and Velvel to meet with the chairman of Commerce Bank, Bill Roberts, to discuss financing.

After analyzing their proposal, he asked, "What kind of seed money do you have?"

Zappala replied, "$5,000." He referred to the $2,500 that he and Velvel kicked in initially to start the project.

"You need more like $250,000," the banker told them. "You need to be able to survive at least two years. It's not a lot of money, really. Look, you can raise $250,000 if you reach the right people." He suggested that they approach area high-tech companies, such as Wang, Digital, and Raytheon. After they did that, then they could come back.

After Velvel and Zappala tried Roberts' suggestion and turned up nothing, Velvel saw only one option left. He withdrew his entire savings from the bank, a total of $20,000, and lent it to the school. In addition, he and Zappala went to the bank and obtained a $160,000 line of credit, using Velvel's condominium as collateral. Now everything Velvel owned was riding on this venture.

*****

Quijotesco. That was the way law student Juan Ortiz saw Zappala and Velvel's efforts to build the law school. It was a romantic, Don Quixote-like notion. Yet to stay at Commonwealth was foolish. That became clear to him and his fellow students.

"Juan, you've got to do this," Zappala said to him, urging him to quit Commonwealth and join their efforts to build a new law school. Oritz trusted Zappala. They had been in a study group with Diane Sullivan, which resulted in a bond among the three that went beyond law studies. None of them were kids. They had experienced all kinds of hard knocks, and legal education opened the door to a new life full of hopes and dreams.

Born in Puerto Rico, Ortiz had moved to the United States when he was 16 and settled in Framingham, Massachusetts. When his father became ill, Ortiz dropped out of high school. To support his family, he worked in a restaurant. At 19, he went to Vietnam, and in combat there he lost hearing in his left ear. Partially deaf, he spoke with an accent that sometimes made it hard for others to understand him.

On the GI Bill, Ortiz attended college, earning As and a degree in literature. "So what's next? A master's? A doctorate?" his professors asked. One suggested law school. Ortiz liked the idea. So when he saw the ad for Commonwealth School of Law, he quit his job with the State Bureau of Special Investigations and signed up.

Following Zappala's advice, in the summer of 1988, Ortiz helped out at the Massachusetts School of Law. The space was open and bare—just a floor and ceiling. Yet, with the enthusiasm of an illusionist, Zappala took prospective students to a spot on the floor and said, "See this. Here will be the library." There was nothing to see, but Zappala could visualize it. When the student prospects asked about books, shelves, tables, and chairs that were obviously missing, he assured them that they were ordered. Everything would be there by opening day, just a couple of months away.

Once MSL had a building, the school needed students. Zappala had calculated carefully. If 50 students transferred from Commonwealth and 50 new students enrolled, the school would have 100 students—just enough to meet expenses. Zappala hoped to attract another 50 students in the spring, bringing the total up to 150 students and putting MSL squarely in the black.

To recruit students, Ahern devised a poster with peel-off coupons attached. Interested prospects could fill out the forms and mail them in, generating a list for the school to use for making calls and mailing school catalogs.

Each day, Ortiz got up early and distributed posters throughout Massachusetts, as well as in New Hampshire and Maine. He placed them in police stations, firehouses, city halls, high-tech companies, senior centers, and colleges—anywhere he could find people ready to make a big change.

Right away, the coupons came back. The mail was full of them. Ortiz placed them in a loose-leaf notebook, pasting as many as could fit on both sides of a page. In no time at all, the notebook was at least three inches thick.

The school also advertised in newspapers. Velvel's son Douglas who had just graduated from Brandeis University, near Boston, sat in the school's building day after day in the hot summer, with no air conditioning, answering phone calls and recruiting students. Everyone had to chip in and help out. That's the only way that MSL could be ready for opening day.

*****

Two months before MSL enrolled its first students, the

Massachusetts Board of Regents met on June 22, 1988, at the
McCormack State Office Building in Boston. Dick Ahern, along
with several MSL students, attended the meeting. They wanted to
see how the Board of Regents voted on Southern New England
School of Law's request for approval of its program. Ahern and
the other MSL representatives wanted to learn everything possible about the state's approval process.

Fifty-two SNESL students were waiting to hear from the
Board of Regents if they would obtain juris doctorate degrees or
not. The school had been mired in problems since its inception in
1981. After failing its first inspection, the school ousted its absen-
tee owner, Dr. Alfred Avins. The Bernstein Group, a consulting
firm, reorganized the school and moved it from Fall River to better facilities in New Bedford. The state inspection, in March
1986, uncovered a few lingering problems. However, school officials submitted a detailed report showing how it would address
each outstanding issue.

Board of Regents Chairman L. Edward Lashman called the
meeting to order. After going over a number of budget issues, the
Board discussed SNESL's juris doctorate program. "This is
somewhat of a special occasion. No law school has been licensed
in the state of Massachusetts for the past 40 years," said Franklyn
Jenifer, chancellor of the Board of Regents. "I recommend
approval. The school meets all of the stated requirements as set
forth in the Code of Massachusetts Regulations."

"Is this program really adequate?" asked Nicholas Boraski,
another Regent.

Jenifer said that expert educators from outside the state had
been brought in to take a look at it, and "they had given it a clean
bill of health." He added, "I'm not going to question their judgment, and I don't think Board members should either."

As if he had some familiarity with the school, Regent Paul S.
Doherty shook his head and said, "I have real reservations with
this school's approval. I have read the regulations and feel that the
school has met them, but I don't like it." Doherty then asked

Jenifer, "Has an ABA visiting team inspected the school?"

"No, just the team sent by the [Board of] Regents."

Doherty asked, "If we grant degree-granting authority, can they [the students] sit for the bar exam in Rhode Island?"

"No. Only in Massachusetts."

Vice-Chancellor Norma Rees rolled her eyes as if she couldn't believe how little the Board knew about law schools. She said, "The Board of Regents isn't the group that determines who will sit for the Massachusetts bar exam. The Bar Overseers determine that."

"Are last year's graduates eligible to sit for the bar?"

Rees replied, "It's my understanding that only those who receive degrees are eligible. Questions concerning the awarding of degrees to students who have already completed the program will be addressed at a later time."

Doherty still seemed unhappy. He shook his head again, "I find the regulations to be extremely vague and new standards, specific to law schools, should be drawn up—something more like what the ABA uses."

The chairman agreed and said that new standards would be drawn up before another law school was approved.

Using his neat parochial school handwriting, Ahern wrote down every word. At a pause in the conversation, he wrote a message, which he would later discuss with the dean: "It is apparent that new standards are going to be drawn for law schools before we go for a vote. I'm not sure how we can do it, but we should attempt to influence these standards."

Just then, another Regent, Susie S. Kim said, "There is no need for more lawyers. There are too many lawsuits already. If you halved the number of lawyers, you would halve the number of lawsuits. I'm going to vote no."

In response, John Theriault, a student member, sitting on the Board for the first time, replied, "There is a need for a law school in southeastern Massachusetts. There is a large immigrant population trying to better itself, and improved access to legal education will be a benefit to them and all residents of this part of the state."

Questions ended, and an 11 to 1 vote gave the school degree-granting authority.

In retelling the story to Velvel, Ahern said, "If need is going to be an issue, then we must do everything possible to go for a vote before Commonwealth." Certainly, if the Board of Regents proved willing to certify only one law school in northern Massachusetts, Massachusetts School of Law had to win that vote first. But Commonwealth already had an inspection coming up in October—just four months away. It seemed far-fetched to think that Massachusetts School of Law would be ready for an inspection by then, but Ahern, Velvel, and Zappala realized that they had no choice. By fall, the school would barely be on its feet. Still they had to try to win the state's approval.

*****

There was a flurry of activity at MSL in the months preceding the school's opening. Karen Edwards, library consultant, donated books to the library. Many were redundant copies that had therefore been discarded by the Middlesex County Superior Court, where Edwards worked as a librarian. Hearing about MSL's need for books, other lawyers and librarians made similar donations. By the end of summer, the school had 5,000 donated books.

Zappala obtained another 4,000 books on a time payment plan, with payments starting in the fall, after students paid their tuition. It concerned him that the school might not have enough books to gain degree-granting authority; however, he believed the number sufficient to carry the school through the first semester or two. The Regents' staff would take account of the fact that, as more money came in, the school would expand its library.

Beyond books, the school needed shelves on which to store them. That was going to cost the school $25,000 or more. Thinking creatively, Ahern had heard that Georgetown

University School of Law was building the "Taj Mahal of law school libraries" and thought that maybe the school would be getting rid of its old shelves. Thus, he called, and the library officials told him that he could have old shelves for just $4,000. He could even pay for them over time if he liked. However, the shelves came with one stipulation. He had to break them down and cart them away.

Before the librarians at Georgetown could change their minds, Ahern and his nephew flew down to Washington, rented a truck, and spent 14 hours disassembling the shelves. They loaded them up and returned to Andover—all in just one day.

Like Ahern, many students jumped in and exhibited a can-do attitude, as if building the school were part of the law program. New students came in, shelved books, and painted walls. Transfer students urged other students to come and help set up the classrooms and hang chalkboards.

Velvel, Zappala, and Ahern turned to their friends and family for help. Zappala's clients who owed him business favors did photocopying for the school. Another friend furnished the school with tables, chairs, and office equipment. Zappala promised that he would pay him in October.

Donations, volunteer labor, gifts, and promises for repayment went far in building, setting up, and furnishing the classrooms and library. Ads and promotions to attract students were paid for with Velvel's loan to the school.

As for the faculty, several professors left Commonwealth to join the new school's teaching faculty. One was Mike Coyne, a Boston trial lawyer who had been an adjunct professor at Commonwealth for two semesters. Coyne knew all about hard times. He grew up in the tough Dorchester neighborhood of Boston. His father had been a lawyer but had died when Coyne was just 14 years old. His mother worked as a secretary.

In order to have any future, Coyne had to work. As a junior in high school, he worked part time in a law office. He earned enough money there, combined with other part-time jobs, to pay for college and then law school. However, by attending Suffolk University Law School's night program, Coyne felt as if he had been treated as a second-class student. That's the way law schools managed their programs. So-called "top tier" students attended day classes and were considered superior academically and financially to "second-class" night students. Coyne considered this unfair. He had grades good enough to be admitted into the day program; he simply didn't have the money.

Coyne vowed, as he left his Boston law firm and later became MSL's associate dean, that he wouldn't let this happen at MSL. He decided that at MSL all students would be considered the same, no matter whether they attended school full- or part-time or nights, days, or weekends.

The building of this law school was an adventure to Coyne. He believed that he, the dean, and the new faculty at MSL were offering something significant in legal education that would change the lives of law students everywhere. For those reasons, he was glad to be a part of it.

*****

On August 22, Boland, Talkington, and Commonwealth's new dean, Judy Jackson, met with former U.S. Senator Paul Tsongas, Lowell City Manager James Campbell, and a politically connected government official, Thomas P. Costin, Jr., from another Massachusetts town, to discuss Commonwealth's impending move to a larger building at 341 Milddlesex Street, in downtown Lowell. By July 1989, Commonwealth planned to occupy the old Burgess-Lang Building, which would be renovated and renamed the Middlesex Building.

The 10-story brick and concrete building, constructed in 1917 for William H. Burgess and Howard W. Lang, had been designed for light manufacturing. Originally it housed small printers, cigar makers, shoemakers, and uniform manufacturers. As industry in Lowell declined, the building emptied. By the late '80s, it was a ghostly neighborhood eyesore. Surrounding it were bars and strip clubs. The Middlesex Building became a convenient flophouse for drunk and homeless vagrants. The building was dangerous and full of trash. An open elevator shaft went from the 10th floor to the ground. A few pieces of plywood loosely tossed over gaping holes in the floors provided minimal protection to anyone wandering around in the dark.

James C. Dragon, a Lowell attorney and trustee for the Athenaeum Realty Trust, the developer, assured those at Commonwealth that all this would soon change. A $6.3 million renovation project was in the works, designed by W. Lewis Barlow IV & Architects.

Athenaeum Realty was the name of a nominee realty trust set up, in May 1988, by Dragon. A nominee realty trust is a title-holding device that enables trust beneficiaries—the real owners—to remain anonymous. While a nominee trust can be used for tax or estate planning purposes, the anonymity also shelters clients from creditors or conceals ownership in business dealings that might be seen as conflicts of interest. It was rumored that a major fundraiser for the Democratic Party, someone closely connected with Governor Dukakis and the Kennedy family, owned the building. Nobody seemed to really know, however.

That day in August, Costin, Tsongas, and Campbell congratulated Boland and Talkington on their decision to move into this building. City officials and boosters said that Commonwealth's move into downtown Lowell would accelerate the city's redevelopment by five years. Tsongas said, ". . . with the presence of Commonwealth School of Law, the University of Lowell and Middlesex Community College, the city will achieve an 'intellectual critical mass' that will fuel it for generations."

*****

That same day, August 22, 1988, classes began at Massachusetts School of Law. There were 94 students—54 had transferred from Commonwealth, and the rest were new. Velvel and Zappala had hoped for more, but it was a good number for starters.

A slightly smaller enrollment translated into less tuition income. Zappala calculated that by the end of the fall, the school would be approximately $50,000 short of its budget. The school could still dip into its $160,000 line of credit, secured by Velvel's condominium.

Since the beginning of August, the school's office staff had received a series of obscene phone calls. By late August, they were wary of every call that came in. One day Pam Pelosi, the Commonwealth secretary, who had quit Commonwealth to work at MSL, answered the phone. She heard on the other end a deep gravelly voice that said, "Hello, this is Santa Claus."

"Who?" Pelosi's eyes widened, and she gestured to the others. She thought it was the obscene caller. They gathered around in an effort to hear.

"Have you checked your mail today?" the anonymous caller asked, growing increasingly annoyed.

"What do you mean?" Pelosi asked.

The caller ordered her to go and look for an envelope, which he described. "It's important," he told her.

Pelosi checked the mailboxes, and, in fact, she found the envelope.

"Open it," he commanded.

She did, and inside she found a check for $50,000. It was unbelievable. A year earlier, Joe Fishelson, Velvel's cousin, had admonished him for being somewhat foolhardy by choosing to work for Boland. Now he had donated this large sum of money without ever being asked or even expressing any intention of doing so. It came as a total surprise and provided the financial cushion the school needed to make it through that semester.

Velvel and the faculty scheduled a state inspection for October 11-12, 1988, just six weeks after the school opened. The inspection team consisted of Dean Howard A. Glickstein of the

Touro Law School in Huntington, New York; Dean Michael J. Navin of the Dickinson School of Law in Carlisle, Pennsylvania; Dean Peter Simmons of the Rutgers Law School in Newark, New Jersey; and Edgar Bellefontaine, librarian of the Social Law Library in Boston. They were accompanied by John C. Weston, the academic program officer for the Massachusetts Board of Regents.

During a review of MSL's financial books, inspectors noted that the school didn't have a cash reserve, other than the $50,000 it had just received. Rather, the school barely had enough money to meet its expenses, let alone survive if the economy slowed and enrollment dropped.

Despite this single criticism, Velvel and the other founders believed that the inspection had gone well. Optimistically they believed that the six-week-old school had met with the inspectors' approval.

*****

Despite all the talk of relocating to a bigger, better building, Commonwealth was in trouble. Each day, the move seemed less likely. In seven months, enrollment had dropped from 183 students in January 1988, when Velvel was still at the school, to just 75 students by fall. No longer could the school's tuition cover the school's operating expenses. Some professors claimed that they weren't getting paid, and vendors complained that the school wrote checks against insufficient funds. Also, the librarian hadn't been replaced.

Being in a race with MSL to receive accreditation, Boland brought in state inspectors on October 18-19, even though the school was clearly not ready. He figured that if the school received approval, it would kill MSL's chances of succeeding. The Board of Regents had made it clear that a school must not only meet inspectors' standards but must establish market need. Clearly the Merrimack Valley region could support only one law school.

Shortly after inspectors left, Commonwealth suffered another damaging blow. An article appeared in the November 7, 1988, edition of the *Lowell Sun*:

Court Orders Lowell Law School Chief to Stay Away from 16-year-old Girl

Michael Boland, president of Lowell's Commonwealth School of Law, has been ordered by a judge to stay away from a 16-year-old Lowell girl.

A Middlesex Probate Court judge issued a restraining order sought by the Department of Social Services, which charged that the 39-year-old Boland has a "questionable interest" in the girl and said it would be in her "best interests" to have no contact with him.

The girl, who was listed as a missing person and a runaway between October 1986 and September 1987, was living with Boland during part of that time, according to an affidavit signed in February 1987 by her mother.

The mother said Boland had visited her Lowell home several times and once offered to buy her a car "if I did not inform the DSS of (her) whereabouts or her involvement with him."

The restraining order marks Boland's latest incident in a series of brushes with the law and controversies involving the unaccredited law school.

The article went on to say that Boland had also gotten into an argument over the girl with a social worker, Cynthia Brennan, and that he had pushed Brennan. The social worker pressed charges, which were later dismissed. The article also said that Boland's brother and sister-in-law had asked the court for guardianship of the girl; however, DSS officials opposed it, saying that this would give Boland "free access" to the girl, who already had a "history of sexual abuse." The reporter also noted that Boland had been previously charged with indecent assault and battery.

If the school's credibility weren't tarnished enough, Commonwealth's second inspection report came in on December 2. As devastating as the report was, Boland painted an optimistic picture, sending the following memo to students:

> We have received the report from the Board of Regents Visiting Team and the news is good! The conclusion of the report was that "Commonwealth School of Law has worked hard to address deficiencies of concern to the prior visiting committee . . . and . . . the school has demonstrated adequate progress . . . and the visiting committee recommends that the Board of Regents approve the school's application . . . ."

Boland had put in the ellipsis and chopped off the end of the final sentence, because in reality it read: "the visiting committee recommends that the Board of Regents approve the school's application when the school provides competent evidence that it has satisfactorily resolved these issues." The inspectors identified four major problem areas, classifying them as "serious." The school needed a full-time librarian, more financial backing, and more student services. The inspectors also criticized the fact that Boland and Talkington had lifetime tenure on the Board of Trustees, and that the decisionmaking powers of the school rested largely with Boland. Despite all this, Boland's language misled students into thinking that the school might have degree-granting authority by January 17, when the spring semester began.

A news release, reiterating Boland's version of the inspection report, was distributed to the news media. Hearing this, John Weston, academic program officer for the Board of Regents, drafted a letter to Boland saying that his statements were "misleading if not untrue" regarding the latest inspection.

"To not include the latter portion of the sentence and then to announce that the process can be completed before the spring semester is obviously an attempt to mislead the students, faculty, and the public with assurances of immediate degree authority," wrote Weston. He also pointed out that Boland had violated a Board of Regents' regulation stating that no institution seeking degree-granting authority can advertise or even imply that such authority would be available soon. He wrote, "Any further publications implying imminent degree-granting authority may jeopardize chances of such authority in the future."

Once again, Boland had been caught deceiving students. When his latest deception was exposed and publicized in the newspapers, he couldn't shrug it off. In a surprise move, he resigned as president. However, he told the media that he would remain on the Board. As he said, he had lifetime tenure and a major investment in the school.

Reading between the lines, Velvel and others at MSL believed that Commonwealth was about to collapse.

*****

Two days before Christmas, Velvel received the state inspectors' report. The team wrote that they had been impressed with MSL's progress to date. They described the school as "a serious endeavor by a group of qualified and dedicated people." In addition, the inspectors wrote that they had "reasonable confidence" that if the school's progress continued, the school would obtain degree-granting authority. However, because MSL was only six weeks old when it had been inspected, inspectors concluded that MSL was "in too early a stage of development to determine whether it will have adequate revenues to carry out its programs. It has admitted only one class and it is premature to predict what the demand for its educational services will be." The site team suggested a follow-up visit in the fall of 1989.

The news crushed Velvel, Coyne, Zappala, and Ahern, who

had worked so hard. Yet they realized that they had been excessive in their hopes. In reality, MSL was a new school with no history and no money. Yet state inspectors considered MSL a serious endeavor and run by competent people, even despite these shortcomings.

The inspection team had criticized the library, which was incomplete and needed a full-time librarian with a law background. As well, the main floor couldn't support the weight of the book stacks except on the main beams. Thus, the floor of the building needed to be reinforced.

Even though the school had not been approved and couldn't grant law degrees to students, the future at MSL looked brighter than that at Commonwealth. Inspectors encouraged Velvel, Coyne, Ahern, and Zappala to keep up the good work. As result, they realized that they had taken a major step in the right direction. They hoped they would achieve degree-granting authority soon.

Immediately after receiving the report, Velvel sent a letter to the student body and faculty, saying that he would meet with all students and faculty on Tuesday, January 3, 1989, in the school's Great Hall. He wanted to explain the results in person. In addition, he placed a complete copy of the report in the library for all to read.

*****

Before MSL's meeting, Margaret Talkington, Commonwealth's new president, held a news conference. She announced that former U.S. Senator and attorney Paul Tsongas would be helping the school. He had been named chairman of its Board of Trustees.

It was a strategic move for the ailing school. Tsongas was a mover and shaker in Massachusetts and son of a Greek immigrant, like Governor Michael Dukakis. They were close personally, as well as professionally. In Lowell, Tsongas was the hometown boy who had done well without forgetting his friends and neighbors. While in Congress, he worked to revitalize "Spindle City," helping Lowell raise nearly $400 million in private and public funds. The money was invested in historic preservation, development of commerce and industry, and cultural and educational improvements.

As these changes transformed the community, the majority of locals not only thanked Tsongas for his help but set him on a pedestal and worshipped him. As in any community, there were a few individuals who were far more cynical about local politics. With tongue in cheek, they sarcastically referred to him as "Saint Paul," implying that not all of his actions were virtuous.

Tsongas was particularly interested in education. He had led Lowell State and Lowell Tech to a merger as the University of Lowell. Later, that school was brought into the University of Massachusetts system and renamed UMass-Lowell. As these changes were made, Tsongas convinced computer guru Dr. An Wang to build his world headquarters in Lowell. The Wang Institute, part of Wang's new business complex, offered master's degree programs in computer engineering and software design. With this addition, Lowell set its sights on becoming a cosmopolitan, diverse educational center.

Tsongas believed a local law school would enhance this goal. Admittedly, rehabilitating Commonwealth would be challenging, given the school's bad health and tainted reputation. For help, Tsongas recruited his political buddies: Bancroft Littlefield, Jr., a professor at Harvard Law School, partner in the Boston law firm of Foley, Hoag & Eliot (also Tsongas' law firm), and general counsel to the U.S. Senate Committee on Labor and Education; Peter J. Aucella, executive director of the Lowell Historic Preservation Commission; Cory Atkins, community leader, faculty member at Middlesex Community College, and wife of U.S. representative Chester G. Atkins; and Lawrence Ansin, a boyhood friend of Tsongas and a wealthy local businessman and former owner of the textile manufacturing firm Joan Fabrics Corporation, located in the heart of Lowell.

Tsongas and the four new members had joined Common-wealth's existing Board, which also included Boland, Talkington, and Donald Berman, who had joined the Board in the fall. Berman was one of four professors who founded the second Northeastern University School of Law after the first one had closed for several years. Some people speculated that he had joined the Board in hopes of becoming dean.

At MSL, Sullivan read this news in utter disbelief. She couldn't believe that these prominent, respected people would lend their names to a school that had been associated with deception and corruption and was on the verge of financial collapse.

Sullivan also wondered if these prominent individuals really believed that they could turn the school around. Though Boland wasn't president anymore, he was still on the Board and, as she saw it, still a threat to the school. But to dismiss him or to think that he had been cast aside underestimated his remaining control over the school. She worried that this new addition to the Board might give students false hope that the school would turn around and become approved.

Then it occurred to her that maybe the new Board could turn the school around. Maybe the members could use their power and political connections with the Board of Regents to obtain state approval. She wondered why would they do this? Did they have something possibly at stake here?

Sullivan knew from growing up in Massachusetts that political powerhouses such as these wove a tight web around themselves that excluded outsiders. They finagled the system and took what they wanted. Clearly the people at MSL were outsiders. As influential as Velvel was with students and faculty, he held no local political clout in the Merrimack Valley region. He had been there just more than a year.

Sullivan wondered what would happen now. What would become of their hard work? They had tried so hard to offer a law school that would be fair to people and would prepare individuals from all walks of life to become lawyers, but, she worried, *would it be for naught?*

Chapter 5

Forged by Fire

On January 7, 1989, as Commonwealth's Board of Trustees met to install the five prominent local individuals as trustees, Boland dropped another bombshell. The school was broke, operating on a budget that would produce a $200,000 deficit. It owed $96,000 in withholding taxes, which the federal government demanded be paid in nine days. The dean and faculty hadn't been paid in two months; they were owed approximately $40,000. Dean Jackson and Steven Kropp were so desperate to be paid that they had filed a complaint in Middlesex Superior Court. As well, the school was $10,000 behind in rent. The trustees were shocked and ordered the school's finances be audited. They realized that they would have to devise a quick strategy in order for the school to offer spring classes.

On January 21, the school's trustees gathered in emergency session. Eight out of the 12 members were present, including the school's founders, Boland and Talkington. Tsongas suggested that Commonwealth merge with MSL. Rather than having 75 students at Commonwealth and 100 students at MSL, the combined school could have nearly 200 students. This would enable it to operate in the black. A merger made sense and would likely win Board of Regents' approval, Tsongas said.

The trustees couldn't argue that point. Tsongas made the motion. Berman seconded it. Unanimously they agreed that they should attempt to merge the two schools. After the meeting adjourned, Tsongas called Velvel.

*****

Tsongas wasn't the first to speak to Velvel about a joint effort. A week earlier, Harold Lawson, dean at Emerson College, had met with Velvel to discuss several cooperative ventures. He suggested that MSL offer a legal course for Emerson students. As well, they agreed to explore team-taught courses, special courses for nontraditional students, and joint degree programs. All were possibilities.

A few months earlier, Velvel and Ahern ate lunch with Lawson and Alan Koenig, Emerson's president. Koenig had told them that he hoped to turn the college into a university. To do that, the school had to offer two doctoral degree programs. Already the school was working on a doctoral program in communications, but it needed another program. A juris doctorate made sense for the school. Emerson already offered several communications law courses, which attracted lawyers wanting to know more about that field. Law complemented Emerson's communications, entertainment, and computer technology programs. In addition, surveys indicated that a percentage of Emerson's graduates continued onto law school. Velvel and Koenig believed the two schools could work cooperatively together. Thus, Lawson sketched out various ideas.

Even though MSL's discussions with Emerson remained open, Tsongas wanted to discuss a potential merger between MSL and Commonwealth. A merger would make licensure a certainty, he told Velvel. Tsongas and Commonwealth trustees Berman and Ansin made an appointment for February 6 to discuss this further with Velvel.

Even though he considered such a merger with Commonwealth to be absurd, Velvel agreed to meet with them. He hadn't recovered from the anger and humiliation caused by Boland. Students still resented Boland, too. He had turned their lives upside down and cost them money and time. Many had used the spring and summer semesters to create MSL. To do this meant delaying law school graduation for six months to a year. They believed that if Boland had not manipulated them and blatantly misrepresented himself and his school, none of this would have happened. It would be difficult to ask them to trust Boland again.

The way Velvel looked at it, MSL was a promising school and on its way to state approval. The dean expected that the school would have it within a year. Velvel couldn't imagine how any of them could go back to Commonwealth.

On the phone, Tsongas reminded the dean that Boland was no longer president. Still Velvel didn't forget what Boland had said: *"I have every nickel invested in this place."* He wouldn't relinquish his power. He enjoyed the many perks of being a law school president, and he wasn't about to give up the power or the perks.

Velvel figured that the merger could only benefit MSL if the school absorbed Commonwealth's students and its library. On the other hand, Velvel and his colleagues didn't want Commonwealth's reputation and wouldn't accept its name, location, faculty, and staff. Already many people confused the two schools.

Velvel knew that the possibility of a merger was a long shot. Yet he felt obligated to meet with Tsongas.

The next day, at 11:30 a.m., Larry Ansin telephoned Velvel as the latter packed for a business trip to Cleveland. Ansin explained that he wanted to be part of the merger discussions, but he would be out of town on February 6. He asked if the two of them could meet earlier, perhaps January 29. Velvel agreed.

Late in the evening of January 25, Tsongas called Velvel in Cleveland. He instructed him to look for an important announcement in the *Boston Globe* the next morning. Tsongas wouldn't reveal the contents of the article, but he told the dean to get the newspaper. The next morning, Velvel read the lead story:

Tsongas to Head State Board Overseeing Higher Education

Warning that the nation must shore up its education system to prevent sliding into second-rate economic status, former Sen. Paul Tsongas yesterday agreed to head up the state's public colleges, thus stepping into his most visible role since resigning from the senate five years ago.

Gov. Dukakis, describing Tsongas as "one of the most able and respected citizens of Massachusetts," appointed the Lowell native as the new chairman of the Board of Regents of Higher Education, which sets policy for the state's colleges and universities.

Tsongas also told reporters that he planned to resign from his positions on the University of Lowell and Commonwealth School of Law Boards of Trustees. As head of the Board of Regents, he would be in charge of approving new schools. (Thus, participating in merger talks between Commonwealth and MSL would be a conflict of interest.)

In reading this article, Velvel couldn't help but wonder, when had this job been discussed with Tsongas? Was it before he became chairman of Commonwealth's Board of Trustees? Was it before Tsongas called him on January 21 to discuss a merger? If so, his comments about "a merger would make licensure a certainty" were likely right.

Local newspapers covering Tsongas' appointment also discussed the law schools' merger talks and speculated on the outcome. At MSL, Al Zappala was pessimistic, claiming "very serious impediments" stood in the way of such a merger. When reporter Dick Dahl of *Massachusetts Lawyers Weekly* could not reach Velvel or Tsongas for a comment, he interviewed the chairman of the Board of Trustees of the University of Lowell, Richard K. Donahue, Sr., Tsongas' personal friend. Donahue said,

"The newer people at Commonwealth are recognizing what everyone has already recognized: that if there's room for a law school in this area, there's room for only one."

Donahue reiterated what Tsongas and other area politicians had said: the Board of Regents would approve only one law school in the Merrimack Valley. The question everyone was asking was which one? Would it be MSL, a school that had received an encouraging inspection report after just six weeks of operation? Or would it be the four-year-old, debt-beleaguered Commonwealth? The answer appeared obvious. Yet Commonwealth held one major advantage. The school, being situated in Tsongas' hometown of Lowell, appeared to be the choice of the Board of Regents chairman.

*****

On Sunday, January 29, Larry Ansin visited the law school and met with Larry Velvel, Dick Ahern, and Joe Fishelson. The latter, an MSL trustee, had flown in from his home in Wooster, Ohio, for the meeting. Beyond lending his financial support to the school, Fishelson, a blunt, outspoken entrepreneur, had embraced MSL's cause. From his perspective, MSL was an exciting adventure, and his participation enabled him to return something good to the public. Thus, Fishelson flew in to make sure that local politicians didn't take advantage of the school in courting such a merger.

Everyone introduced themselves, with Fishelson saying he was from Wooster. Then Ansin explained that he and Tsongas had been friends for 30 years and had worked together in real estate development. In addition, he updated them on what was happening at Commonwealth. He had worked out a deal with the Internal Revenue Service so that the school could remain open. Once the school became state approved, the tax bill would have to be paid.

Fishelson explained that MSL didn't have those problems. It

was a viable school, and there were no obstacles in the way of it achieving state approval, unless there were political ones. He said that Tsongas, as chairman of the Board of Regents, should disqualify himself and not take part in the merger and approval of the schools.

In reply, Ansin said that everything went through Tsongas.

To that Fishelson said, "If he's a gentleman, he will disqualify himself."

"Tsongas will be involved. That is not an issue," Ansin replied.

"You don't see an ethical problem?" Fishelson asked.

With that, Ansin replied that he didn't want to argue. He and Fishelson had different points of view. Ansin said that the only thing that Tsongas cared about was that the combined school be located in Lowell. He called it a "motherhood issue." He didn't care if any members of the staff and faculty were hired by MSL. As for Boland, he was out of the picture, Ansin said. What Ansin and Tsongas cared about was helping Commonwealth students complete their education. Most important, of course, the law school had to stay in Lowell.

Velvel told him that MSL couldn't relocate to Lowell. The school's founders had signed a five-year lease that would cost $500,000 to break.

Ansin remained unmoved. He made it clear that moving to Lowell was non-negotiable. In fact, he said that he already had the location picked out—the Middlesex Building, a 10-story building on Middlesex Street. This was the building that Commonwealth had planned to move into.

Ansin explained that the law school would serve as an anchor in the building, attracting other businesses. Velvel remembered what Ansin had said about being in real estate with Tsongas. He sounded as if he were negotiating a real estate deal. Ansin seemed to place undue priority on filling space in this Middlesex Building. Velvel wondered, but never learned, who owned it. Who were the anonymous beneficiaries in the nominee trust?

Velvel and Fishelson knew that if MSL were to succeed academically, the school couldn't move to Lowell, where it would be vulnerable to being manipulated by Tsongas, Ansin, and other politicians. They would use threats, laws, and administrative actions to control it and force it to do whatever they wanted. To operate a high quality law school and provide opportunity to the working class and the poor, MSL needed to remain free of political control.

"When you lie down with the dogs, you get fleas," Fishelson told Ansin about the idea of moving to Lowell. "What would MSL gain?"

Ansin replied the school had nothing to gain, but it had everything to lose. Both schools could not co-exist, and Commonwealth could get rid of Boland, bring in qualified people, secure loans for the school, and then obtain a license. In other words, Commonwealth could still shut out MSL.

Fishelson, a tough man, an ex-paratrooper who had fought at Anzio and in France during World War II, and who had chased Nazis in Germany after the war, wouldn't budge. He said that MSL was a quality school with excellent instruction, and it would succeed on its merits. If the politicians felt they could stop it, he said, let them try.

Then Fishelson turned to Ansin and said, "I'm willing to back this school with my own money. Are you willing to do the same [for Commonwealth]?"

Ansin said nothing. He had recently sold his business, Joan Fabrics, and was reported to be worth $120 million. He could afford to back Commonwealth, but he made no such offer.

Around 6 o'clock, Fishelson looked at his watch and said, "I've got to leave. I have a plane to catch to go home."

Ansin looked puzzled. "I thought you said that you were from Worcester."

"I am," Fishelson said. "Wooster, Ohio."

Ansin had misunderstood. The pronounciation of the two cities is exactly the same. Ansin assumed all along that he was local. Realizing that Fishelson wasn't from New England, he knew that neither he nor Tsongas held any political control over him.

*****

The next day, Monday, January 30, at 5 p.m., Velvel received a call from Koenig, president of Emerson College in Boston. He said that on Friday, one day after Tsongas was named chairman of the Board of Regents, Tsongas had called Koenig to say that Emerson's plan for affiliation with MSL was a fly in the ointment, and it prevented MSL and Commonwealth from merging. Receiving such a call from the chairman of the Board of Regents, Koenig, who wanted to upgrade Emerson to a university and needed Board of Regents' approval to do so, heeded Tsongas' warning. He said that he would let MSL negotiate with Commonwealth before continuing Emerson's negotiations with MSL.

After 108 years in Boston's prestigious Back Bay, Emerson planned to move to a site seven miles from MSL in Lawrence. Though Andover bordered the city of Lawrence, demographically the two communities were worlds apart. Lawrence was an economically depressed mill city, much like Lowell, that had also been blighted by unemployment, crime, and poverty, but it had never recovered. Andover, on the other hand, was an upscale community and home of Phillips Andover Academy, where George H.W. and George W. Bush both attended high school.

The location itself was of less interest to Emerson College than were the economics behind it. For a number of years, tuition paid to Emerson, a four-year drama and communications school, failed to cover its operating costs, and the school struggled to rise above increasing debt. In 1985, Tsongas unsuccessfully proposed moving the school to Lowell, where property was cheaper and the school could receive financial support. School officials had hoped that a sale of the school's expensive Boston property would generate money to build a new campus in Lowell and pay off nearly all its debt.

The idea made sense; however, Koenig chose Lawrence over Lowell. Lawrence officials had purchased a tract of land along the Merrimack River and drew up plans for a 132-acre park on which Emerson's new campus would be placed. As further support, Governor Dukakis extended a $3.8 million grant to the city to help build Emerson's park and campus.

"I feel wonderful about the decision," Koenig told a *Boston Globe* reporter. "We'll have modern communications facilities . . . we'll have more space, and we'll have a beautiful state park surrounding us."

However, students and faculty felt different. They couldn't understand the logic in moving 30 miles north to Lawrence. In its Boston location, Emerson had access to cultural, arts, and media programs that complemented the school's drama and communications offerings. Not so in Lawrence. Emerson would be removed from professional theater, metropolitan broadcast and print journalism, and documentary film production. None of that was available in Lawrence.

To make their objections clear, Emerson students circulated a petition with 1,200 signatures. They urged Koenig to keep Emerson in Boston. They even tried to convince Lawrence voters to reject the project, explaining that it would cost the city a lot of money. Their pleas were ignored. Lawrence residents wanted the college. They believed it would upgrade the city's image, attract jobs, and, over the long term, bring in more middle-income taxpayers. By a two to one margin, Lawrence citizens voted in favor of the waterfront park and college campus.

In a statement to the media, Koenig said that he realized the students were upset, but he believed in making this move. If the school property, in Boston, sold for $100 million, Emerson would have enough money to build a new campus with upgraded facilities, and it would become a university.

To further that effort, Koenig had tried three times to affiliate with several different area law schools. As of yet, none had worked out; however, his negotiations with MSL were still pending. Of course, Emerson was three or more years away from actually being in Lawrence.

So when Koenig called Velvel and suggested that they halt further negotiations until after he had finished talking with Commonwealth, Velvel didn't mind. In fact, he told Koenig that he thought any merger negotiations between MSL and Emerson were "vastly premature." Thus, Velvel and Koenig mutually agreed that they would postpone their joint-effort discussions until Emerson and MSL both knew where they stood.

*****

In early February, when Commonwealth's audit report arrived, it showed irregularities. In December, when the school was eight months in arrears in paying state and federal withholding taxes, Boland wrote a check to himself for $66,000. He referred to it as a loan repayment; however, there was no record of such a loan being made to the school.

The audit also showed that Boland had submitted false corporate reports to the Board of Regents, to banks, and to the Athenaeum Group, the nominee trust that held title to the Middlesex Building. Further, while the school didn't have money to pay its faculty and its rent, Boland forgave a number of tuition payments, amounting to $10,000. Essentially, he had let friends and acquaintances attend the school for free. Massachusetts Attorney General James Shannon investigated.

Complicating matters for Commonwealth's trustees, a group of 23 MSL students, headed by Dick Ahern, sued the school under the state's consumer protection law. They charged that Boland didn't live up to his promises of winning state approval and enabling the school to grant degrees. Judgment was in their favor, but the school had no money to pay the former students. Thus, a lien was placed against the library. The students, in effect, owned it, unless Commonwealth could pay them.

When the Board of Trustees met on February 11, Ansin told Commonwealth's Board that the likelihood of "opening up next semester is not good." Initially, the new trustees "thought they would be successful in assisting the school in its attempt for accreditation, but we find ourselves now in a Catch-22 situation. Without financial stability, there will be no accreditation. Without accreditation there is no financial stability."

Dean Jackson then said, "But it's the responsibility of the trustees to raise funds."

Ansin replied, "The new trustees did not understand the financial condition of the school. Back taxes were owed. Back salaries were owed. The school survives solely on tuition. In order to remain current on tax liability, money must be paid out of the students' tuition." Plain and simple, there would be no operating money. Ansin said that the school couldn't even obtain a bank loan. What financial institution would lend them money?

Aucella told the trustees that Commonwealth's debt constituted a violation of the law. "I will not remain on the board and place my reputation on the line," he said. He resigned, as did the other board members selected by Tsongas. They rose and walked out the door.

As soon as they were gone, Boland claimed that Commonwealth still owed him $180,000 from money he had lent the school. He demanded that it be repaid immediately. "If you don't," he warned the remaining trustees, "none of you are going to be around."

Clearly, it was a threat. The remaining board members were appalled. They asked Boland to step down from the board. He refused.

After the meeting, the board members continued their discussion about Boland via a conference call. They decided to legally remove him from Commonwealth, if they could.

*****

While Commonwealth struggled to survive in the face of chaos, corruption, and changing leadership, Tsongas continued to look for a way to establish a thriving law school in Lowell. He called Koenig, president of Emerson College, and told him that Commonwealth School of Law was looking for either a merger or a takeover. Tsongas arranged for Talkington, now the school's president, to meet with Koenig and his staff.

For the meeting, Talkington prepared a chart that compared Commonwealth's assets to those of Southern New England School of Law and Massachusetts School of Law. She claimed that Commonwealth had far more books than either of the other two schools—23,000 volumes, worth approximately $500,000. (She didn't mention that there was a lien against the books because of the judgment against Commonwealth.)

As well, Talkington told Koenig and the others that Commonwealth was very close to state approval—much closer than MSL, she said. She had worked on fixing the four problems the Board of Regents had cited, she said. Also, she pointed out that Commonwealth had four years of experience, while MSL had barely been in operation for six months. In conclusion, she told Koenig, "If one accepts the logic that only one law school will be accredited by the Board of Regents in the Merrimack Valley, then there is the potential of gaining 100 students from MSL." The logic was that once Commonwealth became licensed and MSL went out of business, the Lowell school would absorb MSL's students, doubling the school's student body.

Koenig listened and told her, "Emerson has many things on its plate at the moment." He referred to the school's struggles with debt, property sales, and the building of a new campus in Lawrence. "Emerson could only consider such an affiliation if the invitation had the support of the school and community, and if the project could stand on its own financially," he told her. "If we were ever to proceed with this concept, it would have to be tied into the mission of Emerson College."

Talkington understood and agreed to that.

News of the proposed merger quickly hit the newspapers. Tsongas was interviewed and claimed that it was "a logical move." In fact, he claimed that he had been thinking about this idea for some time. Initially he planned for MSL and Common-wealth to merge, and then Emerson could acquire the merged school. It was a concept that neither Tsongas nor his representa-tives had disclosed to Velvel and those at MSL. However, Tsongas said that the Emerson-Commonwealth move "solves a lot of problems."

Koenig told reporters that he "was very excited" about an Emerson takeover of Commonwealth. When asked if this meant that Commonwealth was being considered ahead of MSL, he replied, "Yes, it definitely does mean that." He went on to say that an acquired school would need to complement Emerson's mis-sion and, for that reason, Commonwealth was of more interest to him.

*****

When Velvel read this in the *Lowell Sun*, he was stunned. He believed that he and Koenig had deferred, not called off, their possible joint programs. Now he read in the newspaper that they were to fight head-to-head as competitors. When a reporter asked the dean what he thought about this, he replied, "I find it hard to understand how a gentleman can do this."

It was clear to Velvel that "Saint Paul's" political machine was behind this and that Tsongas had masterminded the negotiations between Commonwealth and Emerson. Tsongas now headed the Board of Regents, which issued degree-granting authority to Massachusetts schools, colleges, and universities. If he had used the power of his position to influence and orchestrate a merger between Emerson and Commonwealth, then he had to be biased towards the two schools. Further, Tsongas, as chairman of the Board of Regents, had been saying that there would be only one law school approved in the Merrimack Valley. If that were true, Tsongas surely saw it as Emerson-Commonwealth—not MSL. Velvel saw Tsongas' actions as an egregious violation of ethics.

MSL had been drawn into a bigger, tougher battle. No longer was the school simply battling Commonwealth but Emerson College and Paul Tsongas, too. What concerned Velvel was that the opposition was stronger and better established. Koenig even bragged that Emerson's long presence in Massachusetts and its educational quality and credibility would make it easier for the law school to obtain degree-granting authority. In fact, he told Emerson's Board of Trustees that the Emerson Law School would be eligible for degree-granting authority from the state Board of Regents, headed by Tsongas, in its first year, and then it could apply for provisional ABA accreditation.

Because freestanding law schools had a tough time competing with law schools at established colleges and universities, Velvel knew MSL faced serious obstacles. It would be hard to beat a college that had vast resources that included personnel, prestige, and money.

Velvel decided to seek advice from John Weston of the Massachusetts Board of Regents' staff. Weston had been a steady source of helpful advice since Velvel arrived in Massachusetts. Because of Tsongas' obvious influence over the licensure process, the dean asked Weston if Emerson's law school could gain degree-granting authority without going through the regular process required of all other start-up schools. In other words, could Emerson obtain degree-granting authority in its very first year?

In Weston's opinion, the answer was no. He said that all schools—big and small—went through the same process. He conceded that Emerson had certain advantages in terms of its structure, registration procedures, and maybe even its finances. "On the other hand, it's no further along . . . regarding faculty, curriculum, and other law school needs," Weston said. This meant MSL still stood a chance to succeed and win.

*****

By summer, Emerson's Board of Trustees approved a plan to absorb Commonwealth School of Law. The board named Don Berman, a Northeastern School of Law professor and Commonwealth trustee, as acting dean. However, Emerson's trustees insisted that none of Emerson's lines of credit be used for the law school. All of Emerson's resources were needed to build the new $80 million campus in Lawrence.

By mid-August, Peter Aucella, head of Lowell's Preservation Commission, helped Berman secure approximately $1.6 million for the school: an $850,000 line of credit, a $500,000 pledge, and a $250,000 loan from the Lowell Development and Finance Corporation. All the while, applications and inquiries for the Emerson Law School poured in. The staff received 1,500 calls and letters and accepted 140 students—many of them from Commonwealth. With registration to take place on September 5, 1989, just two weeks away, the school appeared to be off and running.

However, there was still one big stumbling block. The school didn't have a site. Renovations on the Middlesex Building were going more slowly than expected. Occupancy would still be at least a year away. Complicating matters, Emerson couldn't secure a long-term lease on the six floors reserved for the law school. The Middlesex Building's owners wouldn't give the law school a five-year lease unless Emerson College secured the space with a $3 million note. Emerson's trustees remained adamant. The new law school could not use Emerson's credit.

Thus, the Emerson Law School had no place to hold fall classes. It could hold classes in Commonwealth's old location, the Downes Professional Building; however, Berman and Koenig saw this as a disastrous move. They would be tied to Commonwealth's old stigma. To complicate matters further, Emerson discovered that it couldn't obtain title to Commonwealth's library.

The former students had a lien against it. The IRS also had a claim on all of the school's assets.

The final big blow came to Emerson Law School when Allen Koenig unexpectedly resigned. After 10 years at Emerson, he took a job as president of Chapman College in Orange, California. In a letter of resignation, he talked about being frustrated by a soft real estate market that had delayed the college's property sales. He described it as a "waiting game." Further, he wrote, "I believe that my energies can be more productive there [at Chapman] than at Emerson." As Koenig prepared to leave Emerson, the college trustees spoke out about the school's impending plans, saying that they would continue their move to Lawrence. After all, $7 million had been invested in it already.

Despite the trustees' claims, rumors circulated that Emerson College would remain in Boston's Back Bay.

*****

One week before Emerson Law School was to open, on August 30, officials at Emerson College announced:

> Emerson College will not open a law school in Lowell this September as originally planned. The school is in the process of notifying all prospective students of this decision and returning tuition deposits to students who have been accepted.
>
> The decision not to open the law school was announced today in a memorandum from Emerson President Allen E. Koenig to members of the college's board of trustees. Koenig listed several factors for the decision, including the inability to acquire title to the library and other assets of the Commonwealth School of Law, and the inability to secure a long-term lease for the Middlesex Building in Lowell without use of Emerson College's credit.

Students transferring from Commonwealth felt abandoned and somewhat lost. They had no idea how they could possibly finish their degrees. No law school in the area would accept them or transfer their credits.

Stephen Moses, a former Commonwealth student, sought a restraining order from Middlesex Superior Court to try to force Emerson to open its law school. The judge rejected his motion. Moses told a *Boston Globe* reporter, "[Emerson's decision not to open] threw our lives out the window. People left jobs, sold homes, or took out second mortgages." He said that he and the other students were not done with Emerson. They protested, and they begged officials to find a way to open the law school. They even threatened to sue Emerson, which Moses and other students eventually did.

Tsongas had his say in the matter too. He chastised Emerson, telling a *Lowell Sun* reporter, "I would say it's pretty obvious that Emerson does not have courses in ethics or social behavior. I think the action speaks to a total lack of any conscience and an arrogance that is not present in other colleges and universities in this country." He declared that Emerson had betrayed the Lowell community.

Emerson's decision not to open the law school created much anger and bitterness. However, the angriest person of all was Michael Boland. He was left with nothing. He claimed to still have $180,000, his life savings, invested in Commonwealth, and he accused Emerson of reneging on the merger. With Commonwealth closed, the school's phone lines were disconnected, the students were gone, and Boland threatened to sue Berman for misrepresentation and conflict of interest. He threatened to sue Emerson for fraud and breach of contract.

Emerson paid Boland nothing, though it settled with Commonwealth for what the school calculated it owed Commonwealth for three months' use of its facilities. The college wrote a check to Commonwealth for $36,000.

*****

When the proposed Emerson Law School did not open, MSL suddenly became the only law school in the Merrimack Valley. Though officials at Emerson College continued to express interest in having a law school, they dealt with more immediate concerns: hiring a new president, selling Back Bay property, building a new campus, and soothing hurt feelings among politicians, faculty, and students.

Because Emerson's abrupt retreat left 140 law school students stranded, Velvel offered to help. To benefit both the students and MSL, the Andover law school agreed to admit qualified students and help them catch up on fall classes, which were underway. Fifteen students accepted the offer. Many of the rest continued to believe that Emerson would open, which never happened.

*****

In all aspects, MSL grew and matured. At the beginning of its second year, MSL's student body swelled to 172 students—nearly double its size from the previous year. The school had 40 full- and part-time faculty members, and it offered 48 different courses. There was a full-time librarian, as well as a part-time consultant. In October, when the Internal Revenue Service auctioned off Commonwealth's assets, the tax debt had to be settled before the student lien could be paid. Therefore, MSL bought many of Commonwealth's books, chairs, podiums, tables, and shelves at auction. Commonwealth's books brought MSL's library holding up to 35,000—triple from the year before. The students who had filed a lawsuit against Commonwealth received only a few hundred dollars of what they were owed.

Going into its second year, MSL had addressed most of the state inspectors' concerns. The school's bylaws, curriculum, and procedures had been improved. Enrollment had increased. Thus, the school had become more financially sure-footed. In fact,

Zappala expected the school's revenues to exceed its expenses by $100,000.

One thing had not changed at MSL. The school did not base admissions on LSAT scores. Velvel and his colleagues thought it ludicrous to subject professional people, many in their 30s and 40s, to a standardized test that supposedly assessed their potential but in reality failed to do so. Most of those entering MSL had proven their abilities through personal and professional experiences. The LSAT was intimidating. It required spending money, studying specialized test-taking techniques, and traveling to a test site; thus, it discouraged many individuals from applying to law school.

Instead of using the LSAT, MSL devised its own multi-pronged admission system. To be admitted, students submitted an application and educational transcripts. From their transcripts, the MSL staff learned what kinds of courses they had taken—hard subjects or easy ones—what grades they had earned, and whether their grades had improved over time. They learned what advanced degrees the applicants held and in what fields.

After their applications were submitted, an admissions officer personally interviewed them. Applicants were asked: Why did they want to go to law school? Had they seriously thought about this decision? Did they have family support? Did they have time for law school? Did they have the necessary drive to complete such a huge undertaking?

Sometimes law school candidates were asked to appear a second time before the entire admissions committee. MSL was the only law school in the country that required—or even allowed—interviews, although almost all medical schools required them.

Following the interviews, applicants were asked to write a pro and con essay. Applicants were told to explain why a described person should be admitted to law school. Then the applicant was asked to take the opposite view and explain why that person should not be admitted. The exercise provided a window into the student's thinking and writing skills.

To Velvel and others at MSL, this multi-pronged approach seemed far more suitable and predictive than the standardized, multiple-choice LSAT, especially because legal problems did not come in standardized, multiple-choice packages. In addition, the MSL staff considered the LSAT to be biased, like the SAT, toward white, upper-class individuals who were young and had recently attended the best high schools, prep schools, Ivy League universities, and other Ivy-League-type institutions. MSL was not alone in its view. Many respected scholars and statisticians debunked the LSAT as biased and useless in predicting competence.

One had been Temple University Law School, which, in 1968, developed a Special Admissions and Curriculum Experiments (Space) Program. While Temple's admissions staff looked closely at students' GPA and LSAT scores, they also weighed other factors. One was whether or not students had worked their way through undergraduate school. Temple's mission was to give opportunities to working people who wanted to better themselves. Thus, the school carefully looked at students' backgrounds, particularly their leadership skills. They also gave preference to underrepresented groups, such as Vietnam veterans.

The ABA criticized Temple's Space Program. Peter J. Liacouras, who was law school dean and went on to become Temple University's president, told ABA accreditors, "Wait a minute. Our standards are these standards. We're developing these, and the rest of the law school world should be developing them if they want to do a decent job."

Liacouras also said that "logical skills are fine but the other skills are really what separates a good lawyer from somebody else."

Accreditors made it clear that they didn't like the Space Program. They wanted admissions based on what had traditionally been the basis of law school admissions: GPA and LSAT scores.

Like Temple, MSL sought to be innovative and contribute to

a greater social good by developing a unique law school admissions test, even though the dean and faculty at MSL knew nothing about Temple's experience. In fact, Velvel and the others at MSL believed so strongly in the positive change they were making in legal education that they expected the Board of Regents—even the ABA down the road—to not only accept, but applaud their efforts.

Thus, Velvel and the others at MSL went into the next Board of Regents' inspection with a high degree of confidence. They submitted a 66-page report of changes and improvements that they had made to the school.

The second visiting team came on October 16 and 17, 1989. Legal experts on the team included: Dean Howard A. Glickstein of the Touro Law School in Huntington, N.Y.; John C. Welsh, professor at the Albany Law School in Albany, N.Y.; Dennis Stone, professor and library director at the University of Connecticut School of Law in Hartford; Associate Dean David Cluchey of the University of Maine School of Law in Portland; and Dr. Tossie Taylor, associate vice chancellor for Independent Colleges with the Massachusetts Board of Regents. (Taylor had replaced John Weston, who had left the Board of Regents.) Velvel and the faculty thought the visit went reasonably well, and they expected to be graduating their first class of law students in the spring.

*****

In the fall of 1989, Diane Sullivan entered her last year of law school. She expected to graduate in the spring and sit for the bar in July, as long as the Board of Regents approved the school. For Sullivan, it had been a challenging semester, prompting her to study every night until midnight in the library.

During the last few minutes of October 22, she decided to work even later in the library. Approaching midnight, she decided to study a different subject. She headed to her car to exchange books. Outside, the parking lot was vast, with spaces for hundreds of cars. Only her car and Juan Ortiz's car were there. The parking lot, tucked away behind the mill buildings, sat nearly a city block from traffic, hidden from public view. Despite this, Sullivan didn't feel uncomfortable. The lot was well-lit. Rows of streetlights bathed the expanse of asphalt in a strange, peach-rose hue that resembled candlelight.

On the way to her car, Sullivan heard what sounded like footsteps. She turned around but saw nothing. She listened, hearing only the far away sounds of cars moving down Brook Street. Perhaps, she thought, she had only imagined the sounds, or she had heard her own footsteps echoing in the night. Continuing to her car, she noticed how the streetlights had elongated her shape into a monster-like shadow.

Sullivan stopped. She heard the footsteps again. She was certain this time. The sound traveled from the back of the building. It didn't scare her at first, because she assumed it was a jogger. Being a runner herself, she sometimes ran early in the mornings or late at night.

As the sound faded, Sullivan felt alone. That's when it occurred to her that maybe someone was hidden in the shadows watching her. She picked up her books and ran back to the library.

"I heard something out there," she told Ortiz, the only other student in the library.

He narrowed his eyes.

Before he could reply, she said, "Someone was out there when I went to my car. Listen, I don't want to go out there again by myself. When you leave, I want to go with you."

Ortiz told her that he was leaving, but first he had to secure the building. Having stayed late many times, Sullivan knew the lock-up procedure. They walked through the school checking to see that all the windows and doors were closed and the lights were out.

Once they were certain that everything was secure, they set the alarm, locked the doors, and left MSL. Neither heard strange footsteps or noises. Perhaps they were too tired or their minds were crammed full of cases and arguments. Thus, they both got into their cars and left without looking back.

At 12:38 a.m., a foot patrol officer walking around Elm Square in downtown Andover heard the sounds of his soles slapping the pavement. He stopped and peered into a darkened store window. Then he heard what sounded like a large "Whoom!"

He realized that the sound had been close—maybe a quarter of a mile away. He looked down the hill and toward the train tracks, but the buildings between him and the sound blocked his view. He walked fast in that direction. Something had exploded.

*****

That night, a few minutes later, a phone call awoke Mike Coyne, associate professor at MSL. An operator for the school's security alarm company explained that the school's fire alarm had just gone off.

Coyne dressed and rushed to the school. He arrived to find black smoke rising from the basement windows. Glass was broken, and the air reeked of gasoline. It appeared that the fire was out. All eight heads of the lower floor's sprinkler system had gone off. Four to six inches of water stood on the floor, and water dripped from the ceiling and over all of the books.

Fire and police officials arrived. Police Sgt. Kevin Winters looked around. Outside a basement window he found a five-gallon white plastic joint compound bucket with a screw-on top and a handle. Written on the outside of the bucket in red marker were the words: "water only." Ironically, the bucket smelled oily, like gasoline.

Winters also found a red Butane lighter, the type used to start barbecue grills, and a burned yellow Latex glove. Winters told Coyne that his department would call area hospitals to see if someone had entered an emergency room with hand, arm, and facial burns. Without a doubt, whoever had set this fire had been injured, Sgt. Winters said.

*****

Despite water and smoke damage, the school opened a few hours later. The lower floor of the library had been destroyed. It contained treatises and older case materials, but it was less used than the upper floor. Damage was estimated to be $350,000.

The Andover police department began investigating the fire, and MSL put up a $2,000 reward for anyone with information; however, no one stepped forward.

In the meantime, the Board of Regents sent MSL the report from the latest inspection team. Arriving on December 14, 1989, the report was mostly positive. The team criticized the school's library, the professors' workloads, and the school's use of its own self-devised admission test—its substitute for the LSAT.

"MSL does not require the LSAT examination as a condition of admission to the law school. As noted, it is unlikely that MSL will achieve ABA accreditation if it continues this policy," wrote the inspectors. "We are concerned that MSL has dismissed too cavalierly the importance and relevance of the LSAT examination. It may be that MSL will wish to rely much less on the LSAT than do other law schools. That, alone, is not a basis for not requiring that applicants take the LSAT examination. The LSAT examination provides some objective measure for evaluating the quality of a student body."

Despite those criticisms, the overall report was good. The inspectors wrote, "The 1988 Visiting Committee was impressed with all that had been accomplished at MSL in a very short period of time. The progress that has taken place between the 1988 and 1989 inspections continues to be impressive. It is quite clear that the administration, faculty, and trustees of MSL are committed to developing a quality law school."

Before MSL could be approved, Velvel and the faculty had to go before the full Board of Regents, headed by Paul Tsongas.

There, the Board would finally decide whether MSL should have degree-granting authority or not.

*****

Judy Forgays, one of the original 14 students at Commonwealth, finally approached her last semester of law school. Law school had been a long ordeal for her. Even before Black Saturday, she took a leave of absence from Commonwealth, as she felt uncertain as to where the school was headed.

Once MSL started, she transferred. She found the classes in the new school small and challenging. In such an intimate environment, students and teachers knew each other well. However, Forgays found that she was always under pressure—constantly called upon to stand up, defend her point, and cite cases. The work was tough, but she managed to get through it all and keep her grades up.

One night in January 1990, Forgays took a rare break from her studies. She agreed to meet a couple of friends for drinks at OJ's in Dracut. It wasn't really her kind of bar. It was a tough, seedy place that she referred to as "a biker bar." Still, it was a night out, for a change.

As Forgays and her friends settled into a booth, she was surprised to see Michael Boland sitting with a couple of young people across the room. In his bone Irish knit sweater and khaki pants, he looked like a prep school student. Forgays was tempted to laugh at him. He looked out of place in the smoky room, where everyone was casually dressed in blue jeans and black leather.

"I can't believe he's here," Forgays fumed to her friends. "What would he be doing here, of all places?"

Her friends told her to forget it. She ordered a beer and tried to get involved in their conversation. Still, she couldn't help but notice Boland was still there with a sly grin on his face. It bothered her, and she kept thinking about how he had taken the money her father had spent on her law school education. Boland didn't feel any remorse or regret about that. She realized that she was too angry to have fun. She could not relax with Boland sitting across the room smiling, laughing, and having fun.

Forgays stood up, walked over to him, and shouted, "You scumbag, how could you do this to all of us? How dare you!" Propelled by rage, she shook her head at him, her wavy, shoulder-length hair flying.

"You'd better leave here right now," Forgays told him. Then she pointed to a big burly biker sitting at the bar. "You see that guy? He's going to take care of you, if you don't leave here now."

Though Forgays didn't know the guy who had a pack of cigarettes rolled up in the sleeve of his T-shirt, exposing a snake and skull tattoo on his upper arm, she figured for a beer and a buck or two, he'd help her out.

Boland grimaced and threw a few dollars on the table.

Forgays stared. To her surprise, Boland stood up and left. She had gotten rid of him. He couldn't intimidate her and the other students anymore. At last, she had the peace of mind of knowing that Boland no longer held any power over her or any of her classmates.

*****

Even though MSL still didn't have authority to grant degrees, the school grew. By spring semester, the school had 200 students. Much less expensive than Boston-area schools and a lot more convenient to northern-Massachusetts law students, MSL offered a number of advantages. The school helped students hone their writing and practical skills. Just as Joe Fishelson had said, MSL stood on its own merits.

By May 1990, 14 MSL students had prepared to graduate, as long as the Board of Regents allowed MSL to grant them law degrees.

On May 8, a dozen Regents and a variety of staff people, including Randolph Bromery, interim chancellor, met in Boston.

Bromery, a tall, broad-shouldered man, was nationally recognized as an educator. He was a former president of Springfield College in Springfield, Massachusetts, and a former chancellor of UMass Amherst. He was one of three African-Americans nationwide to hold a Ph.D. in geology.

Also at the meeting was Paul Tsongas, chairman of the Board of Regents. Since he tried to negotiate a merger with MSL while a trustee at Commonwealth Law School, he recused himself from voting. But, as it turned out, he did not recuse himself from voicing his opinion, particularly against MSL.

Regent Nicholas Boraski opened the discussion by saying that despite some negative discussion about the school in a committee meeting, the Board had unanimously decided that the school met the state's criteria for degree-granting authority.

"Will the graduates be permitted to take the bar exam?" asked Paul S. Doherty, the Regent who had been critical of SNESL when it came before the board.

"Yes," said Vice Chancellor Norma Rees, adding that most states allowed only graduates from ABA-accredited law schools to sit for the state bar exam. Massachusetts was one of the few states that allowed graduates of non-ABA schools to take the test.

"Has the staff looked at the question of the importance of taking the LSAT prior to admission?" asked Doherty.

As if Tsongas had been waiting for this opportunity, he interjected, "How can a school that doesn't take the LSAT be taken serious[ly]?"

Stunned, Velvel couldn't believe Tsongas was participating in the discussion. Trying to remain composed and not overreact, he said, "Statistics show that LSAT results are not absolute indicators of performance in law. In fact, the LSAT keeps many potential lawyers out of law school, particularly minorities and nontraditional students."

To that, Tsongas turned to another Regent and said, "I know schools like that. All you need is a check."

Velvel was appalled. Tsongas was not only participating in the discussion, but he tried to persuade the Board to reject MSL. Before Velvel could say anything further, Bromery said, "I think this is to the school's credit that they've decided to take a different approach."

Bromery said that standardized tests, such as the SAT, served as barriers to minority groups attending college and that there was no correlation between a high score on such a test and success in college. In fact, he said that was why Johns Hopkins Medical School (generally regarded as one of the top two medical schools in the nation) stopped using the Medical College Admission Test (MCAT). Bromery had been on Johns Hopkins' Board of Trustees when the medical school made that change. Now, he said, other schools recognized that such tests had serious flaws.

The other Regents agreed, saying that they believed that the LSAT and other standardized tests were elitist and faulty indicators of academic success. To Velvel and Coyne, it seemed as if Bromery had broken Tsongas' hold.

The Board voted. The decision was unanimous among the voting members of the Board of Regents. MSL received the power to grant juris doctorate degrees. Tsongas abstained, though he was clearly unhappy about the Board's decision.

*****

After the Board of Regents granted MSL its license, Judge James R. Lawton, chairman of the Board of Trustees of New England School of Law, in Boston, wrote to James White, the consultant on legal education to the ABA, and expressed concern. Primarily, he worried about how the new, lower-priced law school in Andover would impact the other law schools.

In his letter, Lawton had a specific complaint. He said that Velvel and representatives from MSL had attended the Northeast Pre-Law Advisors conference and set up a booth at the Law School Fair. "The Board of the conference had to accommodate them as the bylaws only indicated that an organization had to be a law school to participate," Lawton wrote. "There was no indication on their school sign that they were not an ABA-approved school." The morning after MSL had set up its booth, the Pre-Law Advisers' bylaws were changed so that only ABA-approved schools could exhibit at future law school fairs.

In reply, White thanked Lawton for keeping him abreast of MSL's activities. He wrote, "What do you think the possibility would be for the ABA-approved Massachusetts law schools to petition the Massachusetts Supreme Judicial Court to amend its rules to require graduation from an ABA-approved law school as a requirement for sitting for the Massachusetts bar examination? I would be grateful for your thoughts and advice on this matter."

Lawton responded by saying that representatives of the American Bar Association needed to pursue this, because other high powered local law schools did not feel threatened by MSL and would not act.

MSL would remain unaware of this correspondence until years later. Velvel and the MSL faculty had no idea that a competing law school and the ABA discussed ways to cripple the school in an effort to shut it down.

*****

On June 3, 1990, a picture-perfect day with sunshine and blue skies, a photographer tried to get the attention of 14 giddy students dressed in black caps and gowns. On the steps of Andover's Old Town Hall, they lined up in two rows.

As if the reality of the moment hadn't sunk in, the students told silly jokes and laughed lightheartedly. Evan Pilavis did his Cary Grant imitation, "Judy, Judy, Judy," for the benefit of fellow student Judy Forgays. Al Zappala played with the tassel hanging over his mortarboard, and the wind lifted Dick Ahern's hat off his head. Before it became completely airborne, he caught it, which evoked more laughter.

"Look this way and smile," the photographer ordered, and the class picture was taken.

"Hey, does someone out there need a lawyer?" Lakin called to people on the sidewalk. It brought another wave of laughter and more clicks of the camera.

"Louise, you are going to put this [the class picture] in the hallway, aren't you?" Lakin asked Velvel's wife.

"You bet I am," she answered.

"Are we done?" someone asked.

"No, Evan's mom wants to take a few more," Lakin said, through a fixed grin. This group had remained together through so many trials and tribulations, they had become one extended family.

When the photo session ended, the students entered the darkened auditorium and fell in step with the brass quartet's march. The trumpets heralded the students' success and beating the obstacles that had held them back, while the French horn alluded to the mysteries of the future.

Judge Isaac Borenstein, an MSL trustee and adjunct professor, stepped to the lectern first. "I thought that my opening remarks would draw from the classics," he said. "But since most of you know me and know how well I know the classics, I thought that I would choose rather the short, but poignant words of Jackie Gleason: 'How sweet it is!'"

The crowd cheered. Several students rose to their feet and applauded. That was the perfect phrase: "How sweet it is."

"There will be many graduations, I know, at the Massachusetts School of Law . . . and yet this is a particularly historic, happy, and indeed sweet event," continued Borenstein. "The class of 1990 is a pioneer class . . . and you . . . are now graduating. We are only at the beginning of a long and important road. The last year and a half of my involvement with this school has raised for me some important themes about dreams that I think are very relevant to the practice of law. They include such things as dreams and goals and ideals and making those dreams come true and taking risks, being persistent, having a commitment, open debate, humor, and a little bit of craziness, too."

When he concluded, Diane Sullivan, the class valedictorian, approached the podium. With a grade point average of 3.74, she was graduating magna cum laude. She had missed summa cum laude by a mere hundredth of a point. (She still holds the highest grade point average ever achieved at MSL.)

Nervous, Sullivan surveyed the crowd, then she spoke emphatically, "How wonderful it feels to stand up here and think back over these past four years and still be able to smile." Laughter among the students, born of recognition, eased her tension.

In composing her speech, Sullivan wanted the crowd to understand the resolute, steadfast determination of herself and her classmates. She wanted them to understand how they had leaped every imaginable hurdle and overcome all of these obstacles just to become lawyers. She asked, "Have you ever wanted something so badly that you could taste it?"

She paused slightly, and then she asked the crowd to recall one thing that they had always wanted—maybe a Mercedes, maybe a dress in the window of Saks Fifth Avenue, or maybe the stamina to finish the Boston Marathon. Then she told them to imagine working hard toward that dream, seeing it draw near, and, just before they grabbed it, they fell to the dirt and saw the coveted prize disappear. Imagine the anguish and the frustration, she said.

"The graduates here tonight know that feeling, but they never gave up," Sullivan said, defiance resonating in her voice. "These individuals have gone beyond difficulty to keep the dream of becoming a lawyer alive. They stubbornly refused to quit. They never blamed fate. But rather, they accepted responsibility for their lives, and now they accept that same responsibility for the lives of others."

She emphasized that these were not ordinary graduates. They didn't decide to become lawyers because of greed. They didn't aspire to work in big firms in Boston or New York. They weren't in search of riches and power. Simply, they wanted a better life and to serve those who had been oppressed or underserved. "Some of us are here because we want to take on issues or causes . . . ," she said, emphasizing that some of them wanted to fight discrimination, poverty, crime, environmental pollution, as well as other social issues. They would pursue cases that other lawyers wouldn't touch, because the other attorneys didn't believe that the small pay justified the hard work.

"We will not become one of the many lawyers," Sullivan concluded. "We'll become one of the few good lawyers."

With that, graduates lined up to walk across the stage. John Lakin, Dick Ahern, Al Zappala, John Cascarano, Diane Sullivan, Judy Forgays, and seven others. One by one they received their diplomas from Dean Velvel.

None of them gave a glancing thought to MSL's future or to whether the school would be accredited by the American Bar Association. They had graduated and had their diplomas in hand. Now they could sit for the Massachusetts bar, even though they couldn't sit for the bar in most other states.

They all figured that the worst was over for them, as well as for MSL. What could be worse than what they'd been through already? They had beaten the odds.

Chapter 6

American Bar Association

When Velvel handed diplomas to Zappala, Ahern, Sullivan, Lakin, and all the other students who had helped build MSL, the dean knew that a seismic shift had occurred in his thinking. These students' path to obtaining a law degree had contrasted in almost every way with his experience. Their parents didn't pay their tuition; rather, they worked hard to earn the money. Rather than being fresh-faced kids, they were adults—mature, with grown-up lives that included spouses, children, and, in some cases, grandchildren. They had experienced a lot in life. Though not financially rich, these students had a wealth of practical knowledge and knew how to make their way through life.

Their efforts and skills enabled them to end up in the same place that all smart, determined law school students end up—holding juris doctorate degrees, ready to sit for the state bar exam, and ready to move on and practice law. Yet because MSL's students had grown up differently from most law school graduates, they reflected down-to-earth attitudes that were sorely needed in the law profession, Velvel thought. They could contribute to social good, just as Sullivan had said in her speech.

At MSL, Velvel had found that most of the students were bright and had common-sense adaptability. If a job needed to be done, they came up with intelligent, practical solutions, as

Zappala had done in obtaining thousands of dollars worth of furniture with a handshake. Other students had reacted similarly in
setting up fundraisers and advertising campaigns for the school.
The students did whatever it took to get the school opened. They
were used to working hard and solving day-to-day problems in
ways that didn't involve extravagant spending or hiring specialists to do the work. They were independent self-starters.

When the school opened, those same students sat down and
studied, and worked hard at learning the law. Now they wanted
to use it to help others. In studying, they enjoyed the intellectual
combat and believed the work would get them ahead a little in
life.

For the most part, the students didn't care that MSL wasn't
Harvard or one of the nation's top law schools. Most of them did-
n't care whether they were at the top of their class or whether they
had the highest GPA. They cared most about becoming lawyers
and practicing law. If they were well-paid for it, that was an
added advantage.

Much of this contradicted what Velvel had been taught. He
was raised to believe that competence and intelligence were
measured by the As one earned, the scores one achieved on aptitude tests, and the schools one attended. One's practical knowledge mattered less, or so he absorbed as a boy. What mattered
was reading at a young age, attending the right schools, getting
high grades, and graduating at the head of the class.

Certainly, he had experienced this elitist thinking in high
school where he was asked to take a National Merit Scholarship
test because of a prior score he had gotten on a similar test, and
where Evanston Township High School's strong emphasis on
academics caused him to take a speed-reading course that nearly
destroyed his future. Velvel had seen it in college, among the jun-
iors and seniors, who measured their worth by their high LSAT
scores and acceptance into the Harvard and Yale law schools—a
summum bonum in their minds. He had seen it among law school
students, including himself, who fixated on high grades and class

standing. As well, he had seen it among lawyers in Washington and among law school professors, who venerated book smarts and academic pedigrees. All around him, in every phase of his life, Velvel had seen human worth measured by academic intelligence.

Fortunately for Velvel, he ultimately measured up to the academic standard. In the early 1960s, he had graduated from the prestigious Michigan Law School near the top of his class. In Washington, he worked in the Department of Justice, then briefly for Senator William Proxmire, before becoming a professor at the University of Kansas School of Law.

But in America's heartland, he questioned whether he had grabbed the academic world's brass ring. His high academic standing at Michigan, his many articles in law school journals, a book on the Vietnam War and civil disobedience, and being a well-liked and admired professor of constitutional law meant nothing next to a Harvard Law School degree. KU was a mid-level law school, and mid-level schools served as way stations for graduates of Harvard, who ultimately moved on to teaching at higher-ranking, sometimes pinnacle, schools such as the University of Chicago Law School or Georgetown Law School. Graduates from schools other than Harvard, such as Velvel, did not often get these opportunities.

What Velvel saw in Kansas existed in Washington, too, although he hadn't seen it or been much aware of it the first time around. When he returned to Washington, however, he discovered that many of the lawyers he encountered were obsessed with being the smartest, best educated, most-credentialed, and best connected. Glad-handing and general pomposity struck Velvel as shallow and pretentious.

Taking the deanship at Commonwealth put Velvel face to face with persons he had rarely seen in law schools or in the practice of law. Many of them had grown up poor or in working-class families. Thus, their lives contrasted in almost every way with the lives of persons in law school academia and in Washington's legal circles. Yet they were bright and would do well in life if given half a chance. That's when it occurred to him that the legal community needed to look beyond academic Einsteins. Good, hard-working people deserved a chance to practice law, in spite of age, LSAT scores, and limited financial resources.

As Velvel understood these students, he realized the falsity and, in fact, the evilness of the elitist philosophy that had been pounded into him and the American legal system. If some of MSL's students had been born Kennedys, he thought, or if they had had born with money and societal advantages, their circumstances would be different. That had no bearing on their intelligence or competence. It spoke merely of money and social class.

Velvel realized that the American legal profession hadn't always been made up of elitists. In fact, prior to the Revolutionary War, ambitious young men studied law through apprenticeships, similar to the way masons, carpenters, and silversmiths studied their trades. They paid for their instruction, as well as for room and board. In Massachusetts, a law apprenticeship lasted five years—reduced by a year if a student already had a year of college. Apprenticeship time varied throughout the colonies.

During the American Revolution and in the new government, lawyers, such as Adams, Jefferson, Hamilton, and Monroe, occupied powerful positions. After the war, law schools such as the one at the College of William and Mary, in Virginia, and the Litchfield Law School, in Connecticut, opened up, and this education took the lawyers away from the "trade" classification. By the early 19th century, the field of law was, possibly, the single most influential field in American society. Alexis de Tocqueville, an aristocratic French politician, writer, and observer, wrote in *Democracy in America*, "If I were asked where I place the American aristocracy, I should reply without hesitation that it occupies the judicial bench and bar."

As democracy set in and manufacturing and commerce started driving the 19th century economy, Americans shunned aristocratic thinking and the landholding requirements for voting. Populist sentiments emerged and a greater cross-section of people participated in lawmaking. "Let the people rule," became the cry of President Andrew Jackson, orphaned son of Scotch-Irish immigrants killed during the Revolutionary War. A model of the do-it-yourself philosophy, Jackson demonstrated that anyone, even the impoverished, could achieve success through persistence, hard work, and self-motivation.

Until about 1880, secondary and college education took a backseat to physical hard work and intellectual self-improvement. Middle, lower, and agricultural classes found no time for college. Self-improvement came from reading or by attending traveling lectures, known as "lyceums." This applied to the law profession, too.

With the nation expanding westward and with a steadily increasing need for frontier lawyers, state legislators changed the parameters for entering law practice. In general, neither education (legal or otherwise) nor apprenticeship was needed. In fact, by 1860, 30 out of the 39 states no longer required lawyers to apprentice. Lawyers studied law on their own.

Abraham Lincoln's success with self-study became an inspiration to people of all classes. Lincoln would say that he "studied with nobody," which was true. He never had more than a year of formal education of any kind. When James T. Thornton wrote to Lincoln and asked how a friend of his should study law, Lincoln responded, " . . . my judgment is, that he read the books for himself without an instructor. That is precisely the way I came to the law. Read *Blackstone's Commentaries, Chitty's Pleadings, Greenleaf's Evidence, Story's Equity*, and *Story's Equity Pleadings*, get a license, and go to the practice, and still keep reading. That is my judgment of the cheapest, quickest and best way . . . ."

But by the turn of the 20th century, American society had changed again. The educated specialist replaced the ideal of the self-made man. Universities proliferated, as did law schools. In

1870, 34 American law schools existed with 1,653 students. In 1920, 143 law schools existed with 27,000 students.

As this movement kicked off, lawyers did not have any type of organization. They didn't operate by a uniform code of ethics nor have a way to discuss national legal issues and how their profession was evolving. Thus, in 1878, 100 lawyers from 21 states met in Saratoga Springs, New York, and created the American Bar Association. The Association's co-founders, Simeon Baldwin, a Yale law professor, and Carleton Hunt, a professor of law at the University of Louisiana (now Tulane), wrote the by-laws. These academics sought to educate the profession. Within a year, Hunt recommended that only law school graduates be allowed to take state bar exams. In the next year, 1880, Hunt proposed a three-year course of study and outlined what courses should be taught: morals, political philosophy, English law, and state constitutional law.

As early as 1894, ABA leaders criticized part-time, night law schools for attracting working students. Knowing that these students had to work to support their families and pay for their education, ABA leaders said that working distracted law students from their studies. These ABA leaders knew that if they could keep the working class out of the law schools, they could reduce the number of immigrants, Irish, Jews, blacks, and other working class people from entering their profession.

In an authorized 1991 historical account of the ABA and the legal academy, *The ABA's First Section: Assuring a Qualified Bar*, Susan Boyd wrote of the legal association's elitist roots: "Bigotry and prejudice permeated the established bar and law school world. There clearly was egregious discrimination against African-Americans, Jews, Catholics, and immigrants from places other than Northern Europe. A great deal of the criticism of night and proprietary law schools stemmed from the fact that these institutions provided access for the vast [cross-] section of the population."

In an attempt to build a wall that would protect the profession from what appeared to be a tidal wave of working-class entrants, John Henry Wigmore, a famous law school dean at Northwestern University, proposed that the ABA insist that law schools schedule their lectures during the day. This would prevent working students from attending.

While no one acted on Wigmore's proposal, and night schools proliferated for another 20 years, the ABA then found another "solution." Once the ABA began inspecting law schools and accrediting their programs in 1923, it did not approve a single night program, even though there were far more part-time night students than full-time day students. The ABA considered night law schools, most of which were independent proprietary schools, to be second-rate institutions. Even law schools that offered both day and night programs distinguished between the two programs by setting different admissions standards. Students who couldn't get into the day program could apply to the night school, which had lower admissions standards as well as lower expectations.

Some of the prejudices against night and part-time schools continued for 60 years in the legal academy. MSL, however, did not have different standards for day or night or full-time or part-time students. Velvel and his colleagues expected high performance across the board. In a sense, the school was extraordinarily tough on students, as if MSL had to prove that it wasn't Commonwealth or a slapdash school that had been the butt of legal academics' jokes. It was readying students for law practice. As Velvel shook hands with each and every student to whom he presented a diploma at the school's first commencement, he reveled in the fact that the students had admirably met the rigorous challenges and had succeeded. To exclude them or others like them from the legal profession, just because they were born less privileged than most students at ABA schools, he considered a moral crime against them and society.

*****

In the fall of 1990, a picture of MSL's first graduating class hung in the school's lobby, just as Louise had promised. In July, many of the 14 MSL graduates took the Massachusetts Bar Exam. Nine passed. With the ability now to practice law, the MSL graduates obtained business cards, acquired business furniture, and rented law offices.

John Lakin married classmate Jo Ann Lanza and became busy setting up a practice in Andover with Al Zappala. John's twin brother Ken would soon join them. Dick Ahern dated classmate Debra Dewitt. They would later open a practice in Lowell and marry. John Cascarano had taken a job as a substitute teacher at Broad Meadows Junior High School in Quincy. It was the same school that he and his best friend, Michael Mattson, had attended some 15 years earlier. Now he was saving his money and planning to open up his own practice the next year.

Diane Sullivan, who had wanted so much to become a lawyer, wasn't headed for law practice right away. Setting up her own firm required money that she didn't have. Though she earned a decent salary as vice president of Commerce Bank in Worcester, Sullivan sent her younger brother to Bentley College and was paying for his tuition. She couldn't afford to take a financial risk quite yet, so she remained at the bank. Bill Roberts, the bank chairman, appointed her to the loan committee, where she participated in major lending decisions. Roberts soon regretted that move. One day, he said to her, "The worst thing that you can do is educate a woman to be a lawyer. Then you can no longer control her."

His words stung like a slap across the face. For many years, Roberts had been the one person at the bank who had really supported her and championed her career. Now, however, he resented her law school degree and the fact that she had developed into a mature, fiercely independent woman with analytical, decision-making skills. She didn't need to look to other committee members to make her decisions. Rather, she acted prudently and judiciously, weighing the facts and making independent, unbiased choices. Sullivan's high principles, however, didn't endear her to the other loan committee members. Roberts' caustic remark and looks from other committee members sent one message to her: she was not welcomed on the committee. She sensed that her career at Commerce Bank was nearing an end.

Coincidentally, Paula Dickinson, law professor and a founder of MSL, called Sullivan and asked if she would be interested in teaching a writing course at the school. Though Sullivan loved learning and thrived in an intellectually stimulating environment, she wasn't excited about teaching. And writing was her least favorite subject anyway. Mike Coyne, now the associate dean, asked Sullivan if she could think of a course that she would like to teach. Sullivan thought. After a few seconds, she replied that she would teach secured transactions and banking. Certainly, she knew the subject well enough; thus, MSL hired her as an adjunct professor.

When spring semester began in January 1991, Sullivan taught her first class. One day, she asked her students, "How many of you have approached the cash register at the grocery store only to realize that you've either forgotten your checkbook or run out of checks?"

There was a show of hands.

"So what do you do?" she asked. Some students said that they went home and retrieved checks. Other used their credit cards or obtained cash from an ATM machine.

At that point, Sullivan held up an orange on which she had written with a felt-tipped pen, "Happy Halloween—$5." On it was her signature with some other numbers.

"Is this negotiable?" she asked the class.

The students looked at her as if she'd lost her mind.

She divided the class into groups and began handing out objects on which various amounts of money and other information were written. To one group, she gave an orange. To another group, she gave a pizza box. To another group, she handed a watermelon. Students were assigned one very simple-sounding task: go out and cash these things. Sullivan told them to convince bank tellers that these were legitimate bank drafts.

The next morning, Sullivan found eight voice mail messages on her machine. All were from bank tellers who wanted to know if she really meant to write a check on an orange or on a pizza box.

Students with the orange said that the fruit had been non-negotiable. Sullivan told them to go back and try again, but be more persuasive. Students with the pizza box had a little more luck. The teller told them they could cash it—demonstrating that a check could be written on anything as long as it had the right information—but because of all of the special handling, she would have to charge them a sizeable handling fee. None of them had that kind of money.

The group with the watermelon cashed their "check," showing that what counted was what was written, not what it was written on. The students bought donuts for the class with their watermelon money.

The lesson was fun, practical, and it left a lasting impression on students. Sullivan liked that, and she discovered teaching to be more fun than she had expected. Soon she realized that students regarded her as more than a teacher. She was a mentor and a role model. Like herself, her students were sons and daughters of mill and factory workers. They looked up to her as an example of what could be accomplished if they tried and applied themselves. She was the result of hard work and perseverance.

This drove home the important role Sullivan served in teaching. Thus, she decided to teach full time. Sullivan worked at the bank until mid-afternoon, and then she worked at the school until late at night. She had two full-time careers. It was a pace that Sullivan realized she couldn't keep up forever. She saw the time coming in which she would have to choose.

*****

Stories like Sullivan's made Velvel realize that, contrary to the elitism he had seen in both the legal and academic worlds, MSL represented a practical exercise in American idealism. It gave ordinary people a chance to better themselves. He and the faculty had taken a fresh look at legal education and approached it in a practical, low-cost, and rigorous way. It had worked, Velvel thought, particularly judging by the quality of the school's graduates and by the school's burgeoning enrollments. By the spring of 1991, there were 400 students, with applications arriving daily.

The public was beating a path to MSL's door, doing so at a rate that enabled the school to save money—enough, in fact, that the school's trustees voted to put $1 million down on a new building. It was an impressive, new three-story brick structure with 90,000 square feet, nestled in the woods, surrounded by trees and ponds and other modern office buildings. The building, originally constructed for high-tech companies, had large picture windows on all sides and a huge parking lot. It wasn't a $30- or $40-million palace like those that some other law schools had. It didn't have tiered seating in the classrooms. The faculty had to work around a few support columns here and there, but that didn't hinder the students' ability to see. The building was exactly what the faculty had wanted: big, clean, airy, modern, and beautiful. The original asking price for it had been $11 million. However, the New England real estate market was in a slump, and the developer sold it to MSL, with the two lower floors built-out to the school's specifications, for $5.4 million.

Faculty members and the dean designed the interior, placing the library on the western side of the ground floor. Ringed by faculty offices, the library served as the school's nucleus where students could meet in study groups, sometimes assisted by professors whose offices were only paces away. Faculty office doors remained open, inviting students to casually stop by and ask questions. The atmosphere within the library was one that promoted idea exchanges and discussions. The accessibility of the faculty was a heartening change from law schools that kept faculty in private inner sanctums. In those schools, students who wished to speak with a professor sometimes found the faculty wing closed and locked.

At MSL, the library improved each year. Insurance money from the fire enabled the school to purchase new books. In addition, MSL acquired Commonwealth's library, as well as a 30,000-volume library from the defunct Boston law firm of Gaston & Snow.

Though plans existed to expand the school's traditional library, the dean and faculty decided to give the students even greater research capabilities by setting up a computer lab with 30 personal computers. The school made Internet and research data banks, such as Westlaw, available to students.

At the same time, the full-time faculty improved their teaching techniques and expanded the number of practical skills courses offered. MSL expected of each professor rigorous, pertinent legal education. To monitor professors' progress and to help them improve, the school videotaped one or more classroom sessions from each professor. The full-time faculty reviewed and critiqued these videotapes, and they also visited other professors' classes and made suggestions. In addition, the dean visited each classroom and analyzed each professor's performance. The dean also circulated memos addressing problems he had seen in the classrooms, and he suggested methods for improving teaching methods. He pointed out new teaching tips and trends.

By the fall of 1990, MSL had added to its faculty, which previously consisted of just four full-time professors. Drawn to MSL were lawyers who always wanted to teach and those who empathized with the school's nontraditional student body and the school's mission to open up legal education to minorities and white ethnic students from working-class families. Many of the professors related to these students because they had grown up in similar situations. Peter Malaguti's father was a gardener. Tony Copani's family had immigrated from Sicily, and his father died just before he graduated from law school.

Phil Coppola's parents were working-class immigrants from Sicily. He was the first in his family to attend college and did so on the GI Bill, attending law school at night. Ultimately he became a public defender. Andrej Starkis' parents and siblings were World War II refugees from Latvia. In 1946, Starkis' mother was six-months pregnant with him when they arrived in America. Starkis started college but went into the Peace Corps and finished later. After college, he worked as a carpenter, and by the time he entered law school, he was 25 years old—older than many of his classmates.

Joe Devlin grew up in a large family in the projects, but desperately sought a better life. He studied hard and made it into the famous Boston Latin High School (as did Starkis and Coyne), before entering Brandeis University and then Boston University School of Law. Kurt Olson grew up in a family that owned a liquor and grocery store. To help out, he bagged potatoes and counted cans, but he dreamed of doing something better with his life, something that would allow him to use his brain. He attended Colby College, graduating cum laude, and received his J.D. from MSL, graduating magna cum laude.

As well, the staff had similar backgrounds. Paula Colby-Clements grew up in a working-class family and after graduating cum laude from MSL, she began directing the school's admissions and career services program. Lynn Bastille Bowab came from working-class roots and started working at MSL part time while she was a student at Merrimack College before becoming director of the school's financial aid department. The dean's wife, Louise Rose, joined the school's staff too, heading up student registration.

A few faculty members grew up with more privileges than others did, yet they embraced the school's reformation effort, too. Tom Martin, whose father had been a dean at Harvard, the school where Martin had attended both college and law school, knew the value of practical skills training and would sometimes say about his alma mater, "It's not all that it's cracked up to be." Connie Rudnick, who lived in the prestigious ocean community of Marblehead, had been a partner in the Boston firm of Gargiulo, Rudnick & Gargiulo for 15 years, concentrating on criminal and civil litigation. From the start, she felt at home with the students and enjoyed teaching at MSL.

There was very little turnover in the school's faculty. Once faculty members joined the MSL group, they usually stayed on and made the school's mission their own. They were a cohesive group, bound together by this vision of offering legal education to those who traditionally were shut out.

With a larger, more experienced faculty, more physical resources, and a beautiful new building, Dean Velvel and Associate Dean Coyne decided it was time to seek ABA accreditation. In the spring of 1991, they gathered scores of books, articles, pamphlets, and documents and began studying up on what they needed to do.

They knew that ABA accreditation would make MSL's graduates eligible to take the bar examination anywhere in the United States. Thus, it would increase students' mobility once they graduated from law school. In 1991, 42 states required newly graduated bar candidates to be graduates of ABA-accredited law schools. Only a few states allowed some—not all—new graduates to take the bar examination and be admitted to practice law if they had attended a non-ABA school. Thus, the ABA had a monopoly in more than 80 percent of the states.

Under Massachusetts' unusual rule, MSL graduates could immediately take the bar in Massachusetts, because they had graduated from a state-approved school. Once they had passed the state bar, they could practice law within Massachusetts. However, they could not take bar exams, upon graduation, in neighboring or relatively close states, including New Hampshire (just 10 minutes away), Connecticut, Maine, Rhode Island, New York, New Jersey, and Pennsylvania.

In more than half of the 42 ABA states, MSL graduates would

never be able to sit for the bar exam, no matter how long they practiced law in Massachusetts. Conceivably, an MSL graduate could be appointed to a high federal court, even the Supreme Court, yet he or she would still be unable to take the bar in more than half of the ABA states. In the states where MSL graduates could ultimately take the bar exam, they would first need to have practiced law from three to 10 years in Massachusetts.

Without ABA accreditation, MSL graduates had limited geographic options in terms of practicing law. This made the school less desirable to a national, non-New England audience looking for low-cost legal study. Beyond increasing MSL graduates' geographic options, ABA accreditation would increase the school's stature. The ABA had told the public for decades that its accreditation process weeded out schools that didn't measure up academically or financially. The ABA said that it accomplished this by making schools live up to a tough set of standards. The premise sounded logical to most people, even to many within the legal profession who had no reason to think otherwise. Being the largest and most powerful professional association in the nation, the ABA appeared beyond reproach.

All of this, particularly the ABA's wide ranging monopoly over those who could take bar exams, placed the ABA in an enormously powerful position, enabling it to control not just the legal profession itself but law students and law schools. The ABA became involved in how students were taught and how the schools would be set up and run. Beginning in the 1920s, the ABA secured this tight grip on legal education as it designed an accreditation program aimed at keeping "undesirable" segments of society out of the legal profession.

The ABA further stepped up its efforts to control legal education and the law profession following World War II. With the GI Bill paying veterans' ways into technical schools, colleges and universities, education enrollments surged. That included law school enrollment, too. Then, in 1952, the ABA persuaded the federal government to make the ABA Council of the Section of

Legal Education (also known as the Section) the federally recognized accrediting body for the nation's law schools. The ABA also aggressively lobbied state courts to permit only graduates of ABA schools to sit for bar exams upon graduation. By the mid-1970s, four-fifths of U.S. states agreed to be a part of this monopoly.

Law schools seeking accreditation faced a laundry list of demands, known as standards, imposed by the ABA. Association officials described them as "must-haves." While many of the rules were written down, some were not; however, deans, who had experience with and talked among themselves about accreditation, knew what was expected.

In fact, since the early 1970s, the whole accreditation process had taken on a collective bargaining tone. In March 1973, a group of individuals, known as the "Ten Wise Ones," met. These individuals included eight past presidents of the American Association of Law Schools (AALS), as well as Michael H. Cardozo, who in 1963 became the AALS' first executive director and set up its national office. Because the AALS maintained close ties with the ABA, Millard Ruud, then the consultant on legal education to the ABA, who was about to become the AALS' next executive director, attended, too. Together these men brainstormed and deliberated about the AALS' future pursuits.

While the AALS was supposed to be a law school organization, in reality it was run by law school academics who sought to preserve and enhance their way of life. These academics sought to improve their salaries, benefits, and working conditions. So, in summarizing the 1973 meeting of the Ten Wise Ones for the *Journal of Legal Education*, Maurice Rosenberg, the AALS president, wrote that the group expressed concern over the way universities were siphoning funds away from the law schools in order to support the entire university program. The "Ten Wise Ones" felt that the AALS should be "defending the fiscal entitlements of legal education." In other words, they believed law professors were being short-changed in terms of pay and benefits.

"This view led to serious discussions about AALS' role in the collective bargaining arena," wrote Rosenberg. Also, "some thought a possible goal might be to develop enforceable standards in support of entitlements of law faculty members as an alternative to trying to utilize the dynamics of the labor-management bargaining arena."

Rosenberg added, "No one appeared to doubt that the association will need to take a more active part in pressing for equitable treatment of law teachers by university administrations and legislatures with regard to tenurial and promotional rights . . . ."

Since the Ten Wise Ones had discussed using "enforceable standards in support of entitlements of law faculty members as an alternative to . . . the labor-management bargaining arena," it is easy to understand why AALS leaders began playing an active role in ABA accreditation and came to control it, many felt. Starting in the early to mid 1970s, the ABA's standards regulated how much professors should be paid, how many hours per week and how many months per year they could be required to teach, how much administrative work (if any) they could be required to do, how many books the library had to have, what constituted a full-time professor, how many full-time professors a school needed to have for its overall number of students (the student-faculty ratio), how much time professors could practice law and still teach, how much paid sabbatical leave professors had to be given, and what courses professors could teach.

The Section of Legal Education sharply limited the number of hours per week and the number of months per year a full-time professor could teach and the amount of administrative work required of any professor. It didn't allow law professors to practice law, except *very* minimally, unlike many medical professors, who practiced extensively and brought their practical experience into the classroom.

The Section also demanded that every law school maintain a low student-to-full-time faculty ratio. For many schools, this student-to-full-time faculty ratio became a complex and disconcerting issue. Only an individual who did nothing else in life but teach law could be considered a full-time professor. This individual couldn't maintain an office elsewhere or even be "of counsel" to a law firm. A full-time professor couldn't perform administrative duties in the school or be a still-teaching emeritus professor.

Further creating an elitist dichotomy and reprising the days when the ABA tried to bar the working class from law school altogether, the ABA did not want full-time law students to work more than 20 hours per week—even if they needed the money to pay for school. It did not matter how needy or how bright the students were. On the other hand, if they volunteered for free in law offices, that was OK. They could work for free for as many hours per week as they wished.

After a close look at all of these rules, Coyne and Velvel wondered how they provided students with sound, quality legal education. It struck them that the standards read more like the demands of a labor union, protecting the income and benefits of legal academic professionals, rather than fostering and promoting quality legal education. In fact, in 1975, the Section of Legal Education and Admissions to the Bar presented a revision of several of the accreditation standards to the House of Delegates. One was Standard 405. As amended, it stated, in general terms, that all law schools had to maintain conditions sufficient to attract a competent faculty. But then it went on to detail, in specific terms, the requirements regarding salaries, academic leaves, and other professional perquisites.

William B. Spann, Jr., a future president of the ABA, spoke about the amendments to Standard 405, saying, "I simply think that we have—if we enact these things as a requirement for accreditation, we have sort of set ourselves up as a collective bargaining agent for law professors against the various Boards of Regents and other educational bodies of the state that control it. [We've] said really that if you don't pay as much as . . . reasonably related to prevailing compensation of comparably qualified private practitioners, government attorneys, and judiciary—it's so broad that we might have a particular accrediting team say, well, if you don't pay these professors as much as the Supreme Court of the state, we're not going to accredit you. I think the general principle of 405 is enough and do not think that we should lay down standards, which may rise to haunt us and, as I say, become a collective bargaining agent for the law professors and this looks very much like a labor contract drawn by a law professor to me."

Demanding extravagant wages, working conditions, and lifestyles for law professors, and demanding plush facilities and libraries, the ABA standards required enormous financial resources. This dramatically drove up costs and tuitions. This in turn excluded the working class, minorities, and midlife career changers. The standards also thwarted innovative new schools, such as MSL, which strived to keep costs and tuitions low.

Velvel and Coyne thought about all this and became alarmed as they realized MSL and its mission did not fit the rigid ABA mold.

*****

A few days after Thanksgiving in 1991, Joe Fishelson had a freak car accident in his hometown of Wooster, Ohio. The Corvette that he had long enjoyed accelerated from a parallel parking space and sped out of control. Fishelson tried to regain control as the sports car hit a number of parked cars. But two weeks later, on December 12, 1991, he died from injuries suffered in the accident. He was 77 years old.

Velvel always remembered the advice his cousin had given him about the school, "You're no good to anyone if you don't survive." At all times, Velvel felt compelled to follow this principle. Too many people depended on the school, not just the students currently enrolled, but students of the future who could not get legal education elsewhere. The school had to survive to serve them and change the system to make legal education available to all who wanted, and had the ability, to become lawyers.

Velvel thought about what it meant to fit the ABA mold. It meant hiring a large, expensive full-time faculty and incurring enormous library and facility expenses. As a result, the school would have to increase its tuition by 50 to 100 percent. The faculty would also have to admit a wealthier class of people than it set out to serve. The school's mission would have to change too.

Rather than do that, Velvel, Coyne, and their colleagues decided to stick with the school's original mission—to offer high quality, low cost, practical legal education to competent, hardworking people who had been excluded from many of the benefits of American life—no matter what adversity they faced. They were not going to forsake the school's mission to satisfy what they considered to be expensive, elitist ABA standards, which had little or nothing to do with good education. The question remained, could they satisfy the Section of Legal Education without sacrificing MSL's mission, without turning it into another expensive, elitist law school?

*****

Velvel found what he considered to be the answer in the ABA's Standard 802, which permitted a variance from the standards. It read, "A law school proposing to offer a program of legal education contrary to the terms of the standards may apply to the Council for a variance. The variance may be granted if the Council finds that the proposal is consistent with the general purposes of the standards."

MSL offered a high quality legal education. Therefore, Velvel and Coyne thought the school's program would be consistent with the "general purposes of the standards." After all, as members of the ABA had said themselves, the whole point of accreditation was to ensure a good legal education. Also, Velvel and Coyne, who had both invested many years in the legal profession, believed the leaders of the ABA were moral people who tried to do the right thing. They believed the right thing would be to accredit a law school that offered a good education, as MSL did.

Still Velvel's concerns mounted as he read more about ABA accreditation, talked with deans and librarians of various schools who had gone through the accreditation process, and tried unsuccessfully to obtain illustrative accreditation documents from the ABA, including sample law school self-studies. MSL also was excluded from the ABA's two-day accreditation workshops, which, the Section of Legal Education claimed, were only for ABA schools seeking re-accreditation. Instead, MSL was admitted only to a single hour-long session of general information for unaccredited schools. That single session was of no help.

Velvel's search for accreditation documents led MSL to Northwestern University, a depository for ABA materials. Upon reading information gathered there, as well as documents shared by other law schools, and a two-inch stack obtained from the Department of Education, Velvel grew increasingly concerned. He could not find a single instance in which the ABA had granted a Standard 802 waiver. In fact, the ABA had not accredited a single school that departed from its key criteria since 1973, the year that James White was appointed the ABA's consultant on legal education, replacing Ruud.

Perhaps the ABA might not approve MSL, Velvel thought. Perhaps Standard 802 was a ruse intended to satisfy the federal Department of Education's criteria requiring diversity of education. Perhaps the ABA was not interested in innovative schools that encouraged working-class individuals.

ABA accreditation officials suggested that Velvel and Coyne hire a consultant to walk them through the accreditation process and show them how to prepare a self-study. Velvel contacted Richardson Nahstoll, an attorney from Portland, Oregon, and an ABA old-timer. However, Nahstoll, who had chaired the committee that drafted the ABA's revised standards in the early 1970s, declined to assist MSL. He said that MSL would never gain approval if it did not use the LSAT.

Instead, MSL hired Ansel Chaplin, a name partner with the Boston firm Chaplin & Milstein. Chaplin made various contacts within the ABA to determine what steps MSL needed to take to achieve accreditation. As a result, James White let it be known that he would be willing to visit the school. Though White claimed to be merely a bureaucrat in the ABA without much power, Velvel had heard otherwise. Deans and professors from other law schools had made it clear to him that White was highly influential.

(Nearly two years later, White was described in an article titled, "Jim Who?" in the *National Law Journal*. Reporter Ken Myers wrote that, while the average lawyer might not recognize the name James P. White, he was clearly the "most important person in legal education." As director of law school accreditation, White influenced the thinking of many individuals in the accreditation process, from site inspectors to those heading the Accreditation Committee. A host of individuals in legal education consulted with him regularly, particularly when seeking advice on appointing deans. Very little happened within legal education without White's knowledge and consent.)

Thus, White was invited to visit MSL, look it over, and offer his opinion about the school's readiness.

White appeared to be determined when he set out for MSL from his home in Indianapolis on January 23, 1992. Weather forecasters had predicted heavy snow. White pressed on anyway, leaving Indianapolis. After his plane had become grounded in Cleveland, he changed planes. He arrived in Andover later that day.

Coyne found this curious. White could have rescheduled his visit. The school wasn't applying for ABA accreditation for another six to nine months. Coyne figured that White wanted to take a good look at MSL and meet Dean Velvel, who was scheduled to speak before the ABA's House of Delegates the following week at the ABA's mid-winter convention in Dallas.

The dean would be speaking in support of a motion put forward by the Delaware Bar Association. The motion requested that the ABA investigate the appropriateness and necessity of using the LSAT, the admissions test that the Section of Legal Education required all law schools to use. The Delaware bar questioned the fitness of the LSAT's assessment of individuals and whether the LSAT in fact predicted an individual's success in law school (let alone ability to practice law). The Delaware bar had asked Velvel to speak in favor of its proposal, and he agreed. No doubt White knew about this and wanted to size up the speaker, Coyne thought.

Still, Velvel ultimately considered that White might have persisted for another reason. Perhaps he was anxious to see the institution that posed a competitive threat to ABA schools. Because MSL's graduates could take the Massachusetts bar exam, the low-priced MSL threatened several ABA law schools located in Massachusetts. Velvel was aware that some law school deans in the area feared the school, even though he hadn't as yet seen the NESL-White correspondence. If the school received ABA accreditation, students could take the bar in states across the country. This would make MSL an even bigger and more widespread threat to ABA schools because of its low tuition.

Upon arrival at MSL, White met for an hour with Velvel, Coyne, library staff, and Larry Blades. Blades had been dean of the University of Kansas Law School when Velvel taught there and had become dean of White's own alma mater, the University of Iowa College of Law. Velvel had invited Blades to be a trustee of MSL.

White, 61, toured the school, speaking highly of the classes he visited, saying they were well conducted, a quality that he didn't find in all law schools. Upon the conclusion of his tour, White addressed the students, who had gathered in a large classroom. One student asked how the ABA viewed diversity of education, and White replied that the ABA's standards encouraged experimentation and flexibility. If law schools across the country appeared to be similar, he said, the fault rested with legal educators, not with ABA accreditation. In fact, White said, the ABA applauded schools that aimed to distinguish themselves by pursuing their own goals, just as long as they maintained a high bar passage rate.

White continued by saying that he thought some schools emphasized the LSAT too strongly in admissions. The LSAT predicted only first-year grades, he said, adding that ABA standards did not require schools to use the LSAT as an entrance exam but did require some type of aptitude test.

Also, White told students that he believed legal education needed to be revamped. He described the average law professor as a stodgy white male who had been at the top of his academic class, worked for a large firm, and persisted in molding students to his own image. Such a professor didn't address the needs of the growing number of women who were entering the profession. Many of these women might eventually have families and be interested in flex-time. This type of professor didn't address the needs of nearly half of the graduates who were destined to open their own practices. White said that law schools needed to keep pace with the times and offer more practical education.

Velvel was stunned. He could have spoken those words, and as he and Coyne sat down with White for a conference before White left, Velvel was willing to think that conceivably his concerns about White had been misplaced.

Velvel then asked White what the ABA accreditors most wanted to see. White gave him a list, placing the school's finances and growth projections at the top. This struck Velvel as peculiar. Why would the accreditors worry about money over academics? Yet Velvel felt confident that MSL would pass such a financial test. The school had been very careful with its finances and had carefully charted its spending, revenue, and growth statistics since the day that he and Al Zappala first sketched out a budget early in 1988. As a result, MSL had always exceeded its growth projections. Already, despite the school's inexpensive tuition, MSL had nearly $2 million dollars in the bank as a "rainy day fund." At the rate that the school was matriculating students, Velvel expected MSL to have as much as $10 million to $11 million in the bank by 1997.

Coyne asked White to clarify a few points, particularly the one of utmost concern: Would the ABA allow a variance in the student-faculty ratio? Of course, Coyne was referring to the ABA's own calculation of student-faculty ratios, which disregarded whether classes were large or small and merely compared the total number of full-time faculty—as narrowly defined by the ABA—to the total number of students.

White told him no, that the ABA wouldn't bend on that.

"We are over 30 to 1," Coyne replied, again referring to the way that the ABA calculated ratios. Coyne knew that 30 to 1 was the maximum the ABA would allow. He continued, "If the idea behind the ratio is to have small classes, we have them. If the idea is to have quality, we have it."

White said, "A variance is never granted on the ratio because the whole future of a school should be charted by the full-time faculty. For a full-time student equivalency of 450, you might get by with 16 full-time teachers for provisional accreditation." By that, he meant that a school might receive initial but merely provisional accreditation if it had one full-time professor for every 33 students. But he said that even that would be a stretch for ABA accreditors. A school would not receive permanent ABA accreditation unless it lowered its ratio to 30 to 1, White told them. But Velvel and Coyne both knew that White pushed schools to hire even more full-time professors in order to lower their ratios to 25 to 1.

Coyne told White that the school had 13 full-time professors. Of course, the school counted full-time professors differently than the ABA did. MSL did not exclude professors with administrative duties or those who practiced law on the side, as the ABA did.

Coyne explained to White, "The problem with requiring 16 full-timers [as the ABA calculated the numbers] is that it would require a sudden jump [in the number of faculty members and costs] that would harm the finances of the school and the collegiality of the faculty. Will the ABA listen to an argument for a variance?"

"The ABA will listen, but the situation is not hopeful if there are 450 full-time equivalent students," said White.

White's firm stance made accreditation for MSL seem unlikely. Replying to White, Coyne said, "But then the standards are rigid and do not, in fact, allow for diversity."

"The standards *do* allow diversity," White insisted.

Probing further, Coyne asked what White meant by *full-time faculty*?

"The standards define them," White said. "You can't have an office elsewhere, be of counsel to a firm, etc."

Velvel knew that if that definition were applied to MSL, the school would have no full-time faculty as the ABA calculated it. All of the school's professors had offices elsewhere, or served as "of counsel" to firms, or were administrators. This not only kept faculty costs down, but it put students in touch with real-life legal experience.

Velvel asked, "Has any school ever been approved that sought a Standard 802 variance from an important issue, such as student-faculty ratios?"

"Not in my time," White replied. "Before my time, Antioch was approved, and we then spent 10 years trying to close it down."

The MSL people knew the story about the Antioch College Law School, based in Washington, D.C. Opening in the 1970s, this practically-oriented law school aimed to groom lawyers for public service. The school started off as a freestanding, proprietary school, unable to obtain accreditation. When it linked with a larger institution, Antioch University in Yellow Springs, Ohio, it became an ABA school. Still, Antioch remained an innovative law school that veered from the standards. The Section of Legal Education, under White, therefore looked for an opportunity to rescind its accreditation. So, when the law school severed ties with its debt-ridden parent institution, the Section of Legal Education, under White, stepped in and disaccredited the school. Enrollment dropped, and the school closed.

White told Velvel and Coyne, "Some variances have been granted, but the basic answer is no. No school has been given a variance from issues that the ABA considers important."

It sounded to Velvel as if White had just contradicted the statements he had made to students. Publicly, he had said to the students that the ABA promoted innovation and diversity. Behind closed doors, he had said just the opposite: the rules were the rules, no deviations were allowed. If MSL wanted to be accredited, it would have to follow the ABA's mandates. To Velvel's thinking, White had just admitted that Standard 802 was meaningless. White had made clear that no waiver was ever granted for anything that mattered. (In subsequent depositions of long-time accreditation leaders, they admitted that they had never heard of any waiver of anything.)

Five days after White's visit, Velvel wrote to MSL's Board of Trustees. He referred to the ABA consultant's publicly-claimed interest in diversity as "humbug." He further wrote, "I think his statements show that the ABA is in violation—I think intentional violation—of the requirements it must meet to continue being recognized as the accrediting agency for law schools by the Department of Education (DOE) and the Council on Post-secondary Education (COPA)."

The reason for White's shell game, Velvel pointed out, was that the Section of Legal Education was in the process of seeking renewal of its official accrediting status from the DOE and COPA. Renewal of recognition by DOE was crucial. As a federally recognized accrediting body, the Section of Legal Education's accreditation of a school meant that the school could offer federal grants, loans, and loan guarantees to its students. Law school tuitions had risen so high that even upper-middle class students found it difficult to pay their way through law school without securing federal grants, loans, and loan guarantees.

But to be recognized as an accrediting body by the DOE, the Section of Legal Education had to allow educational diversity among the law schools it accredited, as well as meet other standards that it had had trouble meeting. As far back as 1978, the DOE questioned whether the Section met the DOE requirement that all accrediting standards must be reliable and fair. In 1983, the DOE asked the ABA to revise its rules. In 1987, when the ABA came before DOE again, the latter aired the same concerns over the Section's non-compliance with department rules and over the ABA's recalcitrant manner in managing complaints, appeals, and guidance. Still, the DOE gave the Section federal recognition status for four more years but asked the Section of Legal Education to submit a follow-up report on the reliability and fairness of its standards.

In 1992, when White visited MSL, the Section had already sought another renewal of DOE recognition. White and ABA accreditors had publicly asserted that the Section of Legal Education promoted diversity of education, which was a DOE requirement. However, what White said to Coyne and Velvel in private contradicted his public statements and made it appear that the Section would not permit educational diversity and would not accredit MSL.

Thus, MSL decided that it had to challenge the ABA's petition to the DOE for renewal of its status as a federally recognized accreditor. MSL would challenge, among other things, the validity of the ABA's standards and its refusal to allow diversity among law schools. This move would, no doubt, place MSL in the lion's mouth, but Velvel couldn't see any other way around the problem. Based on his comments, White appeared to be prejudiced against MSL. Unless the Section of Legal Education thought its accreditation powers might be in jeopardy, it would continue without exception to impose rigid, high-cost standards that benefitted academics but barred students like MSL's from the law schools and the legal profession.

Michael Coyne and MSL's Chairman of the Board Stefan Tucker supported Velvel's decision to challenge the Section of Legal Education in front of the DOE. Tucker, an honors graduate from the University of Michigan Law School, was active in the ABA's Section of Taxation, and a few years later he would be its chairman. He knew how the ABA operated, and he urged Velvel to call Henry Ramsey, Jr. to forewarn him about MSL's plans. Tucker believed this was the right strategy and the gentlemanly thing to do. Conceivably it could even pave the way for some sort of rapprochement.

Ramsey was dean of the Howard University Law School and was also chairman of the Council of the Section of Legal Education that year. Formally, the Council of the Section was the ABA's federally recognized accrediting arm. The Council of the Section was controlled by academics, as was the Accreditation Committee itself, and it reviewed Accreditation Committee decisions. Ramsey himself had been a major player in all aspects of ABA accreditation for many years.

In April 1992, Dean Velvel called Ramsey and explained that, unless it were possible to reach an agreement, MSL planned to go before the DOE and complain about the ABA's imposition of unfair standards that threatened diversity of education. Ramsey replied that the ABA would make no agreement. In fact, he said that it would be inappropriate even to discuss it. Ramsey said the ABA had fairly evaluated and approved other law schools that were different from the norm, including Antioch, CUNY, and Thomas M. Cooley. (Velvel subsequently learned that the ABA required these schools to make drastic changes to meet the standards, and, of course, Antioch closed.)

MSL would be treated fairly, too, Ramsey claimed. However, if MSL needed to file a complaint, Ramsey said, the school should go ahead and do it. Ramsey, an African-American, then added, "Massachusetts School of Law should not try to whitemail us by threatening to oppose the Section's application to the DOE for renewed recognition as an accreditation agency . . . ."

Velvel subsequently filed a 59-page letter with the DOE and gave it to members of the DOE's National Advisory Committee, a group of prominent educators who advised the DOE on accreditation matters. With the letter, he sent a stack of supporting documents. The letter expressed and documented the reasons for numerous concerns about the Section of Legal Education's unfair standards and its lack of diversity of education.

Velvel also sent a copy of the letter to Robert H. Atwell, president of the American Council on Education, and an important figure in higher education. Atwell then wrote to the DOE saying, "Dean Velvel's letter raises important issues bearing on the continued recognition of the ABA. I hope that the National Advisory Committee will give serious consideration to the testimony of the Massachusetts School of Law."

On May 5, 1992, Velvel testified for nearly an hour before the NAC, explaining how MSL differed from other law schools. Under proper, generally accepted principles of accreditation, the school had to be judged not by rigid, inflexible rules but by whether it was meeting its own mission—to innovatively serve working-class and other non-affluent persons, a mission that made it impossible to adhere to all of the ABA's standards. He asked the NAC to advise renewal of recognition of the ABA for only one year, rather than the normal five years, with subsequent renewal if the ABA brought its standards up to the guiding principle of accreditation—that it permit diversity of education and allow schools to achieve their own missions.

Ramsey spoke for the ABA, attempting to allay concerns raised by Velvel. With regard to the LSAT, he told the committee, "The ABA standards do not require that a school make its admissions decisions on the basis of whether you pass or fail the LSAT." But in truth, one could not pass or fail the LSAT; test-takers were merely given scores. Thus, Velvel felt that Ramsey's comment was misleading.

Velvel felt that Ramsey had also deliberately misled NAC

members when he denied the intimate relationship among the Section of Legal Education, the LSAC (which sponsored the LSAT), and the AALS. The three organizations, Velvel knew, shared many of the same leaders, coordinated their goals and actions, and were jointly known as the Big Three of legal education. Ramsey himself had been a leader of both the Section of Legal Education and the LSAC, as well as being active in the AALS. Many other ABA accreditation leaders had also been leaders of one or both or all three groups simultaneously.

In defending the flexibility of the standards, Ramsey said, "Our standards do not say anywhere, and it cannot be shown that it says anywhere, that you must have a particular student-faculty ratio. We say . . . that it is based on the judgment of professionals . . . that if you have a student-faculty ratio of greater than 30 to 1, the burden is on you [the school] to come and show us why it's necessary for you to have such a high student-faculty ratio. There are schools in the country with student-faculty ratios of greater than 30 to 1, and they are approved schools."

This public statement was wholly different from what White had said to Velvel and Coyne in private and from reality, which ABA officials would admit later under oath.

Ramsey continued, "We continue to be and if we are reauthorized, we will continue to be committed to diversity within legal education. There is with one minor exception nothing that Dean Velvel described that goes on at his law school that we would not and do not encourage to go on in law schools throughout the country." This public statement to the NAC was also worlds apart from what White had made plain to MSL privately and even from what was overtly mandated by the standards. In Velvel's opinion, Ramsey had not told the NAC the truth.

Sister Mary-Andrew Matesich, one of two NAC members who had been asked to read all of the materials pertaining to the ABA, including MSL's submission, said that she thought that MSL had raised some "very serious issues." She asked Ramsey about Standard 802. Was this the provision, she asked, under which an institution could seek an alternative if the school had valid educational reasons?

Dean White interrupted and answered, "Yes." He did not disclose that no variance had ever been granted under Standard 802 since he had taken over as consultant in 1973.

Elaborating on White's answer, Ramsey said, "What we are interested in is a diverse academic community that reflects a variety of views and ideas, that is, I think all educators with views essential to their advancement of knowledge. However, we also would—I would add quickly that the law schools of America are the gatekeepers to the profession. We believe that everybody in America who has the qualifications ought to have an opportunity . . . to be a member of the profession if they want." But in reality, of course, the accreditors were keeping competent people out of the profession by imposing expensive standards that raised school tuitions and by elitist academic policies that excluded working-class people, minorities, and others.

At the conclusion of the hearing, the NAC had questions about the ABA's standards but voted to continue federal recognition of the Section of Legal Education for five years. However, the NAC wanted to see an interim report by July 1, 1993, on a number of issues raised at the hearing.

While Velvel believed that Ramsey and White had not spoken the truth to the NAC, he figured that the two ABA representatives must have felt pressured to make their statements in order to retain DOE recognition. Their statements had been transcribed and would appear on a written record. This, the dean thought, might cause the ABA to feel it necessary to live up to those statements.

Thus, Velvel and Coyne returned to Andover feeling that although there was no certainty, there was at least some reason to hope that MSL would be accredited.

Chapter 7

ABA Inspection

In November 1992, MSL self-published a 500-page self-study, in book form, titled *The Deeply Unsatisfactory Nature of Legal Education Today*. Writers included Velvel and five of the school's full-time law professors: Michael Coyne, Peter Malaguti, Joe Devlin, Connie Rudnick, and Sarah Hooke Lee. Bound in a dark blue cover, which was inset with a color photograph of the school's new red-brick building, the self-study was mailed to the ABA's James White, as well as to the deans of the 176 ABA-approved schools.

MSL's Dean and faculty, several of them litigators, minced no words in criticizing mainstream legal education. They accused legal pedagogy of being stodgy, theoretic, and elite-focused. They blamed academics for inflating school budgets and raising tuitions so high that law schools had turned into "upper crust institutions whose student bodies [were] comprised mainly of the economically, socially, and educationally elite." They criticized law schools for preferring students with high LSAT scores, which "worked against and excluded persons from less privileged economic and educational backgrounds. . . . High performance on standardized purported aptitude tests correlates significantly with economic status and high position in society."

As well, the self-study authors denounced law reviews, describing them as badly written and used by professors to obtain higher national profiles and, thus, job offers from other schools, not to speak of tenure and salary increases from their own schools. In support of this view, the authors of the self-study used a quote from James P. White, written in a 1989 article: "The writing style favored by generations of [law review] editors has been found to be overly tentative, pompous, pedantic, and uninteresting; and the content of most law journal articles [has] been held to be little more than in-depth treatment of trivialities."

Beyond enumerating legal education's many shortcomings, MSL's self-study offered countless solutions. The writers showed the strides MSL had made, especially how its conservative, well-managed budget had enabled the school to keep tuition down to just $9,000 a year. (The tuition would remain at that level for eight years, while other schools significantly raised their tuition every year until the median law school tuition in New England became twice that of MSL's.) The school offered pragmatic courses, hands-on legal experience, and courses in practical, clear writing.

Eschewing the LSAT, the school sought a more holistic alternative in admitting students. The school's admissions officer, together with an admissions committee made up largely of faculty members, reviewed candidates' grades, academic improvement, work performance, writing samples, and statements made during face-to-face interviews. This gave the school's faculty and staff broader insights into students' capabilities—more so than isolated numbers on multiple choice objective tests, recognized by many as simply rewarding speed, as well as being racially and socio-economically biased.

The Deeply Unsatisfactory Nature of Legal Education Today fulfilled the written requirement of the ABA's Standard 201, which read: "Through development and periodic re-evaluation of a written self-study, the law school shall articulate the objectives of the school's educational program consistent with the Standards." In reality, however, White and his colleagues demanded something different. They demanded self-flagellating documents that the ABA and the law schools could then use to demand more money from university administrations or Boards of Trustees in order to cure alleged shortcomings. In an effort to show how the law school needed more money to operate sufficiently, self-studies stressed the school's deficiencies rather than its strengths, almost as if they were Catholic confessions of legal academics.

However, in one sense, Velvel and MSL staff wrote their self-study blindly, without aid of a model. Prior to White's visit, Velvel and Ansel Chaplin had asked White, in 1992, to send MSL a sample self-study so that the school could get an idea of what the ABA expected. White claimed that all self-studies were confidential. He wouldn't or couldn't offer an illustrative model of a self-study and wouldn't even let Chaplin look at one in White's office.

At the NAC hearing, Velvel complained about being unable to obtain a sample self-study. To that, Henry Ramsey had said, "The reason we don't put out model self-studies is because we want to encourage diversity within the legal profession. We don't want everybody to be a cookie-cutter school. What we want them to do is come up with their own self-study, not what we say is an acceptable self-study." Ramsey implied that the ABA encouraged law schools to think independently, which was not true.

Not having a model or sample, Velvel and his colleagues prepared the self-study in the manner that seemed appropriate to them. MSL was a school that was attempting to correct shortcomings in legal education and to offer opportunity to the excluded. So Velvel and the faculty wrote about these problems, about how law schools could correct them, and what MSL was doing to correct them.

From his prior stint in education, however, the dean knew that the accreditors were especially concerned with salaries, and they wanted a comparative study of faculty compensation—a chart showing how MSL's salaries compared with those of similar schools in the region.

In one section of the self-study, the school explained MSL's pay structure for faculty. When the school began, the faculty agreed to work for as little as $35,000 per year on the promise that, as long as the school could afford it and the professors performed competently, their salaries would be increased annually. They were told that raises could be as much as 20 percent a year until professors' pay reached a satisfactory level.

For several years, most of MSL's faculty and staff received annual pay increases of 20 percent or close to it. One professor who started off making $35,000 a year in 1988, made $80,000 by 1992. All faculty members who had started in 1988 made over $70,000 by 1992. MSL had doubled their salaries in four years. The school also had continued its policy of starting professors at low salaries, because this put professors in a position of proving themselves in order to move up the salary scale. MSL had considered a salary cap—$100,000 to $105,000, with subsequent cost of living wage increases—but that wasn't in place yet and never would be. The school wanted to remain fair and open-minded in paying faculty. This was important to Velvel, who vividly remembered struggling to support his family on the low salary that he had earned at Catholic University.

However, the self-study didn't contain a detailed chart comparing MSL's salaries with those of other schools. That's because MSL could not obtain detailed compensation statistics from the ABA, which refused to share the information with non-ABA schools, even though it wanted a detailed salary chart. Only ABA accredited schools were given these numbers. "The ABA will not make available to an unaccredited school the highly detailed salary surveys it makes of all accredited American law schools," wrote MSL's faculty. "All that the ABA has been willing to give us are general medians, plus the median information contained in the ABA *Consultant's Digest* for 1992. When compared to the information available to us, MSL's salary level is very respectable." According to the *Consultant's Digest*, the 1991-92 median salary of full-time professors was $74,600. The median salary for MSL's four professors who had been with the school since the beginning was $73,554. This seemed very creditable for a start-up school that had begun with only $20,000 just four years earlier, and whose professors were much younger than those at most ABA schools. They had also spent fewer years in academia.

Researching and writing the self-study took the MSL staff nearly six months. The writers had combed through hundreds of documents, attaching 3,790 pages of exhibits. In the end, the authors were proud of their efforts and considered it a valuable discourse on legal education. Wishing to share their findings, the dean and faculty mailed it to law schools across the country, to some members of the ABA's Section of Legal Education, and to others involved with legal education. (Eight years later, a former dean who was cleaning out his office found a copy and called Velvel to tell him what a great piece of work it was.) The faculty at MSL hoped it might cause some factions within the legal academy to allow others to use different practices than they did themselves.

That wasn't to happen, however. In an article that appeared in the December 7, 1992 issue of the *National Law Journal*, reporter Ken Myers described the MSL self-study as "sharply-worded and candid." He wrote, "How badly does the Massachusetts School of Law want to get its American Bar Association accreditation? Apparently, not enough to go out and wine and dine the ABA powers that be. In fact, one could even conclude that MSL . . . is doing just the opposite." He synopsized the self-study's contents and said that it was "raising eyebrows" in the legal community. White wouldn't comment on it other than to say that he had received "a number of calls about it."

Certainly the critical nature of the self-study and its broad distribution must have surprised the ABA consultant. It contained none of the self-flagellation that the ABA wanted. Rather, it spoke highly of the school's own program, presenting a detailed case as to why various ABA standards should be waived for a school like the Massachusetts School of Law.

The dean and faculty's confidence, as exhibited in the self-study, had been boosted by MSL's runaway success. In the fall of 1992, the school had 775 students—a giant leap from the 94 students in the beginning. That, in part, validated the school and proved that a real need existed for its approach to legal education.

To White, Velvel mailed the self-study, an accreditation application form, an application check for $16,500, and a list of potential site inspectors. For the site inspection team, Velvel recommended well-known legal academics and prestigious academic administrators, some of whom had been involved in law school accreditation. Velvel felt comfortable doing this, as he had learned from Ramsey that site inspection teams were typically jointly selected by White and the law school dean. The deans at the J. Reuben Clark Law School at Brigham Young University, Beasley School of Law at Temple University, and other law schools had done this.

However, White composed his own site inspection team, completely ignoring Velvel's requests. The team included: Dean Steven Smith, chairperson, Cleveland-Marshall College of Law; José Garcia-Pedrosa, attorney from Miami; Professor Jane Hammond, Cornell Law School; Professor Vincent Immel, St. Louis University; Richardson Nahstoll, attorney from Portland, Oregon; Professor Rennard Strickland, University of Oklahoma Law Center; and Associate Dean Peter Winograd, University of New Mexico. The inspection date was set for March 3-6, 1993.

A glance at the list told Velvel that White had lined up the "death squad," as he put it. Based on what he knew about these individuals, Velvel expected them to look unfavorably upon MSL—he was almost certain of this, and an experienced dean of an ABA school wholeheartedly agreed. Nahstoll, a former military man, was one of ABA accreditation's "old guard." He had been chairman of the ABA committee that had drafted the revised ABA standards adopted in 1973, and he had been chairman in 1973-1974 of the Council of the Section of Legal Education. He had refused to serve as MSL's consultant when contacted by the dean. He did not believe the school could be approved without using the LSAT.

Winograd had been president of the Law School Admissions Council, sponsor of the LSAT, from 1988-1990, and Velvel felt certain that he was biased toward using this test. The same could be said of Strickland, a law professor who had been president of the Association of American Law Schools (AALS) and was active in the LSAC/LSAS. Smith had been the chairman of the accreditation team that forced the closure of Antioch Law School in Washington, D.C. and Old College School of Law in Nevada.

The ABA's most conservative and staunchest supporters made up this list, and it was clear to Velvel that White had planned it that way.

Velvel's uneasiness magnified as inspection day approached. White cancelled a pre-site visit by two team members, Smith and Winograd, and in a memo dated February 12, 1993, he suggested to Velvel that the inspection be postponed. White claimed that MSL had failed to complete its application and that Standard 103, specifying that a school operate within ABA standards, had not been fulfilled because MSL sought waivers. Even though Standard 802 provided for waivers, it seemed that applying for them meant facing disapproval under Standard 103 for failure to operate within the standards. Velvel considered it a Catch-22. White even offered to return MSL's $16,500 application check. To Velvel's surprise, the ABA had never cashed it but held it for months. To Velvel, it suggested that the ABA did not intend to inspect the school even though the students and faculty had been anticipating the inspection for months.

Angry, Velvel called and wrote White. He demanded that the inspection continue as planned; otherwise, Velvel said, he would take legal action. The ABA's actions created anxiety among the students, because many hoped to be graduating from an ABA-accredited school in June. Postponing the visit would close off that opportunity. The dean insisted that the ABA stick to its originally planned inspection date.

*****

In the interim, the ABA sponsored a Site Evaluators Workshop on February 26, 1993, in Indianapolis. There, Steven R. Smith, chairman of the MSL site team, conducted a seminar titled, "Participating in a Law School Accreditation Site Visit."

Smith made approximately a dozen key points that day, including several pertaining to salaries. He told site evaluators that "the issue of compensation [was] a sensitive subject with many universities. Many view[ed] professional accreditation (and the ABA/AALS process in particular) as a guild effort to up salaries. It is, therefore, especially important in the exit interview and report to approach funding for salaries as a quality issue." Thus, Smith told site inspectors to "explain the consequences of inadequate salaries in terms of the ability to attract and retain faculty and in terms of its effect on outside employment."

In other words, Smith taught site inspectors that day how to appropriately frame criticisms of low faculty pay so it appeared as an educational quality issue.

*****

A little more than a week later, the site evaluators arrived at MSL. Some of them entered the school's glass, two-story lobby, looking annoyed or at best inconvenienced, as if this trip were a waste of time.

José Garcia-Pedrosa misleadingly seemed on the surface to be an exception. Upon arrival, he reassured students and faculty that he did not come with a personal agenda. A Cuban-American who had graduated from Harvard Law School, he told students and faculty that "it made no difference" to him if MSL attained accreditation or not. Many students appreciated what appeared to be his straightforward attitude and blunt candor.

In a casual moment, speaking with another Harvard Law graduate, MSL Professor Tom Martin, Pedrosa said that MSL had "poisoned the well" in writing what he described as a caustic self-study and trying to hinder the Section of Legal Education in renewing its accreditation status with the DOE. Pedrosa told him that he considered that unfortunate, because he found MSL to be a much better school than he had anticipated. He couldn't understand why MSL picked a fight with the ABA before its inspection. When most schools picked fights with the ABA, it was because they had something to hide, he said.

Trying to make sense of the school's operation, which defied law school norms, Pedrosa said to Professor Martin, "You are taking in students for whom the indicators of success are not very high, and yet you are graduating 85 percent of them. There are only two possible explanations for this. Either the rest of the law school academic world is missing the boat or your school lacks academic rigor."

Martin assured him, "The rest of the world is missing the boat."

Another member of the inspection team, Nahstoll, engaged in a similar conversation with Coyne. Nahstoll, who had a wide reputation among law professors for being abrasive, ironically asked, "Why does your dean have to be so abrasive?" He was referring to MSL's self-study.

Coyne replied that Nahstoll had to understand Velvel before he could understand the school or even the self-study. He explained that the dean felt protective of the students, staff, and faculty. They had been through some rough times.

"You may not at all times like Larry, and you may not at all times like me, but what you have to understand is that we've got the best interest of the school and staff and faculty at heart, and we feel that we have been jerked around in this process," Coyne said.

"You piss people off when you do it that way, and then they come in thinking that it's not a very good operation and that's not true," Nahstoll said.

"We felt that you, the 'haves,' were out to do in the 'have nots,'" Coyne said, adding that he continued to see evidence of the "haves" acting in a superior fashion, even at the inspection.

"But you don't understand. You put people on the defensive, and you've got them antagonized . . ." Nahstoll brought up the DOE hearing.

"You have to understand," Coyne explained. "The only reason we went before the DOE was because Jim White had said that the standards would be rigorously enforced, that there was a fairly strict student-faculty ratio and that, in fact, he would deny us what we thought was rightfully ours. It . . . is a complete injustice."

Coyne opted to speak candidly, "I think there are a couple on the team that may well have been picked because they were set up to do us in."

Though he could name names, Coyne thought better of it. "We had no choice but to go before the DOE."

Coyne mentioned the statements that Henry Ramsey had made at the hearing—about the ABA not having a set student/faculty ratio and about MSL's practices being, with one exception, the type that the ABA liked to see. Coyne said that if those statements were true, "we should be approved."

"I don't know what he [Ramsey] was thinking when he made those unfortunate statements," Nahstoll admitted.

"I don't think they were unfortunate statements," Coyne countered. "It may have been what you now consider as unfortunate to make the representations before the committee that there is no set student-faculty ratio, but at this point you're stuck with it."

Nahstoll only nodded. He did not say anything.

Over the two and a half days, faculty, students, alumni, and staff talked with site evaluators. Some students stopped inspectors in the hallways, asking if they could speak with them. They wanted to personally tell inspectors how pleased they were with the school. Not only did they believe that they had received a good legal education but one that was practical, taught by knowledgeable professors. As well, they wanted inspectors to know that because of MSL's faculty and staff, they were given a chance that no other school had offered—a chance to move up in life and practice law.

Drop-in classroom inspections gave evaluators an opportunity to see professors and students in action. Peter Winograd told Diane Sullivan that she was a fine Socratic teacher. "As you can imagine," Sullivan said later, "I took great pride in his statement because I worked so very, very hard to be as good as my colleagues."

On the third day, the site evaluation abruptly ended, even though the inspection team still needed to review the school's clinical programs, practical courses, and field placement. A major snowstorm had moved in, forcing the dean to cancel classes. Evaluators didn't want to be stuck in New England over the weekend, so they arranged for transportation home.

Thus, they skirted the finale of the three-day visit—the exit interview. Customarily, evaluators presented an overview of their findings at the exit interview. That way, the school wouldn't be surprised when the report came in three or four months later. However, the exit interview didn't take place. ABA inspectors simply packed up and left.

On March 16, 10 days after the ABA inspection team left, the dean and Stefan Tucker, chairman of MSL's Board of Trustees, participated in a conference call, a pseudo exit interview, with some of the ABA inspectors, including Smith and Winograd. When the dean asked for their reactions, they hedged and kept their remarks general. Only one thing could be read into that, he thought. The school would not be accredited. Rather than say anything more, the inspectors said that the school would have a full report by May.

None of this surprised the dean. Just before the inspection, he had read an article about Smith, chairman of the inspection team, in the Cleveland *Plain Dealer*, and Tucker had alluded to the article in an opening meeting with the site team. Smith, dean of Cleveland-Marshall College of Law, was engaged in a bitter battle with Cleveland State University, the law school's parent institution, over funding. Smith's law school had a large budget—a budget 25 percent larger than MSL's. The budget supported seven associate/assistant deans, a total of 23 administrators, and approximately 17 secretaries. In addition, Smith wanted another $2 million in general funding, plus another $1 million for the library. Velvel couldn't help but regard Smith as a self-aggrandizing believer in big bureaucracies and big spending who would not empathize with a school that strived to lower costs while raising educational quality.

On March 22, Velvel drafted a letter to the entire inspection team, which began, "This letter, whose necessity is deeply regrettable, is being sent after lengthy and serious consideration by MSL. The letter largely has been caused by information that did not come to our attention until the week of the inspection at the earliest . . ." Velvel accused certain inspection team members of being biased against the school before they arrived.

Team members had serious conflicts of interests. Velvel wrote, "Chairman Smith's law school . . . appears to follow highly expensive principles at the opposite pole from MSL. Chairman Smith's law school is entitled to run itself any way it wants . . . but it seems self evident that, because MSL does things so much more inexpensively than his own school, Chairman Smith can approve of almost nothing MSL does without thereby undercutting his own school's position . . . ."

Velvel concluded that Smith disapproved of MSL, just as he had disapproved of Antioch and Old College law schools, which he had helped shut down. To the dean, it appeared that he was going to try to shut down MSL, too.

Velvel and his colleagues were not going to stand by and let the school be destroyed that way. He had fought against the unlawful Vietnam War, and he and his colleagues had battled against the wrongdoing of Commonwealth School of Law and against politicians who tried to prevent MSL from winning state accreditation. If necessary, they would fight the ABA, perhaps the most powerful professional association in America. If necessary, they would confront the legal establishment and fight for the existence of a practical, low-cost law school. They believed every American with the capability, rich or poor, had the right to study law in order to try to get ahead in the world through the practice of law or through other professions and businesses where a law degree was helpful. They wouldn't let the ABA take that right away from them, if they could help it.

To win the fight meant battling White, Ramsey, and all the other ABA elites, ultimately in a court of law. As an experienced antitrust lawyer, Velvel believed that the ABA was clearly violating the Sherman Antitrust Act by illegally using its monopoly power to restrict competition. It had forced schools to pay high salaries to law professors, librarians, and deans. It had restricted the hours professors could work, required law schools to build huge, expensive hardcover libraries, required all incoming students to take the LSAT, prohibited law schools from offering a for-credit bar review course, and engaged in other anticompetitive activities.

The faculty at MSL prepared for this battle. Upstairs, at MSL, they set up what would euphemistically be called the "War Room." There they gathered papers, correspondence, and articles regarding the antitrust issues. In this room, they kept the documents that they would need to take on the ABA.

*****

On May 14, 1993, as plans were set for graduating MSL's largest class—101 students—the ABA report arrived. Skimming it at first, the dean felt physically ill. It was worse than he had expected.

He wrote the trustees, describing it as "a semi-sophisticated hatchet job." Inspectors' remarks were offensive, grossly exaggerated, and skewed to make the school look bad, he told them. Nothing about the report reflected positively on the school or its students and faculty.

In the report's summary, written by Steven Smith, the site team recommended that the Accreditation Committee should not extend waivers to the school. In fact, throughout the report, the writers took a cynical view of MSL's programs, referring to them as the dean's sole vision, as if the faculty had no input. In addition, the team criticized the school for not attracting more minority students, ignoring the fact that Massachusetts had only a tiny percentage of minority college graduates, and that minorities from other states could not take bar examinations in their home states if they went to MSL, because the school lacked ABA accreditation. The team not only took a harsh view of MSL's operation, but it criticized its disregard of various ABA standards, particularly the ones regarding student-faculty ratios.

In 1988, the ABA had revamped Standard 402, which dealt with the ratio. Under revised 402 and relevant so-called "interpretations," faculty members "who are 'of counsel' to a law firm . . . may not be considered as full time faculty . . . ." Nor could any professor who allowed his or her name to appear on a firm's stationery or who maintained a law office outside of the school or who listed services in a telephone directory. None of them could be considered "full-time faculty." The ABA's position was hypocritical at best, because some of the nation's most celebrated law schools had professors spending huge amounts of time practicing law. For instance, at Harvard Law School, Alan Dershowitz, Laurence Tribe, and Arthur Miller were well-known legal practitioners.

By ABA criteria, Diane Sullivan (who, during the site inspection, had been complimented by inspector Winograd) could not be counted as a full-time faculty member. Still, she worked 50 to 60 hours per week for the school, far more than most professors work at ABA schools. Inspectors condemned her for working another 40 hours a week in the banking industry. As well, Paula

Dickinson, who spent a third of her time performing administrative duties as the school's controller, could not be considered full-time either. According to Smith, only six of MSL's 84 full- and part-time professors could be considered "full-time faculty."

This distortion enabled inspectors to paint a very bleak picture of MSL. Inspectors had written in the report, "Even using the most favorable application of ABA definitions of full-time faculty, only six individuals at MSL meet the qualifications [of full-time faculty]. With 808 students (633 FTE [full-time equivalent] students after adjusting for part-timers), the student faculty ratio is 105:1 (FTE) or 135:1 (head count). As a consequence of this ratio, there are very heavy teaching loads, a substantial number of courses are taught by part-time faculty or adjuncts, there is limited opportunity for scholarly endeavors, law school faculty governance structures are minimal, faculty have heavy examination loads, there are virtually no seminars, and relatively few small classes are taught by the six full-time [faculty]. It should be noted that of the six individuals who even arguably meet the full-time definition, some have Yellow Pages listings and outside offices."

The inspectors did not mention that when one looked at MSL's student-faculty ratio in terms of the number of actual students sitting before a professor in class—the way such ratios are typically calculated—MSL's was much lower than any ABA school. While the ABA considered 30 students to be a small class, 50 to 60 percent of MSL's classes had 30 students or less. Forty percent had 20 or less, and 30 percent had 10 or less. However, those crucially important facts did not appear in the report.

A faculty compensation chart, comparing MSL faculty salaries with other "New England Law School" faculty, was also misleading. Salaries at MSL, where the professors were almost all young, were made to look low by comparing them with salaries at major schools like Harvard or with salaries at other long-established, university-affiliated schools that had sizeable numbers of highly-paid older professors who had taught for decades.

According to the chart, all of MSL's professors were under-paid in comparison with 1992-93 medians for the area. Comparing professors by academic ranks and years of service, the inspectors claimed that MSL's salaries lagged behind other area schools by $5,798 to $36,539—a big difference from MSL's own calculations.

Using these numbers, inspectors claimed that low salaries prevented the school from attracting good, experienced law professors. Of course, this belittled the quality of MSL's faculty, and Velvel and his colleagues thoroughly disagreed. The school had hired full-time professors by choosing enthusiastic adjunct faculty who had performed well in part-time teaching, instead of raiding other law schools' faculties for older professors who cost more and weren't necessarily as good. Of course, such raiding drove up deans' and professors' salaries, which was perceived as a positive from the ABA's point of view.

In a letter to MSL trustees, Velvel wrote, "One looks in vain for even the slightest overtly stated recognition of a need to make legal education available to the less privileged who surround and attend MSL but are not recognized as minorities by the politically correct academics of today: to Greek Americans; French Americans; Italian Americans from homes where Italian is still the first language; Irish Americans who in prior generations have not wholly shared in the economic and educational good fortune that many of their brethren have attained; Slavic Americans; and immigrants from a host of countries in Europe, Asia, and the Middle East. Instead of recognition of the need to make legal education available to these people, their abilities are denigrated. There is no doubt in my mind—none at all—that in major part this is a class battle. . . ."

Velvel prepared a 90-page reply to the ABA. "Mere English words are insufficient to give the reader a full feeling for, or to enable the reader to truly appreciate, the savagery of the summary," Velvel wrote. "The report uses wholesale omission, selection, emphasis, tone, implication, and slanted statistical interpretation to make MSL look deficient in one respect or another. Chairman Smith's team submitted an unbalanced report that reads like a neon sign telling the Accreditation Committee and the Council that MSL should not receive a variance and accreditation."

With regard to salaries, Velvel wrote that the inspectors had presented a "slanted set of statistics" designed to reflect negatively upon the school. The dean wrote, "It reminds one of the joke that there are three kinds of lies—lies, damn lies, and statistics," referring to the team's salary chart based on statistics that were withheld from MSL but given to 176 ABA schools.

Velvel wrote in his reply, "The report seeks to persuade that MSL's professors have excessive duties, work too hard, and teach more hours per week than they should. Omitted entirely is that MSL's professors do not feel this way; and that unlike so many other schools, where professors complain bitterly to inspection teams about a host of matters where there may be intense divisiveness, which causes faculty life to resemble a circle from Dante's Inferno, MSL's professors did not complain to the team about workloads or other matters, but instead explained to the team that they enjoy working at the school." He and the staff were insulted by the site inspectors' insinuations that MSL was a one-man show.

Though the report had been, in Velvel's eyes, "savage," technically speaking, MSL had not yet been officially denied accreditation. That decision was not for the team to decide, but was initially up to the ABA Accreditation Committee, which met on June 23 at the Brooklyn Law School in Brooklyn, New York. The dean, Mike Coyne, and MSL Trustees Stefan Tucker and Paul Victor attended the meeting on MSL's behalf. Victor had graduated from the University of Michigan Law School with honors and was a major partner of Weil, Gotshal & Manges, one of New York City's largest and most prestigious law firms. He later was a candidate for chairman of the Antitrust Section of the ABA.

"We have stated . . . the report gives short shrift to or omits or downplays a host of matters which reflect well on MSL, while

stressing whatever could be projected rightly or wrongly as negative," Velvel told the committee. He listed MSL's merits that had
been overlooked or ignored: the school's rigorous education,
teaching of practical skills, instruction in ethics, courses on writing and negotiations, and courses on business matters, including
accounting.

Then Velvel told the committee, "It is our collective judgment
that if accreditation is denied to MSL on the basis of this report,
it will show only that accrediting bodies have adopted criteria
that are designed to serve the interests of the law professors and
the law schools, while simultaneously setting their face against a
school which adopts practices making legal education readily
available to persons of all races and backgrounds, from the lower
and middle economic classes, to the working class people of our
area of New England who wish to better their lot in life."

At the end of his speech, which was followed by comments
by Coyne, Victor, and Tucker, the committee thanked and dismissed them. About a week later, a letter came from White. It
read, "Massachusetts School of Law has not demonstrated that it
is in substantial compliance with the ABA Standards. . . ."
Accreditation had been denied.

*****

That same month, Velvel and Diane Sullivan testified before
the Essex County Superior Court. Three years after MSL's fire, a
jury found Michael A. Boland guilty of conspiring to start the fire
in the school's library.

The night of the fire, October 22, 1989, police asked Coyne,
"Who might have done this?" Without a moment's hesitation, he
had answered, "Michael Boland." The former, hot-headed, Commonwealth Law School president had blamed many of his
school's failures upon the dean and his founding of the Massachusetts School of Law.

Boland claimed that he didn't start MSL's fire. He told police that he had no motive. The year before, he had resigned from Commonwealth, which had subsequently folded and fallen into bankruptcy.

Still the circumstance of the fire seemed to implicate Boland, even though no fingerprints or hair turned up in the evidence. Among the items found at the scene were a red Butane lighter, a pair of yellow Latex gloves, and a five-gallon white plastic joint compound bucket—the same kind that Det. Larkham had found in Boland's earlier barn fire. However, to pull the case together, the police needed a witness, someone who had seen something or heard something. At the fire department's request, the school put up a $2,000 reward. The fire department thought that it might entice someone to step forward. Unfortunately, that didn't happen for two years.

After the fire, Boland moved to Daytona Beach. He operated a popular strip club, Molly Brown's, which featured female oil wrestlers. As the trail grew cold, the red Butane lighter and yellow glove were accidentally thrown away when a police officer cleaned out an evidence locker.

In September 1991, when it appeared the case would remain unsolved, Debbie Butkiewicz Mulligan, the high school girl who had been seen driving in Boland's blue Corvette to Lowell High School in 1987, called the Andover police department. She said that Michael Boland, along with his friend, Edward T. Dillon, had set the fire. Boland had admitted it to her.

Mulligan told police the whole story. At age 12, the Department of Social Services had taken her from her home and placed her with Boland's mother, Catherine, who cared for her nieces and grandchildren, who were around Mulligan's age. When the kids looked for something to do, they walked up the street to Boland's stable and rode horses.

There, Boland, then 37 years old, became interested in Debbie. They developed what she described as a boyfriend-girlfriend relationship, which she said included sexual relations. As she grew, Boland treated her to jewelry, expensive gifts, trips, and a car. When seen together, Boland referred to her as "his girl" and sometimes claimed to be her father.

On October 23, 1989, the morning after MSL's fire, Mulligan, who was then 17, found Edward Dillon in Boland's condominium. He looked quite strange. He had a cap pulled down over his hair, which looked singed. Dillon's eyebrows were gone, as if burned off. Even the hair on his arms appeared singed or gone. Boland joked and said that it looked as if a lawnmower had run over him.

Mulligan asked Boland what had happened. Boland replied, "Ed and I burned down the law school." Boland said that he had paid Dillon to do it, but "the stupid idiot [couldn't] even light a fire." He made her promise not to tell. He said that if anyone found out, they would all go to jail, including her.

Mulligan did as she was told and kept quiet. When Boland moved to Daytona Beach, she went with him. There she met Billy Mulligan, a bouncer in Boland's strip club. After a brief relationship, they married. When Boland accused Billy of stealing from the bar, tempers flared, and Billy told his wife to turn Boland in.

Mulligan supplied the details that police needed, and the evidence gathered at the scene fit her story. The motive was obvious. Boland was angry at the dean for establishing a competitive law school and taking many of Commonwealth's students and faculty with him.

On September 17, 1991, Dillon was arrested in North Chelmsford. He pled guilty to arson and was sentenced to serve three to 10 years in prison.

As for Boland, he was in Florida, where local police were monitoring him. In addition to running a strip club, he worked for an 89-year-old woman, supposedly providing her with nursing care and managing her money. When investigators entered her home, they found Boland's dancers and oil wrestlers posing as nurses. A check of the elderly woman's finances found $500,000 missing.

On September 25, 1991, Boland was arrested and charged

with abuse and exploitation of the elderly and brought to jail, where he was expected to remain for some time. However, a year later, he was released from prison on a legal technicality. As he walked out of jail, wearing a Molly Brown's t-shirt, Massachusetts state troopers took him into custody and brought him to Salem.

In June 1993, the Salem Superior Court held an eight-day jury trial for Boland. The prosecution showed how all of the evidence could be traced back to Boland, particularly the white bucket, which had contained the accelerant that had started the blaze.

Several years after his Tyngsborough barn had burned down, Boland sold the property. Larkham, who had investigated the 1986 fire, asked the new owners if he could look through debris in the back—trash leftover from the fire. Larkham thought he might find evidence that might explain how the fire had started. In the trash, he found more of the same white buckets that he had seen the day of the fire. There were several of these buckets, all labelled in red felt-tip pen: "water only," "brushes only," "grain only," and so on. Larkham took one. It looked just like the bucket found at the MSL fire. It seemed obvious to everyone that the bucket found at the MSL fire scene had come from Boland's former horse stable.

In addition, numerous inculpatory statements, made by Boland, came up during the trial. Ronald Krenn, who had been Boland's business partner in Florida, testified that he had asked Boland whether he had burned down MSL. In reply, Boland said, "Ron, you go into the 7-Eleven and you rob it, you come out and I drive you away. Who's guilty?" Krenn said that he had told Boland that they both would be guilty, but Boland didn't see it that way.

Also, Boland told Krenn that he didn't believe his former girlfriend, Mulligan, would testify at trial. "She's too scared of me," he had said. Boland also claimed that Dillon wouldn't talk either.

Between the evidence and the testimony, jurors found Boland guilty of having conspired with Dillon to start the blaze. In sentencing him, Judge Charles Grabau described Boland as "selfish and vengeful" and sentenced him to eight to 10 years in the Walpole state prison.

*****

The pressing concern on the minds of Velvel and the faculty in 1993 was how to obtain accreditation from the American Bar Association. On July 19, 1993, Velvel wrote J. Michael McWilliams, president of the ABA, and told him that MSL was prepared to sue the ABA on antitrust charges. With his letter, the dean sent a 75-page legal opinion prepared by the law firm Weil, Gotshal & Manges of New York City. Paul Victor, an MSL trustee, supervised its preparation.

In the letter to McWilliams, Velvel accused a small group of people, led by James P. White, of controlling the ABA accreditation process and using it as a labor union to increase professors' wages and benefits. The dean wrote that ABA accreditors had enforced criteria that have "caused law tuitions to increase by hundreds of percents in recent years—sometimes by up to 450 percent . . . ." Velvel explained that these high costs barred working-class people, minorities, and second career seekers from entering law school. He told McWilliams that this had social ramifications. Because most working-class people were unable to obtain legal education, relatively few moved into politics, sought lawmaking positions, or served as judges. In addition, he accused the ABA of operating in a conspiratorial manner and using its monopoly status unfairly.

"The time has now come when MSL can no longer continue to merely endure what has been shown to be a wholly unavailing accreditation process filled with illegal cartel requirements and unlawful procedures. MSL must now take action," he wrote. "However, prior to filing suit and presenting the matter to the Antitrust Division of the Department of Justice, MSL is placing the matter before the ABA's Board of Governors, which has the power to act for the House of Delegates when the House is not in session and which can therefore overturn decisions of the Section of Legal Education. If the Board of Governors desires to enter an appropriate settlement on behalf of the ABA, MSL will forego its antitrust suit and other proceedings. If the board does not desire to enter an appropriate settlement, MSL will shortly begin proceedings."

*****

In August, the dean and faculty appealed their denial of ABA accreditation before the Council of the Section of Legal Education. At that meeting, Dean Velvel spoke at length about the school, and Council members posed questions that were similar in many ways to the questions raised at the Accreditation Committee meeting.

Then Council member Erica Moeser, who would later become chair of the Section of Legal Education and president of the National Conference of Bar Examiners, said that a waiver might be appropriate for a school with exceptional circumstances. Still, appearing dubious, she said, "I'm trying to understand if your arguments for waiver are, in fact, an argument that you have exceptional circumstances."

She asked, "Are there principal bases for distinction of your school from other schools which might also not be in compliance with the standards? That is, can we distinguish MSL from other schools that might come before us acknowledging that they do not meet as many standards as you presently concede that you do not meet?"

To Velvel, Moeser's concerns were obvious. If the ABA waived the standards for MSL, other schools would claim exceptions, too. He knew that this went to the heart of the Council's long-standing fear of opening the door to schools that might not meet its rigid standards. Replying to Moeser, Velvel explained MSL's position and what he felt was at stake: "It has been represented to the Department of Education that the standards promote diversity . . . if a program is of high quality, then in the name of diversity it can be approved, even though it does not meet the standards. The foreword to the standards speaks of diversity; the policy for teams speaks of diversity; documents submitted to the Department of Education speak of diversity. According to your standards, there can be a waiver in order to achieve diversity. . . .

"Obviously, the problem with law and regulation is that sometimes people have to make considered judgments as to when a waiver might be worth it or desirable and when not, or else all you're left with is rigidity in the name of uniformity and in the name of never diverging from the standards.

"Now, we are asking you, Ms. Moeser, to take into account, if you wish to look for specific factors that can be taken account of to give our school a waiver, while not opening your door to giving all schools the same waiver, which I take to be the problem inherent at the bottom of your question."

Moeser replied, "Principal distinctions was the phrase that I used."

Velvel said, "There are not a lot of schools in this country that are making a concerted effort to make education available to white ethnics, to racial minorities, to mid-lifers, to low-middle class people and to lower economic class people by keeping costs down and keeping tuition the same year after year after year, instead of raising tuition annually by amounts that Dean White has said in certain 10-year periods have amounted to 250 percent. And we know of schools where it's 450 percent."

Tuition at MSL was just $9,000 for full-time students. It had been raised only once since the school started (and in future years it would remain half of the median tuition of other New England law schools). The dean told the Council that "we have . . . an academic mission and a social mission that we are attempting to perform, and under your standards that mission cannot be performed. The inspection team, when confronted with this ugly fact by members of our adjunct faculty, had no answer. A hush fell over the room . . . .

"When our people said, you know that under your standards, if they are fully applied here, we cannot serve the economic classes of people we wish to serve because they can't afford the school, a hush fell over that room and there was a period of silence until somebody mercifully changed the subject. We know of no answer to what we are saying."

When MSL was finished making its presentation, the Council turned the school down. Velvel later said that like the Bourbons, the members of the Council forgot nothing, learned nothing, and therefore could do nothing except maintain a rigid status quo.

*****

After the Council refused to grant MSL a waiver, the next ABA forum for appeal was the ABA's Board of Governors' meeting set for November in Savannah, Georgia. At the Hyatt Regency Hotel, MSL's representatives assembled once again. Based on conversations Velvel and Coyne had had with James Halverson, who was a partner in the New York firm of Shearman & Sterling and an ABA Governor, they believed the Board of Governors understood the school's antitrust case.

Joining Velvel, Coyne, Paul Victor, and others from MSL was Harold Kohn, the school's outside counsel. A spry 76-year-old, Kohn was a well-known plaintiffs' antitrust lawyer and had practiced law for 55 years. He wanted to speak before the Board of Governors. Beyond being a name partner in the Philadelphia firm of Kohn, Nast & Graf, he served on an advisory board of the prestigious University of Pennsylvania Law School.

Standing in the ballroom of the Hyatt Hotel, Halverson outlined the proceedings to MSL, saying that MSL would be given 20 minutes to spell out why the Board of Governors should hear its case. After that, the Board would go into executive session and decide whether to hear the case.

Velvel appeared before the governors and explained that a

small group of individuals, headed by James White, had taken control of the law school accreditation process and run it with an iron fist for the last 20 years. They had barred schools such as MSL, which sought to serve capable individuals from lower-middle and low-income classes, as well as those seeking to change careers in mid life. By making schools adhere to standards that significantly increased the schools' operating costs, the White Group, as Velvel called them, had forced tuition, in 1993, as high as $15,000 to $20,000 per year in most law schools. (Today the median law school tuition in New England is more than $24,000 per year, while MSL's is $12,300.)

Velvel then turned to the heart of the matter: "Accreditation Standard 802, the diversity standard, specifically provides for accreditation of a high-quality school like MSL that varies from certain of the other standards. 802 specifically says variances from other standards can be granted when a program 'is consistent with the general purposes of the standards.'"

But as Velvel pointed out, "the controlling group" would not "permit diversity unless a school first [complied] with the standards. It is as if 802, which allows variations from the standards, does not exist. Diversity has been deliberately eliminated in favor of uniformity." To conform to the ABA's standards, law schools had to invest huge sums of money in bringing the library, the professors' salaries, and facilities up to highly expensive levels insisted upon by ABA accreditors. Law schools paid for this by raising tuition beyond what any lower-middle or lower-class students could afford. To break that vicious cycle, Velvel pointed out, a school such as MSL could not comply with the ABA's rules.

"MSL offers high quality [education] while operating efficiently, and keeping tuition low, and teaching the skills needed in practice. It therefore stands convicted of violating accreditation criteria that one, limits the hours a professor can teach to eight per week in a work year required to be no more than nine months," the dean said, now outlining the grounds for the antitrust case. "Two, precludes professors from being required to contribute to their schools by doing significant administrative work.

"Three, requires professors to be given paid leaves to do research and writing that the controlling group claims is part of their regular everyday jobs anyway. Four, intentionally creates more full-time jobs for law professors by ratios demanding a high number of full-time professors on every faculty and by narrowly limiting the use of adjunct professors . . . ." As well, he pointed out, professors could not be involved in the admissions process or teach courses that prepared students for the bar exam.

Velvel concluded by saying, "MSL stands convicted of violating these work-reducing criteria, although the controlling group had to admit to the Department of Education that many of these criteria cannot be justified."

Following Velvel, Victor spoke to the governors, saying that he had joined MSL's board as a way to contribute something of value to the profession and society. However, he was shocked in reading over the ABA's accreditation standards.

"These standards are more like a code of protection for law professors, deans, and librarians. Their intent and purpose is to feather the nests of the suppliers to the legal education process, not to improve legal education," Victor said. "I mean, can you imagine if there were standards that said a law firm can only get ABA approval to practice law if it provided minimum salaries, gave three-month vacations, and limited the amount of time associates could work, if it had a fixed ratio between partners and associates?"

Victor continued, "These criteria don't have anything to do with the quality of legal services. They have everything to do with protecting lawyers' salaries and working conditions. And if they were in effect, they would severely limit competition among law firms, plainly increase the cost of practicing law, and by no means enhance the quality of legal practice."

Kohn spoke last, urging the governors to talk with the school now, before MSL filed an antitrust case against them. "I think everybody in this room would be making a terrible mistake if you decide that we can't at least talk to each other," Kohn said. "And if this has to go through another level of the American Bar Association, then you're going to have to talk after the complaint is filed, instead of before. . . ."

By that time, MSL's 20 minutes were up. Velvel, Victor, Coyne, Kohn (who mistakenly left his hat and briefcase in the ballroom), and the others were ushered to an anteroom while the governors discussed whether or not they would hear MSL's case. The MSL crowd stood outside the double doors of the ballroom and could hear a ruckus going on inside. Shouts and yells escaped through a crack between the doors. Someone emerged from the inside and led them farther away, beyond another set of double doors, where the commotion could no longer be heard.

After 30 minutes, Darryl DePriest, the ABA's general counsel, pushed through the outside double doors. He carried Harold Kohn's hat on top of Kohn's briefcase, in front of him, horizontally, as if he were serving the hat on the briefcase, which acted as a tray. Had tension not been so thick, the MSL representatives would have laughed. It reminded them of the old joke, "Here's your hat. What's your hurry?"

"What happened?" Coyne asked him.

DePriest looked at him as if the answer were obvious. "Your request has been denied." The Board of Governors had decided not to hear the case. MSL would have to take its case before the House of Delegates, which would meet in February.

Coyne stared in disbelief. No member of the ABA Board of Governors came out to say "good-bye," or wish them well or even feebly offer some kind of explanation. They had been summarily dismissed. Coyne considered this cruel. Until then, Coyne was not convinced that anyone within the ABA had really conspired against MSL, though he had felt disheartened that ABA officials were reluctant to step out from their ivory towers to see the social significance of offering affordable legal education.

However, he perceived this action as a slap in the face. It was a shabby way of treating people. No one who cared about social justice would treat people that way, he thought. After that, he looked at the ABA quite differently.

*****

On November 23, 1993, MSL filed a complaint in the U.S. District Court for the Eastern District of Pennsylvania, in Philadelphia. The school could have filed suit in New England or even Chicago, where the ABA was headquartered, or in a number of other places. The school chose the Eastern District of Pennsylvania because one of the defendants, the LSAC, was located just outside Philadelphia. As well, Philadelphia was a semi-centrally located spot, with respect to all of the organizations in the case, and the Eastern District of Pennsylvania was the jurisdiction of the Third Circuit Court of Appeals, which in past years had a decent record in antitrust cases.

The complaint named the ABA, the Law School Admissions Council/Law School Admission Services, Inc., the Association of American Law Schools, headquartered in Washington, and 22 individuals, including the inspection team, James P. White, and Henry Ramsey of violating the antitrust laws by manipulating accreditation standards to maintain high pay, high benefits, and soft working conditions for law professors and law librarians. The actions of these collective associations and individuals, MSL said, had restricted competition and kept out lower-priced, competitive schools.

In other words, the ABA acted like a cartel preserving what the dean and others at MSL saw as a cushy academic life—a lot of pay, but little work, supported by generous sabbaticals and vacations. The ABA's insistence on these working conditions mimicked the actions of a labor union, which the ABA was not. While labor unions' actions aimed at improving a group's pay, and working conditions were exempted from the antitrust laws, professional associations' actions were not. The ABA's actions violated the Sherman Act, which stated, "Every . . . combination . . . or conspiracy, in restraint of trade or commerce among the several States . . . is declared to be illegal."

Velvel knew all this as an antitrust lawyer. Also, in 1978 he wrote an article for the *Catholic University Law Review*, titled "The Legality Under the Antitrust Laws of Wage Statistics Compiled by Professional Associations." His article weighed whether the compiling and use of wage statistics constituted price fixing, the most culpable of all antitrust violations. The ABA demanded and compiled extensive salary statistics from all schools. Then it used comparative salary charts to drive up, and fix at high levels, the price of salaries for professors, deans, and librarians at all schools. This was price fixing. As an antitrust lawyer, Velvel knew the courts would take a dim view of this, because they often sent price fixers to prison.

In its suit, MSL sought damages of $90 million, covering past and future lost revenues caused by the ABA's refusal to accredit the school. It also sought attorneys' fees.

MSL's case was reported in newspapers across the country. When speaking with reporters, some ABA representatives made light of the case. Pauline Schneider, chairwoman of the Accreditation Committee, told a *New York Times* reporter, "This is not a close case. MSL's claim of a special mission is invalid. There are many other schools meeting such a mission."

As well, James Halverson told a *Boston Globe* reporter that many schools did not receive accreditation the first time around, and that MSL's appeal was not over. It could still go before the House of Delegates in February.

Some deans of ABA schools saw the seriousness of the issue. In speaking with the *New York Times*, Colin Diver, dean of the University of Pennsylvania Law School and former dean of Boston University's law school, said, "If the bar association loses the suit, the whole house of cards falls apart." Diver said that he didn't know if MSL deserved accreditation or not, but he thought the school had "raised vital legal and philosophical issues." He said that the ABA's accreditation standards "[had] gotten too protectionist and [drove] up the cost of legal education, and tended to make it essentially impossible for alternative models of legal education to develop."

*****

Filing its own antitrust suit was only one part of MSL's challenge to the ABA. MSL also contacted, sent initial evidence to, and met with the Antitrust Division of the U.S. Department of Justice, which then opened its own antitrust investigation into the ABA's accreditation activities. On January 5, 1994, Velvel wrote a 22-page letter to the U.S. Department of Education, asking Secretary Richard Riley to terminate the ABA's status as a federally recognized accreditor. Velvel attached 400 pages of related documents to the letter. He accused the ABA of not only ignoring DOE rules but of misrepresenting its actions when ABA officials appeared before the DOE, in 1993, to request that the ABA's federal accrediting status be renewed for five years.

Velvel requested a full hearing. He listed 16 grievances against the ABA under the DOE's governing regulations. Velvel believed that the ABA ignored the DOE's rules and regulations, misrepresented its own actions, treated schools inconsistently, and thwarted diversity in law schools.

*****

On Tuesday, February 8, 1994, in Kansas City, Dean Velvel and his colleagues from MSL appeared before the ABA House of Delegates. The House of Delegates, which sets policies for the ABA, was made up of 500 lawyers. If the delegates voted against MSL, all normal channels within the ABA system would be exhausted.

Realizing that MSL had already brought the antitrust case

against the ABA to court, ABA officials could either continue to deny MSL accreditation and spend a lot of money on the court case, or they could accredit the school and settle with MSL. Of course, the latter action might prompt other schools to step forward and do the same thing that MSL did. Also, accrediting MSL meant overriding the Council of the Section of Legal Education and the Accreditation Committee, which the House was reluctant to do.

Being a pessimist, Velvel figured that the ABA wouldn't accredit MSL, for he believed that the ABA's influential Section of Legal Education feared an accredited MSL. Accreditation meant that MSL's graduates would be free to take bar exams anywhere in the country. If students from the low-priced MSL were free to take the bar everywhere in the U.S., this would adversely affect many high-cost law schools, make them look bad, and might even run a few out of business. It could also result in more competition in the legal profession, possibly driving down fees.

The House of Delegates gave Velvel, his colleagues, and Paul Victor approximately one hour to speak. They divided the time between them. Velvel spoke first, reiterating some of the same points that he had made before the Board of Governors and at prior meetings. "It would be literally impossible to start the type of law school which MSL is and aspires to be and to accomplish the educational and social mission it seeks to accomplish while adhering to each and every ABA standard," he said.

Norman Redlich, a long-time leader of ABA accreditation who was dean emeritus of the New York University School of Law, stood up before the House of Delegates and said, "The issue . . . can be simply stated: Is MSL in substantial compliance with the standards? The answer is no." He had never visited MSL, and now he claimed that the school refused to hire full-time faculty and said it offered no financial aid to students, had a student-faculty ratio in excess of 100 to 1, and had the lowest bar passage rate in Massachusetts. His statement contained serious distortions and misstatements, e.g., MSL did have full-time faculty members, did help students financially, did not have the lowest bar passage rate, and did have low student-faculty ratios, if one counted how many students were in a given class.

Velvel listened to one ABA speaker after another make prejudicial misstatements about MSL. Pauline Schneider, chair of the Accreditation Committee and a private practitioner in Washington, spoke for 10 minutes.

She attacked MSL's student faculty ratio, falsely claiming it was as high as 135 to 1 or 105 to 1. From this statement, she falsely concluded that MSL lacked student-faculty interaction. She then said that a lower student-faculty ratio enabled more student-faculty interaction and collaboration between teachers and students. "Where classes are large because of high student-faculty ratios, consultation is difficult and tends to create a climate in which only the occasional or exceptional students seeks the benefit of personal conferences with a teacher. And, I remind you, this is a school by its own admission who seeks students with special needs," she said.

Velvel knew Schneider's comments were not only harsh but deeply wrong. MSL's in-class student-faculty ratio was much smaller than that at most ABA schools, because MSL was designed, in fact, to have a high degree of interaction between students and faculty. Structurally the school was designed to encourage faculty-student interaction, which occurred daily.

When Coyne spoke, he addressed the criticisms of the speakers. "It is very hard to sit here and listen to a depiction of our law school that is not entirely accurate," he said. "I carry a full-time teaching load, and I hold the position of associate dean. Although I teach as many courses as any other full-time professor at the law school, I am not considered a full-time faculty member because the interpretations prohibit it. It is on this basis that our student-faculty ratio is alleged to be in excess of 100:1."

Likewise, Diane Sullivan addressed the ABA's narrow definition of full-time professor. She told the House of Delegates that even though Peter Winograd, of the site inspection team, had praised her for being a fine Socratic teacher, she could not be considered a full-time faculty member.

"Do you know why?" Sullivan asked the delegates. "I was employed at a bank, the same bank that I had worked at throughout law school. Imagine that, I never worked less than 60 hours per week [for MSL]; oftentimes I worked up to 80 hours per week, and I was not to be considered a faculty member at all."

Sullivan told the House that she had approached the inspection team and told them that their policies were discriminatory. She had gone up to them and asked, "You mean to tell me that if I worked 35 to 40 hours per week at the law school, but then I spent my non-school hours at home, raising a family, taking care of a home, I would then be considered a faculty member?" They told her, "Yes."

"House members, the professors at Massachusetts School of Law, like all of you here today, work very, very hard. We set a good example for our students . . . I brought 20 years of banking [experience] to my classroom. We provide practical expertise that is lacking in many law schools today," Sullivan said.

After nearly two hours of back and forth debate, a motion passed to close the discussion.

When asked if he had any final words, Velvel, who felt like a condemned man, had only a few parting words, "All I can say is to reiterate the famous statement of Daniel Webster to the Supreme Court of the United States [in his argument of the Dartmouth College case in 1819], 'It is a small school, and yet there are those who love it.' Regardless of what happens in this body, where the opposition brought out the artillery, which we cannot hope to equal . . . [p]residents of the past, presidents future, chairs past, chairs future, people who know nothing about our school, who have never been there, who don't know our professors and don't know our students . . . there will be another day, regardless of what happens here."

Chairman Anderson then put the issue to a voice vote. "All in favor of the appeal of the Massachusetts School of Law, signify so by saying aye," he said.

A few ayes could be heard.

"All opposed, say no."

MSL's representatives heard hundreds of no's.

"Dean Velvel, would you like a count of the vote?" Anderson asked.

"No," he replied. He knew that the fix had been in from the start, and the ABA's decision was clear from the overwhelming chorus of no's. It was over.

Velvel and his colleagues left the building with one resolve. They would try to right this wrong. They would fight to have the ABA's decision overturned; they and society owed it to the students, to the faculty, and to all those in society who deserved a second chance.

Chapter 8

MSL vs. ABA

In addition to filing an antitrust lawsuit against the ABA and formally complaining to the Department of Justice, MSL wrote to the U.S. Department of Education. The school asked the DOE to terminate the Council of the Section of Legal Education's status as the nationally recognized accrediting agency for law schools. In a 110-page letter-memorandum, and later in a 103-page memorandum, MSL described the school's bid for accreditation and how James White and his band of ABA accreditors and officials (the White Group) had set up obstacles and roadblocks. MSL wrote that the White Group planned to keep MSL from accreditation all along by using conspiratorial practices. What the ABA had done to other schools was now happening to MSL.

MSL showed how the ABA had suppressed information about the accreditation process and how the White Group had misrepresented facts. The misrepresented facts included the alleged granting of waivers (none had ever been given), ostensibly promoting educational diversity (the ABA claimed to encourage diversity but enforced standards that made true diversity impossible), and supposedly allowing law school applicants to take an aptitude test other than the LSAT (in fact the test had to be the LSAT).

With regard to the LSAT, ABA Standard 503 read that "all [law school] applicants . . . should be required to take an acceptable test for the purpose of determining apparent aptitude for law study." The standard didn't actually say the test had to be the LSAT, yet law school deans knew that the LSAT was the only test that would be allowed by the Accreditation Committee or the Council. Every law school approved by the ABA used the LSAT. This didn't happen by coincidence, thought Velvel. Several leaders of the Law School Admission Council (LSAC), which sponsors the LSAT, were also leaders of the White Group. As well, millions of dollars annually were garnered from the LSAT, and some of this money provided regular luxurious travel benefits for law professors, including members of the White Group.

In a letter to Karen Kershenstein, director of the DOE office that deals with accrediting bodies like the ABA, Velvel wrote that, in discovery in MSL's antitrust case, the LSAC said MSL "mischaracterize[d] the LSAT as an aptitude test." Contradictorily, the LSAT and the ABA publicly claimed that the LSAT fulfilled Standard 503's "aptitude test" requirement for law school admissions.

Addressing the claim that the LSAC made in discovery, the dean wrote: "If the LSAT is not an aptitude test, then what is it? The answer is in an LSAC Research Report. The report makes clear that 'acquired academic skills [are] measured by the LSAT.' It is obvious that the better one's elementary school, high school, undergraduate school, and graduate schools were, and the closer one is to the time when he or she underwent that academic training, the better one is likely to do on the LSAT. This in turn means that the less privileged of all backgrounds, African-Americans, Hispanics, members of the working class, white ethnics, and mid-life persons—all of whom generally have lower quality prior schooling or have been away from academia for a significant period—will do less well on the LSAT and will be denied entrance to law school. And that is exactly what happens."

What Velvel showed in his correspondence to Kershenstein

was that even though White and Ramsey had presented themselves before the DOE as flexible, open-minded, and accepting of diversity and innovation, they weren't. Instead MSL found them rigid, narrow-minded, and poised to squeeze out independent, non-conforming schools. MSL thus urged the DOE to terminate the ABA's status as a nationally recognized accrediting body.

Kershenstein responded to MSL's letter by writing, "You raise serious questions about the compliance of the ABA with the Secretary's requirements for the recognition of accrediting agencies." Further, she told MSL that her office would be investigating its complaint. She would report the results and the DOE's follow-up action, she said. But, as matters turned out, the DOE never took effective action. Instead, Kershenstein and the DOE became the handmaidens of the Council of the Section of Legal Education.

Because the ABA's denial of accreditation to MSL discouraged new students from enrolling, MSL hoped its antitrust case would proceed quickly, which can happen if a judge feels the need to expedite the litigation. Thus, MSL asked the judge assigned to the case, J. William Ditter, Jr., to give immediate attention to the case to prevent further financial harm to the school. However, Ditter did not move quickly. He did not hold a pre-trial conference for five months. Based on Velvel's experience as an antitrust lawyer, he considered this very unusual and did not think this augured well for MSL.

During this five-month delay, Ditter did one thing. Pursuant to a motion made by the defense, he dismissed as defendants the individual ABA accreditors—the ABA members of the White Group—whom MSL had sued. Thus, the LSAC, the AALS, and the ABA individuals most responsible for the accreditation actions of the ABA would not be brought to task or have to pay damages. Only the organizations would be made responsible if MSL won its case. Velvel regarded this as another bad sign.

On March 14, 1994, five months after MSL filed its lawsuit against the ABA, all parties gathered for a pre-trial conference in

Philadelphia. In a dimly lit, modern courtroom, Velvel, Coyne, MSL's "outside" attorney Harold Kohn, and Kohn's assistant Joanne Zack sat at the plaintiff's table. Behind them sat MSL professors Peter Malaguti and Connie Rudnick. On the other side sat the ABA's inside general counsel Darryl L. DePriest and outside counsel David T. Pritikin, who was from a huge national law firm based in Chicago. Sitting with them were other lawyers representing the LSAS/LSAC and AALS.

Ditter entered the courtroom. In his early 70s, the judge had a reputation for holding conservative, pro-government views. His father, J. William Ditter, Sr., had been a Pennsylvania representative in the U.S. House. In 1943, he was killed in a plane crash. The next year, a naval destroyer—the U.S.S. J. William Ditter—was named in his honor.

His son J. William Ditter, Jr. had been a naval aviator during the war. He went to law school after World War II, and in 1970, President Richard Nixon appointed him as an U.S. District Court judge. He had served on the bench some 24 years. After being assigned MSL's case, the judge sent a letter to the defendants and plaintiffs saying that he had some prior, minimal involvement with the ABA:

> As was the case with many young lawyers at the time, shortly after my graduation from law school in 1948, I joined the American Bar Association. More or less by habit, I continued my membership. In 1992, I decided not to pay any further dues and to permit my membership to expire. Despite several reminders from the ABA, I paid no dues in 1993 and do not intend to renew my membership. This decision has nothing to do with any of the issues that are involved in this case, issues about which I had never thought until this suit was brought.
>
> I have never held any office in the ABA, never served on any of the committees, and so far as I can recall, never attended any of its meetings. If you think

> that this case should be assigned to another judge,
> please make that fact known to the Clerk of Court.

From what the judge had written, MSL didn't perceive Ditter as biased toward the ABA. Velvel realized that most lawyers and judges of Ditter's generation, as well as his own, had belonged to the ABA at one time or another. What MSL wondered was whether the ABA would consider Ditter prejudiced because he had dropped his ABA membership. However, the ABA lawyers didn't ask Ditter to recuse himself, so he remained on the case.

Ditter started the pretrial conference on March 14 by making some introductory remarks. Then he said, "I had some initial problem in reading the complaint to know just what is alleged. In other words, I'm not quite sure who is alleged to have done what to whom, and when it is alleged to have been done." Ditter suggested that MSL revise its complaint, propose limited discovery, and try to reach a joint statement with the defendants on whatever matters both parties "can agree to disagree upon."

Kohn, a long-time Philadelphia lawyer, didn't question the judge. Rather, he said that he would work with the defendants to reach some kind of joint statement and if not, he would submit a statement of the points of disagreement. Velvel had a reaction different from Kohn's. MSL's complaint, he thought, was very clear—and quite accurate—on what was being alleged. Rather, Velvel believed the judge's claim of not understanding the complaint was a device typically used by judges to show favor to the defense counsel. After two years of trying to reach an agreement with the ABA, Velvel knew there was no way the two parties could reach a mutual understanding now.

Pritikin, the ABA's counsel, commended the judge, telling him that this made a lot of sense. In fact, Pritikin said, once both parties had made limited discovery, "the case may well be subject to summary disposition." In other words, Pritikin suggested that after limited discovery, the judge would see that MSL did not have enough facts to bring this case before a jury. Instead, the

judge himself would decide it for the ABA. Therefore, the more
that the ABA could withhold information from MSL by means of
only limited rather than full discovery, the more likely it was that
Pritikin's prophecy would become true.

Ditter responded to Pritikin by saying he would like the parties to reach a joint agreement on issues, but "certainly it occurred
to me that summary disposition might be the eventual formal
route that you take."

The dean studied the judge. Despite MSL's request for expe-
dition, Ditter had delayed the pre-trial conference for five
months. He had dismissed the individual defendants from the
case. Now he allowed MSL only limited discovery of facts and
was encouraging the ABA to file a summary judgment motion,
which the ABA would likely win because of the limits Ditter was
putting on discovery of facts. To Velvel, it was clear: Ditter
planned to do in MSL.

"May I request a five minute recess to confer with Mr. Kohn
and the plaintiff group?" Velvel asked.

"Confer all you want."

Velvel, Coyne, Kohn, and the others from MSL left the courtroom and entered a small room with a conference table.

Velvel told them that he thought the school was in big trouble.
He explained why he thought the judge intended to rule in the
ABA's favor.

Kohn and Coyne didn't see it that way. Rather, they believed
that they needed to educate the judge and show him how the ABA
had violated the antitrust laws. Kohn flatly refused Velvel's
request to strongly object to what Ditter was doing. They returned to the courtroom, and Kohn told the judge that he would
submit something within a 20-day period.

Ditter concluded, "I don't think the baseball season is open
yet, but I will be around."

Ditter's comment struck Velvel as insensitive. Further, it
demonstrated an antagonistic attitude toward MSL. The judge
seemed to mock the hours and money the school had invested in

the case. He seemed oblivious to the weight of this matter—that the future of MSL and its students were riding on this. He joked about ball games.

After the hearing, Ditter granted another ABA motion. He disqualified MSL's in-house lawyers: Velvel, Coyne, Rudnick, and Malaguti. He said that these attorneys could not serve as the law school's advocates at trial because they would likely serve as witnesses. It was yet another legal maneuver in the ABA's favor. Disqualifying the opponent's lawyers meant that the opponent would need to spend more money, hire more lawyers, and educate them quickly.

In this particular case, by removing MSL's in-house lawyers, who were the most familiar with the school's case, MSL had to rely more heavily on outside lawyers who charged far more money and needed to be educated about the school's position.

MSL's lawyers objected by saying that many other MSL personnel could equally well be witnesses, so the in-house MSL lawyers did not have to be. In addition, much of the evidence would come from documents rather than witnesses, as is typical in antitrust cases. But Ditter would neither listen nor relent. He continued to disqualify them, which hurt MSL immensely.

As news of MSL's case against the ABA appeared in national newspapers and circulated among academics, law school deans and professors told MSL of their own woes in obtaining ABA accreditation. The dean of Columbia University Law School, Lance Liebman, told a *New York Times* reporter that the ABA's accreditation policies were "too detailed, too specific, like the number of chairs you have to have in your library, the number of books on the library shelves, which doesn't make sense at a time when students can get much of this information electronically on computer."

Hearing about the case, James W. Doig, chair of the Committee on Law and Public Affairs Education at Princeton University, wrote Velvel. Doig told him that 20 years earlier, Princeton had tried to create a different kind of a law program that would combine legal training with political, economic, and management studies. However, when the ABA's standards arrived, Doig saw that Princeton's proposed program would not meet the ABA's stringent criteria. The bulk of the Princeton law school faculty would have to have law degrees, which would defeat Princeton's innovative idea. Also, to design a law school that would meet the ABA's standards would cost Princeton far too much money.

"This standard would make it extremely difficult for our new enterprise to be innovative," Doig told Velvel. After reading the standards, the Princeton committee dropped its proposal. Doig wrote, "I recall thinking . . . that the accrediting standards did provide a form of monopoly control . . . ." Doig sent copies of this letter to Liebman and Colin Diver, dean of the University of Pennsylvania Law School. In receiving this letter, Velvel was deeply struck by the fact that even Princeton—certainly a wealthy, elite, and powerful school—was stymied by the ABA when it tried to be innovative.

Six weeks after the pre-trial hearing in Philadelphia, a group of 14 law school deans, many from the nation's top law schools, wrote a letter to the deans of the ABA's 175 approved schools. The 14 asked for the others' support in changing the ABA's accreditation process. "We find the current process overly intrusive, inflexible, concerned with details not relevant to school quality (perhaps even at odds with maintaining quality), and terribly costly in administrative time as well as actual dollar costs to schools," wrote the deans in their letter, dated April 24, 1994. Though drafted on the letterhead of Ron Cass, dean of Boston University School of Law, it was signed by Cass and the law school deans at Harvard, Boston University, the University of Chicago, Cornell, George Mason, Nebraska, Northwestern, the University of Pennsylvania, Southern California, Stanford, Texas, Vanderbilt, Virginia, and Willamette. The deans insisted that law schools needed greater independence in order to offer variety in legal education. One school might specialize in professional training and practical skills, while another might excel in presenting theoretical and scholarly issues.

"Our varied visions of legal education focus on the results of the educational process, on the outputs of legal education—about the graduates we produce, about the sort of lives they will lead, about the consequences of our writing and teaching. In contrast, the ABA's accreditation process increasingly concentrates on inputs—how many seats are there in the library, for example—and often on trivial inputs or inputs only haphazardly connected to the quality of our outputs," wrote the deans. They accused the ABA of having a "one-size-fits-all" attitude and discouraging diversity within the legal community.

The letter was an indictment of the ABA's accreditation process. The deans' charges were similar to those made by MSL. Certainly they demonstrated how dissatisfied the legal academic community had grown over ABA accreditation. Within a month, a total of 40 deans had joined Cass' group, which they named the American Law Deans Association (ALDA). They urged the ABA to make changes. In just a few years, ALDA grew to 120 deans.

Even Robert Stein, chairman of the Council of the Section of Legal Education, admitted in a letter to the ABA law school deans that some members of the ABA's House of Delegates thought the standards to be "too protective of law faculty . . . particularly as to such matters as maximum teaching loads, sabbatical requirements and compensation . . . ." A commission would be appointed to study the accreditation policies, he said.

Stein appointed Rosalie E. Wahl to head the commission. She was, however, a leading member of the White Group, as Stein himself had been. Stein described her as "one of the real giants in the legal profession," since she had been the first woman selected for the Minnesota Supreme Court, and one of the leaders of the ABA group that produced the MacCrate Report. That report said that law schools needed to offer more practical training. As a result of that report, the ABA passed a resolution encouraging law schools to offer more skill-oriented courses.

Practical training, of course, was MSL's specialty. The school had hired working judges and lawyers as adjuncts to teach from experience, helping to fulfill the MacCrate ideal of practical training. Ironically, the accreditors condemned the school for using adjunct professors. The accreditors didn't consider adjuncts to be real faculty—a designation they reserved for full-time faculty who performed few administrative duties and did not practice law in the real world. Thus, none of MSL's adjuncts were figured into the school's student-faculty ratio by the accreditors, making its student-to-professor ratio appear absurdly high. In reality, MSL specialized in small classes—more so than any ABA schools did. Not figuring adjuncts into the ratio was yet another guild-type practice used by the ABA to pressure law schools into hiring more full-time faculty with high salaries, tenure, and extensive benefits. It had nothing to do with the quality of the education that students received.

*****

That spring, D. Bruce Pearson, an antitrust lawyer with the U.S. Department of Justice, visited MSL to take a look at the school. Velvel figured that he wanted to be certain that MSL was not a shoddy little school that would embarrass the DOJ if a lawsuit resulted from MSL's complaint.

Pearson had gained national attention when, in 1989, he investigated a price-fixing practice used by the Massachusetts Institute of Technology, Ivy League schools, and other elite schools, known as the "Overlap Group." The schools' admissions officers met once a year to discuss student candidates. At the meetings they compared their financial aid packages, making sure one school didn't offer a prospective student more money than the others. After the Department of Justice's investigation began, most of the "overlap" schools changed their financial aid practices and signed a consent decree barring them from colluding on financial aid. However, MIT fought the case. After losing in the federal District Court, the school took the case to the U.S. Court of Appeals for the Third Circuit in Philadelphia. The Court of Appeals remanded the case to the District Court for a more elaborate analysis of the problem. But before the District Court acted, the DOJ and MIT settled.

In analyzing MSL's complaint, Pearson couldn't help but think about the "Overlap Group." The DOJ lawyer interviewed law school deans across the country and inquired about ABA accreditation practices. When he arrived at MSL, Pearson looked over the law school's facilities. The DOJ attorney seemed struck by MSL's modern building. The red brick structure made a far better impression than indicated in the ABA's site report, which criticized the school for its lack of tiered classrooms, a few non-obstructive pillars, and a central office described as crowded and congested. The minimal flaws had been greatly exaggerated, the dean thought, especially since the inspectors mentioned none of the positive physical features of the school, including its naturally lit classrooms, its spacious library ringed by professors' offices, its modern computer lab, and its beautiful park-like setting.

That kind of misrepresentation was part of the problem MSL had with the ABA, Velvel explained to Pearson that day. He also told him how law school deans used these lists of alleged faults to leverage more money from university administrations to build bigger, more expensive buildings, costing as much as tens or scores of millions of dollars. In turn, students paid for this through higher tuitions.

When Pearson visited MSL, he asked Velvel which judge would be hearing MSL's case. Velvel told him J. William Ditter. At that, Pearson mentioned that Ditter's son had attended the Delaware Law School (DLS) in the early '70s. Pearson seemed aware of the DLS story.

The dean recalled that Delaware Law School had been an inadequate institution, and that the ABA Accreditation Committee had turned down the school four times when it applied for accreditation. The school's founder, Alfred Avins, fought fiercely with the ABA. Velvel couldn't help but wonder if Ditter had been involved in any way with that accreditation fracas.

In the beginning of this case, Ditter had written to both MSL and the ABA: "[T]he issues that are involved in the case [are ones] about which I have never thought until this suit was brought." Velvel wondered about this. If Ditter's son had been at Delaware Law School during the time Pearson suggested, the judge might have been exposed to the accreditation brouhaha there. He might well have thought about his son's future and about wasting money on an education that could prove to be worthless. He would have known that lack of ABA accreditation would have caused the school to close. This should have concerned any parent of a DLS student at that time. Presumably it would have greatly concerned Ditter, a judge.

But DLS' story was strikingly different than MSL's. DLS parents acquiesced to the ABA's demands, forced out the school's founder, Alfred Avins, and hired a new dean. At the ABA's insistence, the school merged with Widener College and was subsequently accredited by the ABA. Considering the tumult that had gone on at the new, initially independent law school attended by Ditter's son, MSL wondered whether this was known to Ditter and, consciously or subconsciously, affected his attitude towards MSL.

On June 20, 1994, Ditter ruled on pending motions. He dismissed MSL's case against Carl C. Monk, director of the American Association of Law Schools (AALS), though he said that he would hear the case against the AALS. This meant that Monk would not be personally liable for any damages, and thus would be less likely to advocate that the AALS itself should settle before trial. In his opinion, Ditter wrote, "MSL has alleged that the object of the conspiracy was to maintain high salaries for law school faculty, restrict faculty output, raise tuition, and make law school education inaccessible to people in lower socio-economic classes."

Then he added an odd footnote, "This may be one of the few cases on record involving an employers' trade association conspiring to raise wages paid to its members' employees, restrict their production, and limit sales to potential customers. When university trustees, who have to foot the bills resulting from high salaries, low output, and restricted sales, learn what has been going on under their very noses, heads may roll. In the meantime, it is reassuring to know that the schools making up the AALS do not teach economics or logic, only law."

Clearly Ditter had misunderstood. The AALS, though ostensibly an association of schools, was in reality run by and served the interests of law professors and deans—not the university administrations, as Ditter had thought. The AALS was regarded, in fact, as the trade association for law professors. Thus, it made sense for AALS to seek higher pay and perks for its professors and deans. One thing Ditter did understand: the AALS wanted to raise professors and deans' salaries, while decreasing their workload.

MSL's antitrust case moved onto its next phase, discovery. Routinely in antitrust cases, the plaintiff asks for discovery documents that show how harm was done. In turn, the court orders the defendant to turn these documents over to the plaintiff. In this case, the dean and his colleagues asked for specific documents that showed how the ABA had conspired against small, cost-cutting schools such as theirs. MSL knew that the ABA had forced law schools to hire more full-time faculty (and less adjunct faculty) and build expensive facilities that included huge hard copy libraries. They also knew that the ABA required law schools to provide faculty with paid sabbaticals, higher salaries, lighter workloads, and other perquisites.

Some of these ABA requirements were published. Others were not. Law school administrators knew about the latter rules either by word of mouth or by receiving a negative ABA inspection report that told them how the school must be changed if it were to maintain ABA accreditation. MSL needed these correspondence and inspection reports between the ABA and various law schools to show how the ABA had operated in a conspiratorial manner. Obtaining such documents was considered standard procedure in an antitrust case involving a conspiracy. However, though the school continuously asked the ABA for documents, the ABA sent nothing. The Association even made clear that it would not send anything unless the court made it. And Ditter didn't.

By contrast, when the DOJ launched a full-fledged investigation into the ABA's anticompetitive conspiracy, it obtained 544,000 pages of material from the ABA. Obviously, the Association was afraid to snub the Department of Justice. But MSL needed the same material the DOJ had.

Because the ABA had refused to provide MSL the documents it needed, MSL used another technique common in antitrust cases. The school asked the judge to order the ABA to turn over all of the documents that it had given the DOJ, which was investigating the same conspiracy charges leveled by MSL. In antitrust cases, federal judges had always granted such requests; MSL couldn't find one case in which it was ever refused. Thus, the faculty at MSL wrote to Ditter, "[I]t is relatively common in antitrust cases for defendants to be required to produce to plaintiffs the documents which the defendants have been required to produce to the Department of Justice."

The judge denied MSL's request. He granted discovery only of documents pertaining to MSL itself and its denial of accreditation. Also, the ABA was to send documents related to the history of ABA standards. He refused to require the ABA to send MSL documents pertaining to any other school—the precise evidence that proved that the ABA was engaged in a nationwide conspiracy. In addition, Ditter denied a pared MSL request—for documents pertaining to just 75 of the ABA's 175 schools.

As far as MSL was concerned, Ditter acted in a way no other judge in the history of American antitrust had ever done. He had refused to compel the defendant, the ABA, to produce documents that the ABA had been required to produce to the DOJ in a case making the same charges.

Among the incriminating documents that Ditter refused to require the ABA to produce were two notebooks that were kept in Jim White's office. MSL had learned of them in a deposition of one of White's assistants. The school had informed the DOJ of them, and the DOJ had gotten them from the ABA. These two notebooks were arranged school by school for every school the ABA had inspected. For each school, the notebooks listed all of the ABA's findings and actions subsequent to a school inspection. After examining them, the DOJ told MSL that the school needed the notebooks: these two notebooks themselves proved the illegal conspiracy, MSL learned. But Ditter refused to order the ABA to turn them over to MSL.

This hurt MSL's case. Outside of the court's discovery process, the school obtained documents from a handful of other schools. Several schools had experienced problems similar to MSL's and, therefore, disliked the ABA and were eager to share their materials. A few publicly funded schools were subject to state Sunshine Laws and voluntarily agreed to forward their documents. All this evidence, however, was only a fraction of what MSL should have received in discovery. Certainly it was infinitely less than that received in most antitrust cases.

The documents that the ABA provided were limited in scope and were provided in such a way that they were almost impossible to use. For instance, MSL needed documents relating to given individuals in order to formulate questions to ask at their depositions. The ABA would sometimes make the documents available at the last moment, when MSL would have no time to read them. Once, six banker's boxes of the documents were made available at 8:30 in the morning for a deposition that began at 9:00 a.m.

*****

Once Bruce Pearson pointed out Ditter's connection to the Delaware Law School, Velvel and his MSL colleagues did research to find out when Ditter's son had been there and what role, if any, the judge played in the school's accreditation dispute.

They learned that Alfred Avins had founded DLS in 1971. (Subsequently, he established the Northern Virginia Law School, in Alexandria, and the Southern New England School of Law— the school in southern Massachusetts that Boland had attended and had used as the model for creating the Commonwealth School of Law.) When he opened DLS, Avins' first classes were taught in the Wilmington YMCA.

Three years later, after the school had 665 students, Avins filed for ABA accreditation. Inspecting DLS were James White, then the new ABA consultant, and Millard Ruud, the former ABA consultant and the new executive director of the AALS. They wrote a devastatingly negative report. In it, they said that the school had many inadequacies, adding, "The most important deficiency is an intangible one: there is an academic ennui that pervades the institution. The intellectual spark is missing in the faculty and students."

As harsh as the report was, Avins remained resolute that he would obtain ABA accreditation. Two months later, the ABA sent new inspectors to the school. Like White and Ruud, the new inspectors reported that the school still had problems. They included inadequate faculty, a high student to faculty ratio, questionable admissions practices, low professorial pay, and concentrated power in the dean. Site inspectors claimed that the dean ran the school himself without input from the faculty or a Board of Trustees. The site inspectors' criticisms of DLS weren't all that different—were sometimes identical—to the false ones made against MSL nearly 20 years later, when White controlled ABA accreditation.

As it turned out, Ditter's son, J. William Ditter, III, had attended DLS in 1974-1975, at the peak of the accreditation controversy. Because of the accreditation problems, more than eight judges and lawyers, who had children enrolled in the school, formed a committee headed by Judge G. Fred DiBona, a judge on the Court of Common Pleas of Philadelphia. Known as the Judges' Committee, the goal of this group was to assist DLS in obtaining ABA accreditation. Judge J. William Ditter, Jr. sat on that committee.

In July 1974, Avins, DiBona, Ditter, and Charles Peruto, a lawyer who sat on the Judges' Committee, met at Luigi's Restaurant to discuss the accreditation. Avins, who described himself as "the most conservative constitutional law historian in the country," admitted to being a "stumbling block to accreditation." He told those at the dinner table that his manner, his controversial nature, and his behavior had antagonized the ABA.

A few days later, DiBona flew to Hawaii to attend an ABA meeting, and there he discussed DLS' accreditation problems with Jim White and others. They told DiBona that Avins had to resign before they would accredit the school.

When DiBona returned, he asked Avins to step down as dean. Avins refused. He claimed that there was nothing wrong with the school, but DiBona, the Judges' Committee, and students continued to pressure Avins into stepping down. When the students threatened to strike, Avins finally resigned. In September 1974, Arthur Weeks took his place.

Though the school had a new dean and had made improvements, the ABA once again refused to accredit DLS. ABA officials told Weeks that the school needed to affiliate with a bigger school. Thus, negotiations began with Widener College in Chester, Pennsylvania. In 1975, just before DLS' first class was to graduate, the ABA granted the school provisional accreditation. DLS became Delaware Law School at Widener College (which subsequently became Widener University).

Eight lawsuits grew out of the dispute. Avins sued White for defamatory remarks that, he said, caused parents and students to lose trust in him and subsequently oust him as dean and professor at DLS. After a three-week jury trial, the U.S. District Court for the District of Delaware ruled in Avins' favor. On the defamation claims, he was awarded $50,000 in compensatory damages. However, the U.S. Court of Appeals reversed the defamation charges upon appeal and remanded for a new trial.

What concerned MSL was that Ditter hadn't revealed this story when he took the case. The similarities between the DLS and MSL cases were striking. The ABA accrediting body had turned down both schools for many of the same reasons, and both schools had fought against the ABA's anticompetitive policies.

Certainly White may have remembered that Ditter had been involved in DLS' accreditation battle and had taken the ABA's side. If White recalled this, then he would have had no reason to ask the judge to recuse himself. Likely he would have regarded Ditter as a plus for his side.

Unlike DLS, MSL fought to remain innovative and independent. Velvel thought back to that first pre-trial conference and how the judge had looked at him. Although they had never met, Ditter didn't seem to like Velvel, and Velvel's colleagues thought they knew why. When the judge looked at him, he thought of Avins— an intellectual, outspoken law professor who started up his own independent law school that appealed to individuals normally shut out of legal education. But Ditter had a negative experience with that type of law school and that type of dean. It seemed entirely possible, even probable, that, consciously or unconsciously, he drew parallels between the two schools and the two deans and despised what MSL stood for.

That fall, MSL filed a motion requesting Ditter to disqualify himself because of his affiliation with DLS. At the very least, he *appeared* to be biased.

In an opinion issued on December 20, 1994, Ditter denied having played a "leading role on the Judges' Committee," as MSL contended, or even being active in gaining accreditation for DLS. He claimed that he had not participated in the DLS site inspections, had not read the site team reports, and did not read newspaper reports about the school, although some of them appeared in *The New York Times*. Though he had attended no fewer than eight of the Judges' Committee meetings, he claimed to have missed so many that he had to be "filled in on some of the details."

"I have had no reason to think about these matters for almost 20 years . . .," wrote the judge in his published opinion. "No reasonable person could view those events of 20 years ago and conclude they would affect any ruling I might make in this case . . . . There is no basis for my disqualification in this matter." Ditter referred to Velvel's charges as erroneous and claimed that MSL overstated his involvement in DLS' bid for accreditation. Thus, he remained on the case.

MSL could not agree with Ditter's putative assessment. He did not deny that he had sat on a committee set up specifically to assist DLS in becoming accredited, nor did he deny that he and the committee had sided with the ABA, insisting ABA standards be met, and forced the dean to resign. It seemed reasonable that such an individual might be biased and should not be judging a similar case. Yet Ditter remained.

*****

By 1995, the ABA had "spent more than $1.1 million in legal fees in defense against antitrust litigation brought . . . by the Massachusetts School of Law," according to a report written in the *Chicago Daily Law Bulletin*. "That amount already exceeds the entire [yearly] budget—allocated for outside counsel fees . . . . The ABA's total annual budget for that year [was] $118 million, according to an association spokeswoman." The ABA had hired two major law firms, Sidley & Austin of Chicago, and Pepper, Hamilton & Scheetz of Philadelphia, to represent the Association.

As the DOJ investigated the ABA, the Wahl Commission— mostly members of the White Group—ostensibly looked at the ABA's accreditation standards. Patrick Hetrick, dean of the

Campbell University School of Law in North Carolina wrote to Wahl objecting to the type of scrutiny law schools underwent during site inspections. He wrote in his memo, "Sometimes one gets the impression that a labor union for faculty members and law librarians has entered the building to negotiate salary increases, additional staff, and benefits."

Other deans and experts in legal education made similar observations. One was Robert Stevens, author of the book, *Law School: Legal Education in America from 1850's to the 1980's.* He said in a deposition, "The idea of outside groups telling law schools how much they can pay professors and intimidating them if they do not pay them a certain amount, seems to me appalling. The idea of an outside body telling you how many hours you can teach seems to me very strange indeed. It is the kind of thing that George Meaney [the long time head of the AFL-CIO] would have dreamt about, but the law professors have actually achieved."

As well, Peter J. Liacouras, who had been dean of Temple University's Beasley School of Law, had a lot to say about the ABA's practices in a deposition taken by MSL. Liacouras, son of Greek immigrants, had been a natural at leading the law school, before moving on to become the University's president in 1982. Temple, located in a tough urban Philadelphia neighborhood, fought for social justice for its students and worked hard at giving underrepresented segments of society a better chance.

However, Liacouras found that many of ABA's standards thwarted the school's mission. In fact, he found that many of the standards intruded upon law school management. "Accreditation is supposed to assure that there's not consumer fraud; that there's a certain minimal level of quality that is achieved through the school's education of students . . . ," Liacouras said.

"What happens though is that areas, such as working conditions—essentially [a matter] between the employer and the employees—is invaded by the accrediting body, the ABA," Liacouras said. "They tell you [that] you can't teach more than a certain number of hours, [and that] your students can't work more than 20 hours a week. Now, that of all the silliness and noblesse oblige views that were somehow made up [by] all of these rich descendents of the robber barons and not of the immigrants and those who have to work their way through and for whom $20 is a big deal. . . ."

Liacouras also criticized the ABA's definition of full-time faculty. He claimed that rules that said that faculty could not perform administrative duties and handle an academic load greater than eight or 10 hours was "an intrusion into management affairs." In addition, he criticized the ABA's classroom ratios and its close monitoring of professors' salaries. "Of all the areas that the ABA had the least . . . justification to use in the accrediting process, it's salaries," he said.

Despite the criticism leveled by scholars and academic leaders, the ABA remained committed to using standards that denied innovative, independent law schools accreditation.

*****

Once MSL's motion to disqualify Ditter was over, the ABA's lawyers filed a motion for summary judgment. They had said that they would do this at the pre-trial conference, and Ditter had indicated that he supported it. Throughout the case, Ditter appeared biased against the school. So the time seemed right for the ABA to end this case. The AALS filed a similar motion.

On May 13, 1996, Ditter ordered an *ex parte* hearing for May 16 with White and the ABA's antitrust lawyers. MSL was not informed of the hearing. Even if MSL and its lawyers had known of the hearing, they would not have been admitted. An *ex parte* hearing is when one side is allowed private time with the judge. Such hearings are so rare in the midst of a case that they are largely considered to be nonexistent.

The subject of this hearing was whether MSL's salaries had been discussed at two meetings in which ABA officials talked about MSL. The first meeting was on June 22, 1993, at a dinner

attended by White; Nina Appel, chair of the Council of the Section of Legal Education; John Ryan, chair of the Accreditation
Committee; Claude Sowle, draftsman of the Accreditation Committee's action letter on MSL; Cathy Schrage, executive assistant
to White; and David Stewart, one of the ABA's outside counsel.
The next day, many of the same individuals met privately for 15
minutes before MSL was to address the Accreditation Committee. Though Ditter had permitted MSL discovery regarding
the school's denial of accreditation from the ABA, including
information showing whether the ABA had used salary data, the
ABA refused to reveal the contents of those two meetings. The
Association claimed attorney-client privilege.

On May 23, following the *ex parte* hearing, Ditter wrote:
"Based on Mr. White's affidavit and the testimony I received at
the hearing on May 16, 1996, I find that there were no discussions related to MSL's faculty's salaries at either the June 22 or
23 meetings. Therefore, MSL's waiver argument does not entitle
it to any additional discovery from the two meetings in question."

MSL, being barred from the hearing, could not cross-examine
ABA personnel as to whether there had been discussions of
MSL's salaries either at those two meetings or at other times. As
well, MSL could not cross-examine them about documents that
clearly showed that data about MSL's salaries had been part of
documents considered by the accreditors.

Ditter's handwritten notes were the only record of the hearing.
There was no stenographic transcription, which is rare. Ditter
ordered his notes sealed and impounded and not to be "opened or
transcribed except upon further order of the court."

Velvel and Coyne believed Ditter had engaged in serious misconduct by holding a "hearing" about antitrust issues crucial to
MSL's case and allowing only the ABA and its counsel to attend.
Such conduct, which prevents cross-examination or refutation, is
so fundamentally unfair that it is nearly unheard of in the judicial
system.

This was only one of numerous incidents that led Velvel and

the MSL faculty to believe that they could not win this case, though MSL had fought bitterly to do so. The law school's faculty repeatedly wrote that the defendants were seeking to have the school's case dismissed before it received the discovery to which it and every antitrust plaintiff had a right and which would prove its charges of a widespread conspiracy enforced against every law school seeking accreditation. It pointed out that the DOJ had told it that the government had received two notebooks that showed every action the ABA had taken against every law school—those notebooks themselves proved MSL's conspiracy charges. MSL pointed out that the information it had received from a few schools outside the discovery process strongly supported its claims that it had been the victim of a conspiracy to force all law schools to follow practices that benefitted professors.

All this was to no avail. Ditter threw out MSL's case, just as Velvel knew he would do from the first pre-trial conference. After that conference, all of MSL's lawyers had ultimately come at various times to the same conclusion as Velvel—Ditter intended to do in MSL. He had made it plain by disqualifying MSL's inside counsel, refusing time and again to require the ABA to provide MSL with the discovery to which it had a right and which it needed to prove its conspiracy charges, refusing to require the ABA to give MSL the documents it had provided the DOJ, which was investigating the same charges, refusing to disqualify himself despite having been active in the DLS controversy where his group had adopted the ABA's line, assailing MSL's dean and outside lawyers, and holding an *ex parte* hearing from which MSL was barred.

In throwing out MSL's case, Ditter said that MSL had sought to "bluff, bluster, bludgeon and bully" the ABA—i.e., he claimed that the young, small, non-affluent MSL had tried to bully the wealthy, powerful, 370,000-member ABA, which had lawyers, state and federal judges, senators, congressmen, and law school deans as members.

He also wrote, "The ABA has a reputation for being good at what it does," and supposedly is regarded by states as "quite good at setting standards for legal educators." That most states had utterly no idea of what the ABA's standards and procedures were, and therefore could not possibly know whether the ABA did a good job or not, was a fact that utterly eluded Ditter. To Velvel, Ditter's comments about the ABA's quality, though couched in what other people allegedly thought, in fact showed Ditter's favoritism toward the ABA.

Making comments antagonistic to MSL and favorable to the ABA, Ditter also said that, if the states' reliance on the ABA operated to "freeze out lower income people," disgruntled parties can petition the state legislature to abandon its reliance on the ABA." Ditter's comments, Velvel thought, not only showed his lack of sympathy for the poor but that he had failed to grasp a critical issue in the case. Ditter failed to understand that, in 90 percent of the states, it was state courts, not state legislatures, that gave the ABA the authority to determine who could take the bar exam.

After Ditter threw out its case, MSL took an appeal to the U.S. Court of Appeals for the Third Circuit, headquartered in Philadelphia. MSL hoped the Third Circuit would prove to be more open-minded than Ditter was. When preparing for the appeal, MSL held two mock oral arguments before two prominent retired Third Circuit judges, each of whom had been chief judge of that court. Each of those judges read the briefs of the parties and, after the moot courts for MSL's counsel, they were convinced that the school had the better of the case.

Their opinions did not matter. The Third Circuit was not about to overturn its own trial court judge by reversing him in a case against the representative of the legal establishment, the ABA, or by reversing its previous failure to disqualify Ditter. Thus, the Third Circuit upheld Ditter on all points. It upheld him even where it was implicitly forced to concede the weakness of his position: for example, with regard to his denials of discovery. And it upheld him even where this required it to write astounding law: for instance, when it claimed that the active governmental supervision which the Supreme Court said was required to immunize a private body like the ABA from antitrust, was unnecessary here. The Supreme Court had said that the active governmental supervision needed for immunity required serious hearings before state bodies on the private body's anticompetitive rules to determine whether the state approved of them. But here there had been no such hearings in any state, and in fact state judges usually had no idea at all about the content of the ABA's rules—its publicly announced ones or the ones it followed as a matter of secret enforcement practice. There was no active governmental supervision here.

*****

On St. Patrick's Day in 1995, Velvel, Coyne, and Paul Victor sat in the foyer of the West Wing of the White House. Looking at big, burly men roaming the building, Coyne assumed that an Irish event of some kind was going on. One of the men looked closely at them, and they recognized him as Mark Messier, center for the New York Rangers. The President had invited the team members there because they had won the Stanley Cup the previous spring.

The MSL representatives were at the White House to meet with Deputy White House Counsel Joel I. Klein. He would soon become deputy assistant attorney general in the Justice Department's Antitrust Division and would assume responsibilities for the potential case against the ABA. Pearson and several other DOJ representatives joined them in the meeting in a tiny, west-wing basement room that was very cramped with about 10 people sitting around a table.

Klein had been a Washington lawyer in private practice, with relatively little antitrust experience. In 1993, following Vince Foster's suicide, he took Foster's place as deputy White House counsel. In that position, he dealt with an assortment of Bill

Clinton's political problems, including Whitewater, Travelgate, and the mysterious circumstances surrounding Foster's death. To Velvel, it appeared odd that Klein, who was not an antitrust lawyer, would now suddenly be moved to the Antitrust Division and be put in charge of the Division's case against the ABA.

Velvel and his colleagues explained to Klein how the ABA had engaged in a sophisticated form of price fixing. During a school's inspection, the ABA would compare that school's compensation statistics with those of ten or so comparable law schools. If the school's compensation fell below the mean of this comparison group, the school would be told to raise its salaries to at least the mean. Once that school adjusted its pay, its salary rank would usually be above the mean. The school that had previously been at the mean would now have slid below the mean, and all the schools below it would have slid further down from the mean. Then the ABA would chastise and threaten those schools for not paying their professors and deans enough money. Next, those schools would have to raise salaries to the mean, and so on. This was an ongoing leapfrog game. Schools had to constantly surpass each other in order to meet ABA edicts. Under antitrust laws, this is considered to be price fixing.

MSL representatives also explained that the ABA had forced schools to require lighter teaching loads and overall workloads, to give paid sabbaticals, and to provide more full-time faculty jobs. Sometimes these practices were part of its published rules, and sometimes they were part of its secret enforcement.

At first, it seemed that Klein had a limited knowledge of the case. But as Velvel, Coyne, and Victor explained the case, it appeared that Klein began to understand what it was all about. In fact, at one point Klein responded that it sounded as if the ABA were operating like a labor union. That was exactly the point. It was acting precisely as a union acts, though it was not a labor union and did not qualify for the so-called labor exemption from antitrust.

The meeting went extraordinarily well. Velvel had brought a

list of talking points, but he didn't even refer to it. All the points that he wanted to address came up naturally in the conversation. After leaving the White House, Velvel and Victor felt more optimistic than they had felt in a year. Klein had seemed to understand what had happened to MSL and other law schools. Later that day, Velvel communicated his enthusiasm to Kenneth Hart, of the prominent New York City antitrust law firm of Donovan & Leisure, which now represented MSL. He wrote, "After the meeting, I personally felt, without exaggeration, that it had been the best meeting I had attended in my entire career." Four and a half months later, Velvel was disappointed to hear that the Antitrust Division agreed to a consent decree that was weak, ineffective, and did not even come close to solving the problems.

Following his meeting with MSL, Klein met with ABA officials, who believed that they faced a serious problem. A DOJ lawsuit would mean a long, costly fight. Additionally, a suit by the DOJ would mean that all the incriminating evidence it had collected would become public instead of continuing to be hidden, and it would be available for use in lawsuits against the ABA. Such lawsuits would likely proliferate, especially because the ABA's accreditation rules had harmed so many schools and so many students, who had had to pay much higher tuitions or who had been excluded from law school altogether. So on June 7, George E. Bushnell, Jr., president of the ABA, wrote to Anne Bingaman, assistant attorney general of the Antitrust Division, to try to dissuade the DOJ from bringing a case. Bushnell told Bingaman that:

> In order to be responsive to the issues raised by your office, the Board [of Governors], following consultation with the Council of the Section of Legal Education and Admissions to the Bar, determined that changes in the accreditation process should be made and that those changes should be communicated to the chief justices of the states, the presidents of universities, and the law school deans.

Bingaman suggested that the ABA enter a consent decree, but Bushnell claimed that it wasn't necessary. The ABA was complying with the law by amending its accreditation rules, he said. Further, he brought up the ABA's fear that a consent decree would make the ABA vulnerable to private, treble damage lawsuits. "The ABA has spent a great deal of money defending the Massachusetts School of Law case and lacks the resources to defend additional major private lawsuits that might challenge accreditation activities," he told Bingaman.

Notwithstanding Bushnell's plea, a few weeks later, on June 27, 1995, the DOJ filed a complaint formally charging the ABA with fixing professors' salaries and other violations. Using a common antitrust technique, the DOJ's complaint was simultaneously accompanied by a consent decree agreed to by the ABA. In other papers accompanying the complaint, the DOJ said that it could prove its charges (it had gotten 544,000 pages of evidence from the ABA). It also said that the accreditation process had been in the grip of a small, permanent group of insiders—academics who had used accreditation to further the self-interest of professors instead of improving education. In regard to salaries, Klein told the press, "They began a process that became steadily more guild-like," which led to "ratcheting up the salary data." Anne Bingaman said, "The ABA's accreditation process required that universities raise salaries to artificially inflated levels and meet other costly accreditation requirements that had little to do with the quality of education they provided. The settlement reached today stops this anticompetitive conduct."

By agreeing to a simultaneously filed consent decree, the ABA avoided having the DOJ's evidence exposed to the outside world in pre-trial briefs and later at a trial. This was important to the ABA. The more public the DOJ's evidence became, the more vulnerable the ABA was to lawsuits by other law schools affected similarly as MSL, by law school students whose tuitions had been exorbitantly raised, and by persons who had been excluded from law schools because of ABA standards. With the DOJ's evidence remaining secret (which occurs when a consent decree is filed with the complaint), the ABA could avoid such suits. Potential plaintiffs would find necessary evidence inaccessible. They would face the same roadblocks MSL had faced: unavailable, unproduced evidence, an opposing legal juggernaut that would fight to the death, and a federal judiciary sympathetic to the ABA.

The Department of Justice knew this. Nevertheless, it agreed to a consent decree that would keep the evidence secret from the victims. MSL repeatedly asked the DOJ not to do this and requested that the courts not permit it; however, the school's pleas were ignored.

*****

The DOJ's complaint, accompanying papers, and consent decree did stop the ABA from continuing its practice of salary price fixing. But as MSL warned both the DOJ and the courts, the DOJ's actions were far too weak. Even after the consent decree, the ABA continued to require schools to hire huge, expensive full-time faculties who had light teaching loads, to build expensive buildings costing millions of dollars, to have a huge and expensive hard copy library even though legal materials are available on-line, and to demand high LSAT scores from applicants. The decree did nothing to open law schools to persons who had been unfairly excluded.

MSL complained to the DOJ and to the courts, but to no avail. Thus, law school tuitions continued to rise, reaching an average of $24,000 per year at private ABA schools. Such schools make up approximately 60 percent of all law schools and predominantly exist in urban areas where millions of poor and minority persons live. In some rural areas, ABA schools are the only law schools within a large geographic area. Thus, the poor and minorities remain excluded.

MSL was not alone in thinking that little or nothing had changed. The American Law Deans Association believed that many of the problems had only been glossed over. The ABA still required all law school applicants to take and do well on the LSAT, still forbade schools from giving a for-credit bar review course to help students pass the bar exams, still demanded elaborate and expensive buildings, and still required large, expensive hardcover libraries. Tom Leahy, one of two dissenters (from the prevailing views of the White Group) on the Wahl Commission —the two dissenters had been placed on the large Commission as tokens—was dissatisfied. He thought that the ABA's continued emphasis on full-time, academic, non-practicing professors (and continued limits on adjuncts) contrasted diametrically with the Wahl Commission's own determination that more "training from front-line practitioners" was needed.

Ron Cass, the other dissenter on the Commission, questioned what effect the consent decree would have. Richard Posner, not only the most influential and famous federal court of appeals judge in the country, but a law professor at the University of Chicago Law School, gave a speech saying that a major problem of legal education arose because it was a "cartelized and regulated industry, rather than one in which the consumer is sovereign." Were it not for the requirements imposed under the cartelization, Posner said, law schools, like business schools, might have "matriculation at a later age, schooling often interrupted, two years at most, weekend and night programs even at the best schools and more rigorous attention to both skills and theory."

The cartelized education created by the ABA's accreditors, and not affected by the consent decree, was thus subject to much criticism. But the ABA continued to stridently defend it. Stopping at nothing in this defense, ABA General Counsel Darryl DePriest later expressed contempt for the view that the ABA's expensive rules were driving up costs and tuitions. In 1998, in the midst of continuous annual rises in law school tuitions, he told the *Christian Science Monitor*, "There is no competent evidence I have seen that the accreditation process of the ABA is driving up the cost of law school. We've looked at the issue and we've seen nothing that supports it." Apparently DePriest and the ABA felt they defied the economic law that states that increased costs require greater revenues (tuitions, in this case) to pay for the increased costs.

Responding to Velvel's view that the consent decree had accomplished little, DePriest also told *The National Law Journal* that MSL's dean "makes the Unabomber seem lucid." Thus, DePriest resorted to character assassination when all facts, reason, and logic stood against him.

*****

The DOJ, in addition to taking weak and ineffective action in its consent decree, made other serious mistakes that allowed the ABA to continue to prevent working-class people and minorities from entering law school. MSL protested these mistakes both to the DOJ and to the courts, but once again its protests fell on deaf ears.

Instead of banning certain practices outright, like limits on using adjunct professors, the DOJ let the Wahl Commission make the initial decision. This commission, however, was mainly made up of members of the White Group—the people whom the DOJ had called a small, permanent group of insiders that had used accreditation for self-interested purposes. Thus, the commission adopted recommendations that were merely cosmetic and that offered no real changes. These were approved by the ABA and, generally, by the DOJ.

To allow the people who had violated the law to decide how they should change their behavior was an unprecedented move in antitrust. In this case, it was like putting the fox in charge of the hen house. Still, the DOJ and the courts did this.

Among the supposed new rules mandated in the consent decree was that the ABA had to have a mix of membership on its major committees, such as the Accreditation Committee and the Council of the Section of Legal Education. Half of these members had to be non-academics. What the DOJ thought to be a new rule wasn't new at all. Non-academics had always made up half of these committees. The problem was that ABA leaders ensured that the non-academics were academic-friendly individuals. Many had been legal academics and had served as active accreditors when they were academics. Now they were judges or practicing lawyers; thus, they could be counted as non-academics. In this sense, the DOJ's new requirement did not change the make-up of these committees. Even when MSL pointed this out to the DOJ and the courts, they did nothing.

*****

Nonetheless, the DOJ's case, which charged the same conspiracy and the same illegal actions as MSL did, vindicated MSL's views. Before the government's case, with its broad-ranging allegations and charges, many people thought MSL's claims about the ABA were frivolous, or at least ill taken. After the DOJ's case was filed, many more people accepted that what MSL had said was true.

But while the government's case was wide sweeping, the remedies it settled for in its consent decree were weak and inadequate. They did literally nothing to change the nature of legal education. They did nothing that opened the door to accreditation of and competition from low priced, innovative schools like MSL that wanted to provide legal education and societal opportunity at affordable costs to working-class people, minorities, poor people, and immigrants, but could not if they had to follow high-cost, academically exclusionary standards. The question in MSL's mind was, why did the DOJ settle for such a wholly inadequate and ineffective consent decree, which accomplished little or nothing, when it had charged and in its papers had said it could prove a wide-ranging conspiracy?

MSL thought the answers to this question were both plural and obvious. To begin with, the DOJ was comprised of lawyers. So was the ABA. Indeed, the ABA, and the Section of Legal Education itself, had federal judges as members. The DOJ was not going to go hard on an organization of fellow lawyers and judges, MSL thought. A few years after MSL's complaints, DOJ lawyer Bruce Pearson conceded in a letter that the DOJ was not enthusiastic about assailing an organization that included federal judges.

Just as the dean and MSL's faculty had thought, the DOJ had handled the ABA lightly in its antitrust case as a "professional courtesy" to fellow lawyers and judges. After all, the lawyers in the DOJ had themselves been connected with the ABA, and they, like other lawyers, considered the ABA's leaders to be honorable people who would do the right thing once they had been made aware of anitrust violations. This was understandable because Coyne and Velvel had initially felt that way. Unfortunately, they were all mistaken.

Certainly politics played a role in the DOJ's actions, too, Velvel and MSL's faculty believed. President Bill Clinton was a Democrat and the entire administration was also Democratic. One could not get past the fact that the legal profession was the largest contributor of any business or profession to the Democratic Party. Also, the Democrats depended on the ABA for its powerful lobbying help on administration and other Democratic bills. And many Democratic leaders, right up to Hillary Clinton herself, had been deeply involved in the ABA and were very friendly with ABA leaders, including its 1995 president, Patricia Ramo.

Then, too, Joel Klein, who had negotiated the consent decree for the DOJ, had been counsel to and had handled major political problems for President Bill Clinton. At the time he had been assigned the ABA case, Klein was relatively inexperienced in antitrust matters. However, he was known to be ambitious with high aspirations. For the highly influential ABA, Klein became an easy, pliable mark in terms of negotiations. That's what Velvel thought. Even when he and the faculty of MSL complained about the weaknesses of the decree, Klein said that he wouldn't renege on his deal with the ABA.

*****

MSL had lost its antitrust case, though it believed it was right (a view the DOJ's complaint vindicated). It had also seen the DOJ's case end in a weak and ineffective decree that resulted in no change in legal education. These results were major disappointments to MSL. They also were very harmful. Because the ABA was not curbed, and therefore would not accredit MSL, the school's student body declined, and so did its finances. The student body dropped from a high of 825 to 450 students. This drop represented a multi-million dollar annual decline in revenues. Instead of having large annual surpluses that were put away into an endowment, as had occurred in the school's early years, it was losing hundreds of thousands of dollars every year.

MSL was fortunate that in its earlier years it had saved money that it put into what it called a "rainy day fund." It did this because Velvel rejected the conventional academic wisdom of the 1970s and 1980s that the good times will roll on forever. He believed that good times are followed by bad, and he had seen schools face disaster when they had spent recklessly instead of saving and planning ahead for the proverbial rainy day. When the ABA had inspected MSL, the accreditors had objected to this philosophy. They accused MSL of not spending enough money. Ironically, it was because of the problems created by these accreditors that MSL experienced the very kind of problems its rainy day fund was designed to help with. Velvel was glad that he and the school's founders had had the foresight to create an endowment.

Though disappointed by the outcome of both its own case and the DOJ's, MSL forged ahead in the courts. In 1995, the school filed a case against the ABA under state law in the state Superior Court of Essex County, Massachusetts. The defendants in this case included the ABA, members of the White Group, the AALS, and a competing law school, the New England School of Law ("NESL"). The charges included fraud, deceit, breach of contract, and unfair and deceptive trade practices. MSL alleged that the ABA, in effect, promised schools that it was an honest accrediting body that worked for the betterment of education, but this was in reality untrue. To accomplish their aim of benefitting faculty (rather than improving education), the accreditors conspired among themselves and with others to injure and, if possible, destroy schools like MSL that would not do what they wanted.

MSL claimed that NESL had played a role in this because it had wanted to ward off competition from MSL. It therefore had conspired with Jim White to try to have the Supreme Judicial Court of Massachusetts revoke the right of MSL's graduates to take the state's bar exam. MSL's claim was based upon the correspondence between NESL and White, which had come into its possession during its federal antitrust case against the ABA. In that series of letters, the chairman of NESL, James Lawton, had written to White warning that MSL students would now be allowed to take the state bar exam because MSL had been approved by the Board of Regents. He falsely stated that MSL had been approved by the Board of Regents because Paul Tsongas, who headed the Board, was "for all intents and purposes the 'principal'" of MSL and had gotten it approved by means of political clout.

White had replied by urging Lawton to enlist the ABA schools in Massachusetts to persuade the state's Supreme Judicial Court to revoke the right of MSL's graduates to take the bar. Lawton then told White that he was afraid those law schools would not cooperate because they did not care about MSL, which was not a threat to them. Instead, Lawton urged White to enlist major ABA figures in Massachusetts—including past and future ABA presidents—in an effort to persuade the state's Supreme Judicial Court not to allow MSL graduates to take the bar. "It is my opinion," he said, "that those individuals who have had close ties with the American Bar Association on a national level should be recruited as a leadership team to inaugurate a campaign to discourage the further expansion of new and unaccredited law schools."

Nothing came of the correspondence between Lawton and White. However, MSL thought it showed what lengths White and NESL would go to in order to try to get rid of MSL. This had even occurred three years *before* the ABA denied MSL accreditation.

MSL had brought a case in the state courts because it alleged state violations. Also, it hoped that state judges might prove to be more open-minded than the federal courts were, since state judges were not as uniformly tied in with the ABA as federal judges are. The ABA, in fact, feared that state judges might be more receptive than the federal courts were. So the ABA "removed" MSL's state law case from the state court to the federal court under a new, opaque Congressional law relating to switching accreditation cases from state courts to federal courts. MSL requested that its state law case be "remanded" back to the state court. However, the federal judge ordered that it be heard in his own court. Eventually, he threw the case out. He said that the claims MSL made in Massachusetts should have been put forth in its Philadelphia case, under federal law. The judge's opinion was upheld by the federal First Circuit Court of Appeals in Boston. The judge stonily concluded, "David does not always best Goliath."

Chapter 9

The Tide Starts to Turn

As MSL battled the ABA in various courts, it also continued asking the DOE to revoke the Council of the Section of Legal Education's status as a federally recognized accrediting body. In doing so, MSL sent lengthy memos to Karen Kershenstein, head of the DOE office that deals with accrediting bodies. Her job was to recommend to the Secretary of DOE whether an accrediting body should be federally recognized. MSL regularly sent her memoranda, pointing out how ABA standards violated various DOE regulations and how the Council of the Section acted as an elitest gatekeeper to legal education, discriminating against minorities, working-class people, second-career seekers, and others who wanted and deserved a chance to study law.

Since 1978, the DOE had asked the Section of Legal Education to prove that its standards were reliable and fair, and in July 1994, new DOE regulations were in place requiring accrediting agencies' standards to be "valid and reliable," which the ABA's were not. With the new regulations in place, the DOE staff told the Section of Legal Education that it had not complied with them. However, since other agencies hadn't complied yet either, the department granted the ABA more time to meet the requirements of validity and reliability. Recognizing that this delay might cause some schools and students, such as MSL and its students, to be harmed under invalid or unreliable accreditation standards, DOE officials wrote:

> Department staff also recognizes that . . . some institutions may be denied accreditation or placed on probation, and/or forced to take corrective action to come into compliance with standards that may in fact prove not to be valid and reliable measures of educational quality. For this reason, Department staff believes it is critical that the [Section] keep the Department thoroughly informed of its progress in assessing the validity and reliability of its standards and the results of that assessment. Specifically, the [Section] should provide the Department with an interim report in each of the next two years, and that report should include complete reports of each meeting of its Standards Review Committee, including any proposed changes in Council standards that are under consideration . . . .

Thus, the DOE allowed the Council of the Section to continue operating as the official accrediting body for law schools but requested that it submit progress reports in 1995 and 1996. However, the DOE had been doing this for a long time with regard to the ABA. Rather than demanding specific changes in ABA standards, for years and years the DOE merely asked for additional interim reports. One of the reasons this continued to happen, Velvel believed, was that the Democrats were now in power and DOE Secretary Riley was a Clinton appointee. Because the legal profession contributed huge amounts of money to the Democratic Party, Riley and his staff didn't want to arm-twist the ABA or revoke its status as a federally recognized accrediting body.

Nearly a dozen times MSL appeared before the National Advisory Committee, which advised Kershenstein and the Secretary of Education about accrediting agencies. Riley had appointed 15 prominent outside experts on higher education to the committee. They included Dr. David Adamany, a former law professor who was the president of Wayne State University in Detroit, and later the president of Temple University in Philadelphia; Tom Salmon, a lawyer who was the former governor of Vermont and had been president of the University of Vermont; Alfredo G. de los Santos, Jr., vice chancellor for Student and Educational Development at Maricopa County Community College District, in Arizona; and Dr. George Pruitt, president of Thomas A. Edison State College in New Jersey. Many of these individuals criticized the ABA and sympathized with MSL and its mission.

This became apparent on November 28, 1995, when Joel Klein, head of the DOJ Antitrust Division, appeared before the NAC to explain the Division's findings. Klein said that "it was our conclusion based on elaborate analysis of the evidence that, in fact, the ABA process . . . had become captured by the people who were actually immediately affected by it in a way that they were able to further their own what we consider guild concerns at the expense of the legitimate accreditation issues." In other words, the DOJ had found indisputable evidence of a "salary fix." He added that this "led us to become concerned about other areas such as student-faculty ratios, such as your quality of physical plant and so forth." Further, he added that the ABA's standards were "faculty driven, not a quality education driven enterprise."

In response, Adamany said, "I think this is one of the most restrictive and most anti-competitive arrangements that we have in academic life that significantly works to the detriment of law students."

Further, he added that "by way of example, the whole discussion of student-faculty ratios has certainly as much of an anti-competitive aspect to it as do salaries when only full-time faculty are counted in calculating student-faculty ratio, and indeed the regulations are so restrictive that students cannot be given clinical opportunities with practitioners. I could not send a student in our law school to work with Mr. Pearson to learn about antitrust unless a full-time faculty member were going to supervise that arrangement."

To that, he added that restrictions on student-faculty ratios and the manner in which they are counted "prevent effective clinical education for American law students, and also, of course, compel the hiring of full-time faculty and hence create what I believe is a form of academic featherbedding." That, Adamany asserted, contributed to the enormous law school tuition hikes that they had seen.

The idea of faculty devising better lives for themselves, inconsiderate of the cost and restrictions it placed on less-privileged students, appalled Adamany. He was the son of Lebanese immigrants. His father had come directly from Lebanon, and his mother had emigrated from Lebanon via Canada. Adamany had worked in his father's restaurant.

In 1953, the year before Adamany was to graduate from high school in Green Bay, Wisconsin, Nathan Pusey became president of Harvard University. He came from Lawrence University in Appleton, Wisconsin. This background gave Pusey a different view of Harvard admissions. He believed that Harvard could not become a great educational institution unless it accepted graduates of public schools and students throughout the United States.

So, when Adamany graduated from high school the next year, in 1954, he and seven or eight other Wisconsin kids were admitted to Harvard. Prior to Pusey's arrival, Harvard had only admitted one or two Wisconsin students. This affected his vision as a university administrator and as a spokesman on the NAC. Pusey's broadening of Harvard's admissions policies "suggests that universities ought to be thinking about the world that will be in the next generation, rather than the world as it is in the present generation," said Adamany in an article in the Winter 2001 *Temple Review*. In particular, Adamany believed that Harvard, Wayne, Temple, and the many American law schools needed to consider how they could encourage a more diverse student body.

Others on the NAC, including de los Santos and Pruitt, agreed with Adamany's concerns. Pruitt said that when the ABA first came before the NAC, he saw

> interlocking webs of interest that went beyond, way beyond what we traditionally see from disciplines. I saw the accreditation tied to who was allowed to sit for the bar exams and who controls the bar exams, and I remember asking the group would Clarence Darrow be able to practice law today, and I was told clearly he would not. And I'm not sure how the public's interest got served by not allowing or excluding a contemporary Clarence Darrow from being able to participate because he wouldn't have been allowed to sit for the bar exam. And I was very much concerned that what I saw was a pipeline that was very tightly welded from the accreditation process, from the law school, then to who got to, and you had to come out of one of those law schools to even be able to sit for the exam . . . I mean there was a guild of institutions, and that to sit for the exam, you had to come out of the guild.

In response, the ABA pleaded for more time to comply with the DOE regulations, which was granted. When the ABA appeared again before the NAC, in 1996, the committee warned the Council of the Section that it had become the extreme example of the "gatekeeper of the guild," according to Pruitt. "I can't think of any other group that comes before this body where the interrelationship between the educational structure and the ability to practice in the field is so closely aligned."

Governor Salmon said that limiting adjunct professors, in the ways it had, negatively affected minorities. He explained that he had just visited a New Jersey college that served "young men and women from the inner city. It has adjunct faculty whose numbers are double what its full-time faculty is, and it is making a difference, I believe, within its enclave, which is dedicated to a mission that this gifted leader has identified as central . . . namely to create opportunity . . . ."

To Salmon's comments, Pruitt added that ABA accreditation shuns many deserving people. "My sense is that your profession is very tightly controlled," Pruitt said. "You can't become a lawyer—I think I am right—in most states unless you are a graduate. You can't even sit for the bar unless you are a graduate of an accredited law school . . . . So it is very tightly controlled by who gets in the profession."

At subsequent hearings, these prominent educators continued blasting the ABA. The list of highly critical comments made at earlier and later hearings was huge. Adamany said that the ABA's standards are one of the most anticompetitive arrangements in academic life, are detrimental to students, often have no relationship to academic quality or results, are the product of an "old boys network," drive up the cost of education, and are based on indefensible assumptions. He also said that the LSAT had become a "dangerous weapon" that was being used against racial diversity, that the ABA had taken far too long to cure its violations of law, was a "blind cartel," and was denying accreditation to MSL though the latter was "running a successful enterprise for disadvantaged Americans" and had "measurable results."

Despite such comments from prominent educators, the DOE merely instructed the ABA to file interim reports. Therefore, the ABA continued stalling. The DOE itself did nothing of consequence, and time and again the stalling continued.

*****

The consent decree that had been signed by ABA leaders had embittered many members of the Council of the Section of Legal Education. They believed that the ABA had conceded too easily and quickly to the DOJ's accusations. In fact, Joseph Bellacosa and Pauline Schneider, the heads of the Council and the Accreditation Committee, respectively, temporarily resigned.

Those accreditation leaders who remained on the Council sought a way to circumvent the decree or weaken it.

The DOJ stipulated in the consent decree that the House of Delegates had to oversee actions of the Section. Kershenstein agreed to this because, in her opinion, the Section of Legal Education operated separately and independently from the ABA. This was an important point, especially since the enactment of amendments to the Higher Education Act in 1992. The Act insisted that all federally approved accrediting bodies, such as the Council of the Section of Legal Education, had to be "separate and independent" from their trade association affiliates. This rule prevented accrediting bodies from placing association members' interests ahead of sound educational principles. For instance, a trade association might pressure an accrediting body to limit the number of new schools accredited, thus limiting competition. In part, that's what the ABA had done.

Though the ABA and the DOE were satisfied with the Council being under the watchful eye of the ABA House and Board of Governors, Council members resented it. They still wanted ABA funding, but they didn't want the ABA House and Board of Governors to dictate their actions.

Thus, they figured out, with the help of ABA's in-house counsel Darryl DePriest, a way to obtain more automony and to even solicit the help of the DOE. In 1998, Council members explained to Kershenstein that the ABA's House of Delegates made the final decisions in accrediting individual law schools; thus, the Section and House were not separate. Publicly, Kershenstein professed to be surprised at this news, even though years before Velvel and Coyne had explained this to her and her colleagues.

Still, Kershenstein said that this information was new to her and now insisted that the ABA House of Delegates and the Section of Legal Education were not separate and independent. To meet DOE's regulations, ABA leaders would have to give up control over the Section, Kershenstein said.

"This epiphany is astounding since the ABA's accreditation

procedures have been in place for over 50 years," wrote Gary Palm, a University of Chicago law professor who had been a prominent ABA accreditor. He had served seven years on the ABA's Accreditation Committee and six years on the Council of the Section. He strongly objected to cutting the Section loose from control by the ABA's leadership. In testifying before the DOE, he described the Council as a political machine and said, "Apparently the Department of Education's interest was first aroused by the consent decree and from entreaties by the leaders of the Council of the Section of Legal Education and Admissions to the Bar for help from the DOE in obtaining relief from the consent decree."

Palm was very critical of the Council, claiming that it accredited schools it favored and withheld accreditation from those it didn't. In testifying before the DOE, Palm said that he had seen this happen on the Council and believed that because of this, some members had reacted unfairly to MSL. Someone on the Council had even admitted bias against the school to him.

Palm suggested that leaders of the ABA, the Council of the Section, and DOE had met privately and discussed how they could modify the consent decree. That's when they approached DOE regarding the ABA and Council's relationship. "I think it's in violation of law and particularly in violation of Judge Richey's consent decree here in the District of Columbia Federal Courthouse," Palm said in response to removing the Council from the ABA's supervision.

Like Palm, MSL opposed the way ABA leaders gave up control over the Section of Legal Education, but it happened anyway. ABA leaders conceded to act in a merely advisory role to the Council of the Section of Legal Education, rather than to supervise it or to have any control over it.

*****

Despite views expressed by prominent educators on the

National Advisory Committee, Kershenstein and the DOE continued to allow the Council of the Section to continue operating unchecked and to thwart DOE rules.

The Council's unchecked standards caught the attention of Dean Scott Bice of the University of Southern California Law School. Dean since 1980, Bice was the third most senior dean of any ABA-accredited school. During his tenure at USC, he doubled the size of the law school and became president of the 120-member ALDA.

At the NAC hearing in 1998, Bice supported MSL by saying that "when I read through the list of reasons [why] the ABA has refused to accredit the Massachusetts School of Law, I must say I personally find each and every one of those reasons an illegitimate reason to deny accreditation—faculty sabbaticals. I mean, what do faculty sabbaticals have to do with the quality of the legal education? When I go down [that] list, I would say each one of those to me personally is not legitimate."

At that NAC meeting, many of the committee members expressed their frustration with the ABA in not complying with the Higher Education Act, particularly in terms of showing validity and reliability of its standards. Thus, Adamany made a motion that the NAC recommend to Secretary Richard Riley that the ABA "be required on each occasion when it cites its recognition by the Department of Education as an accrediting body, to report also that the Department of Education has found that the American Bar Association's accreditation policies are in substantial noncompliance . . . ." He wanted the ABA to make full disclosure of its noncompliance with DOE regulations.

Adamany explained the reason for his motion. One third of U.S. states permitted unaccredited law schools to seek approval from the State Supreme Court to have its graduates take the bar exam, according to Adamany.

"The ABA goes into those state courts, opposes the law school that attempts to be recognized by the State Supreme Court and cites DOE recognition. It is a unique case. We do not have other accrediting agencies going before state agencies or the state judiciary citing DOE recognition as a reason why they should not accept for the licensure exams the graduates of institutions," said Adamany.

"I concur," Salmon said and seconded his motion. "This may be an exceptional motion, but we have an exceptional problem, a problem of deep neglect, a problem of piling on a little law school in Massachusetts that does a hell of a job for its students. I know that to be the case, because I have been there."

As well, Pruitt thought it was a great idea, particularly since the ABA had used its "accreditation status in the context of litigation." He said, "The other thing that I think that makes this so important is that there is a predatory aspect to this. The profession has said that the gatekeeper for competency is the ability to pass the exam, but this says you cannot even get a shot at the exams."

Pruitt added that he remembered the first time he sat on the NAC, asking the Council, "could Clarence Darrow practice law today? I was told no. I do not think that is in the public interest."

Adamany's amendment was adopted and submitted to Secretary Riley. However, the Secretary of Education refused to implement it. In a follow-up letter to James White, Riley wrote that he did not concur with the NAC's opinion pertaining to the manner in which the ABA and the Council "describe their recognition status." He asked that the Council submit an interim report by September, but it would continue as it had before.

*****

Because the DOE refused to take any action against the ABA, MSL turned to Congress for help. Congress was preparing to renew the Higher Education Act. Velvel and the MSL staff had numerous meetings with a total of 45 Congressional aides. MSL discussed the need for new HEA provisions to address problems such as those raised by the ABA's actions. The school was the only institution or person to discuss such problems with Congress. It met several times with Senator Ted Kennedy's staff. Considered by most people to be one of the four or five most powerful senators in the history of the Senate, Kennedy could single-handedly effect changes in the renewed bill that would require the DOE to force the ABA to comply with the HEA or be terminated as a federally recognized accrediting agency.

Kennedy convinced the Congress to change the HEA in two ways. First, it reordered the statutory criteria, which had to be met by federally recognized accrediting bodies. Originally, fostering student learning had appeared halfway down the list of statutory criteria. Kennedy pushed it to the top, making student learning—the so-called "outputs" of education—the number one priority of accrediting agencies, instead of expensive inputs of resources being the first priority. The Senate Report on this said, "As the National Commission on the Cost of Higher Education recommended, accreditors should be focusing more on measures of student achievement and less on resources, particularly in the light of widespread concern about the cost of education."

To the NAC, Kennedy wrote:

> All accrediting standards should be considered in the light of their effect on student achievement. I am concerned that some accrediting standards rely too much on traditional and easily manipulated "inputs," such as volumes in the library, which may have little or no relationship to real student learning. Also, some traditional standards might stifle innovation in education as well as contribute to excessively high costs.
>
> Like many of my colleagues in the Congress, I am concerned about the cost of higher education. Given the significant gap in education between high and low income students, standards that unnecessarily raise costs may undermine Congress' efforts to ensure that higher education is accessible and affordable to all qualified students.

The second provision gave accrediting bodies a maximum of one year to comply with DOE criteria. Extensions were to be granted only rarely and briefly. About this change, the Senate Report said, "The [National Commission on the Cost of Higher Education] is concerned about reports that the Secretary of Education has been reluctant to find agencies in violation of the statute and has allowed long periods of time for them to correct possible violations." In fact, the ABA had already been given more than six years to comply—five years more than Congress said it should have been granted. Yet the DOE then gave the ABA still another two years to bring its standards into compliance.

The first amendment, as Kennedy said, insisted that accrediting agencies judge academic institutions by the quality of their education rather than by resources such as the building, the library, or the number of faculty. However, the DOE ignored this. In fact, the staff and officials of the DOE claimed that the amendment had no effect on the evaluation of accrediting agencies. They said that accreditation bodies could still consider inputs, as the ABA did. To MSL, it was clear that DOE had decided to eviscerate the new HEA amendment. It is not uncommon in Washington for the federal bureaucracy to vitiate congressional action.

By December 1999, Velvel and Coyne had appeared at nine NAC hearings in seven years. The committee stated at its last meeting that it had lost patience with the ABA, which refused to reform its accreditation standards. It had violated the bill passed by Congress stressing that accrediting agencies had to focus on outputs rather than inputs. Yet the DOE refused to terminate the Section as an accrediting body, which was incomprehensible to Velvel and Coyne except as a measure of DOE weakness, incompetence, and susceptibility to political influence.

Velvel told the NAC that during the last seven years, "law school tuition [had] increased 75 percent. The average college tuition during the same period has increased by only half that much." Congress had changed the Higher Education Act "in the light of widespread concern about the cost of higher education." Yet legal education continued down the same path that lawmakers feared and had tried to remedy. The ABA was more concerned over a school's resources—over how many full time professors it had, its building, how many books it had on its shelves, and so on—than with what students were learning.

Deeply discouraged, Velvel said, "I don't know that we're going to come back here anymore. I have finally learned . . . that we are not able to rely on government to solve the problem. And we have other things that we can do that will be more beneficial and constructive. We have television programs. This coming Friday, we have a one-hour television program on Robert McNamara's new book, *Argument Without End,* that will be seen in 1,200 cities. The panel will be Eugene McCarthy, Daniel Ellsberg, and McNamara's biographer, Deborah Shapley. We have programs of that character every month. We have legal programs every two weeks." Velvel and the faculty realized that they didn't need and could not rely on the DOE or the DOJ. They didn't need ABA accreditation, either. The school had established itself in other ways. It could exist quite well without the ABA, DOJ, or DOE.

When Velvel finished speaking, he thanked the NAC members for their time, support, and attention to the school's concerns. He said, "I think in the future, unless I change my mind or unless the faculty insists that I continue coming here, as they say, I don't see the point any more. I remind myself of Nixon having lost the governorship of California and saying that you won't have Nixon to kick around. And of course, as soon as possible, he made sure that we did have Nixon to kick around."

There was a chuckle from the NAC and the crowd.

De los Santos and Adamany looked on. They had both been sympathetic to Velvel and the issues he had raised. Adamany had left Wayne State University and moved on to become the eighth president of Temple University. Located in urban Philadelphia,

Temple was a school designed for common people. Its law school had innovative admissions policies, a part-time program, and it offered legal classes to non-lawyers.

Once Velvel had finished speaking, Adamany and de los Santos approached him privately. They believed that he and MSL had made a valuable contribution to the NAC, and they hoped MSL would return.

*****

Because the DOE would do nothing, and had eviscerated Kennedy's amendment, MSL returned to Kennedy's office to seek further help. The Senator himself had invited this when Velvel had run into him in the Washington, D.C. airport one day. MSL thought that legislation, which would ensure the right of its graduates to take bar exams anywhere in the country, would be the best solution to its problem. Velvel believed Congress had the power to enact such a law under several constitutional provisions, but especially under its power to tax and spend. For it spent, or provided loan guarantees for, billions of dollars annually that supported legal education provided by states and by private law schools. When it provides financial support, it can attach conditions to that support. One such condition, thought Velvel, would be to require all states to allow MSL graduates to take bar exams. This was no different from attaching the condition of standardized tests to Congress' spending in support of grammar school and high school education in states. Nor was it any different from the Solomon Amendment that cut off federal monies to any university that refused to allow campus military recruitment, even though many schools objected to the military's discriminatory policies against homosexuals. (Even Harvard had to accede to this amendment in 2002.)

As invited by Kennedy, Velvel arranged for this meeting, which included himself, members of Kennedy's staff, Mike Coyne, several Washington lobbyists who were helping MSL at that time, and another MSL professor. To Kennedy, Coyne suggested that he put pressure on the ABA.

"You just piss people off when you put pressure on them." Kennedy surprised them by shouting back.

Coyne and Velvel sat back in their seats—shocked. They had never seen a political figure talk in anger like this to his constituents. But Kennedy had a habit of losing his patience and speaking forcefully. On October 2, 2002, in Washington, the Capitol Police Department was summoned to the meeting room where Kennedy had exploded at R. Thomas Buffenburger, president of the International Association of Machinists and Aerospace Workers, who made the mistake of criticizing the Senator. Obviously, he had hit a nerve, just as MSL had.

When the Senator calmed down before the dean and MSL representatives, he said that his office would help them, but they would have to do it his way, not by legislation. Kennedy's office made inquiries at DOE and the ABA but did not take effective steps in aiding MSL. The office worked closely with the ABA on many legislative issues, on which it supported the ABA and vice versa. These were critical issues to the liberal agenda, and Kennedy wanted continued cooperation with the ABA. This allegiance proved to be more important to the Senator than helping MSL.

*****

For years, MSL had fought for recognition before the ABA, the DOE, the DOJ, the state courts, the federal courts, and even the U.S. Supreme Court. Millions of dollars and thousands of hours had gone into these campaigns. The school's professors had traveled around the country attending hearings and obtaining depositions.

Velvel and the others at MSL believed in the beginning that the courts would be fair. Even if one judge were biased, the next one wouldn't be, or a change of law or an amendment to rules would alter the school's circumstances. Unfortunately, none of this had occurred, and Velvel and Coyne had come to think that their initial belief in the good faith and honesty of judicial and governmental bodies was pure naivete. After years of battling, MSL was no closer to ABA accreditation. As a result, its student body was only half the size it had been, and MSL had lost millions of dollars per year in revenue. To remain solvent the school had to ultimately increase its tuition, a step that Velvel despised having to take even though the new, higher tuition was still only half of the average tuition charged by the ABA schools in New England.

Despite the disappointments and setbacks in courts and before the DOE, MSL refused to stop fighting for its students and its mission. Even after MSL's request for intervenor status had been refused in the DOJ's antitrust case against the ABA, the school filed an amicus brief in the U.S. Court of Appeals for the District of Columbia. MSL asked the court to overturn Judge Richey's approval of the consent decree, which MSL correctly said was inadequate to open the door to innovation and competition in legal education, and the judge's refusal to allow MSL to intervene in the case. The government and the ABA both objected to MSL's requests, and the appeals court therefore denied them.

Though MSL continued to try to persuade the DOE to revoke the federally recognized accrediting status of the Council of the Section of Legal Education, and though it repeatedly but unsuccessfully asked the DOJ to take further antitrust action, Velvel and Coyne quickly realized that the school might never get anywhere with any of this continued effort. It might never gain ABA accreditation or recoup its financial losses by judicial or administrative action. Thus, they focused on other ways to make the school exceptional so it would be regionally, and even nationally, appealing.

Persuading states outside of Massachusetts to open their bar exams to graduates of MSL, even though it was not accredited by the ABA, was one way of increasing the school's appeal. To do that, the school petitioned individual states to change their rules governing who could take bar exams. In June 1995, the New Hampshire Supreme Court granted MSL's petition and amended its rules to allow MSL graduates to take the state's bar exam as soon as they were admitted to practice in Massachusetts. At the next New Hampshire bar exam, one fourth of the bar test-takers—a total of 28 lawyers—were MSL alumni. When the New Hampshire Bar Examiners announced the results, the largest number who had passed the state bar came from MSL.

Having success there, MSL tried more than a dozen other states. So strong was the ABA's monopoly, however, that nine of the states denied the school's petition without even a hearing. In Maine and Wisconsin, the Supreme Courts did grant hearings and then allowed MSL graduates to take the bar exam after being admitted to the bar in Massachusetts. In Rhode Island, MSL had a hearing before the bar examiners rather than the Supreme Court, and its petition was denied. Events surrounding the hearing made it clear to the Dean that the examiners favored the ABA from the beginning.

With regard to Connecticut, visiting inspectors examined the school on behalf of the bar examiners, who subsequently granted MSL graduates permission to take the bar exam immediately upon graduation. At the next Connecticut bar exam, nine MSL graduates took the test. Seven passed, giving MSL a first-time bar passage rate of 78 percent, matching or exceeding the rate of Boston University, Quinnipiac, New England School of Law, Seton Hall, and SUNY—all ABA schools. Once again MSL proved that expensive input-driven legal education did not create smarter lawyers.

The school also needed accreditation from a federally recognized accrediting body in order for its students to obtain low-interest, federally guaranteed loans. Nearly every student attending the school needed financial aid. Wholly private, nonfederally guaranteed financing was expensive. Thus, it became obvious to Velvel and the others that MSL's survival depended upon obtaining the necessary accreditation from a federally recognized body.

MSL applied to the New England Association of Schools and Colleges (NEAS&C), a prestigious regional agency recognized by the federal government. The NEAS&C was infinitely more reasonable than the ABA. It did not judge institutions by expensive inputs. In 1997, the NEAS&C inspectors visited the school. The team included a prior college president, a current one, a Harvard University financial officer, and an ABA law school dean. As the team's report showed, it was impressed with many aspects of MSL, such as its mission, faculty, teaching, ethics, and attention to students. After the report was issued, the NEAS&C approved MSL for five years. This enabled MSL to offer students Stafford Loans and other types of federal financial aid.

MSL forged ahead in many other ways, too. Beginning in 1994, MSL began producing a magazine, *The Long Term View* (LTV). Rather than the typical pompous law journal published by most law schools, MSL offered intellectual articles from thinkers, writers, and scholars in a readable format. Each issue of LTV explored a single topic that MSL faculty felt the media had largely ignored. The topics included, among others, history in America, medicine in the 21st century, the competency of the press, socioeconomic stratification, whether educators have forsaken critical thinking, responsibility for the plight of minorities, whether sports in America are a distortion or a reflection of life, sources of morality in politics, assessing competence in the professions, misconduct of American judges, legacies of the Vietnam War, and, especially apt for MSL, failures and reforms in higher education. Persons who authored the articles or whose interviews appeared in LTV included a legion of prominent names in academia, politics, and journalism, as well as rising talents. University and law school libraries around the country subscribed to it, and it was sold at many Barnes & Noble and independent book stores.

The school also became a strong competitor in the annual mock trial competition sponsored by the American Trial Lawyers

Association (ATLA). Annually a team of four students prepared a mock case and tried it before a mock jury. Professor Tony Copani groomed students for the competition, which pitted MSL's team against those from Harvard, Boston University, Vermont, Franklin Pierce, Suffolk, and others.

One of the shining stars on the ATLA team was Daniel DeBruyckere, who was in his 40s. However, in 1998, the student told Copani that he could no longer participate. A hard-working student with three kids and a mortgage to pay, he said that he needed to work, in a court or law firm, so he could make money and gain some practical law experience before he graduated in the spring.

Copani liked DeBruyckere. He was not only a smart student who took the ATLA team seriously, he was also an interesting individual. In 1976, DeBruyckere had bought a service station in North Andover, Massachusetts. He made a success of that and evolved another business out of that—a software company for service stations and garages. Though DeBruyckere proved to be a success at that, he had higher ambitions. He entered New Hampshire College (now Southern New Hampshire University) and graduated in 26 months with a bachelor's degree. He was at the top of his class, graduating summa cum laude.

DeBruyckere planned to go to law school; thus, he applied to Suffolk University Law School. The school told him that they'd put him on a waiting list. However, he didn't want to wait. He had a family, and he couldn't waste time. He needed to study now and move on with his life. Thus, he entered MSL. DeBruyckere became editor of the *Writ*, the school newspaper, and joined the ATLA trial advocacy team.

Copani told DeBruyckere, "Look, I'll make a deal with you. If you stay on the ATLA team, I'll put you to work in my office." It was a great offer. He stayed on the team, where Copani coached him and his teammates, Michael Belanti, August Gangi, and Kenneth Byrd. They practiced hard for months and prepared for the competition.

"We had something to prove," DeBruyckere said about the ATLA experience. "We set out to prove that we were just as good." They knew that they would be facing students who had had all the opportunities, who attended the schools that had either turned them down or put them on waiting lists. DeBruyckere and the members of the MSL team saw this as their opportunity to shine and show that they had the smarts and the capabilities to be a formidable force in the courtroom.

At the ATLA Northeast Regional Competition, DeBruyckere's team first made the semi-finals. They argued head-to-head with Suffolk and, in the end, won the Regional Championship.

"It was such an achievement," DeBruyckere remembered. "But there was no magic involved. It was hard work and a great coach, and we were far better prepared than they were." From there, DeBruyckere and the others went on to the national competition in Washington D.C. There they competed against teams from across the country and placed midway among some of the nation's best schools. DeBruyckere and his teammates were proud of their achievement. They had stood up well against students from the nation's most prestigious law schools.

As Copani promised, DeBruyckere got a job in his law firm. DeBruyckere stayed in Copani's firm after he graduated from MSL, finding he could serve a community that he knew quite well.

The ATLA team, under the direction of Professors Copani and Tim Cagle, continued to show strength. In 2002, MSL beat all but two teams in the regional competition. The winner was Harvard, and MSL tied with a second Harvard team for second place. When the tie-breaking vote was cast, Harvard was named the second place winner. The presiding judge of the competition (who was unable to cast a vote) told the MSL team later that he was stunned. He believed that the MSL team had performed much better than the second-place Harvard team.

About this, Cagle would say that MSL's students proved "that not only do we belong, but we are a factor to be reckoned with and in many cases feared because of what we can do in a courtroom." Looking at the broad-reaching implications of this factor, he then added, "The most satisfying fact is that this has remained constant, whether the American Bar Association accreditors choose to agree or not."

*****

After a few years at MSL, Diane Sullivan resigned from the bank and dedicated herself solely to teaching at the law school. Like the other professors, she accepted various administrative tasks at the school. Regularly, she, the dean, and their colleagues discussed new ideas or brainstormed about new teaching approaches or better ways to run the school.

One day when the dean called Sullivan to his office, Velvel explained that he had been thinking about starting a regular, nonlegal television show. Not only would it elevate the school's visibility, but it would serve as a way to explore scholarly and other viewpoints on topical, nonlegal issues. It would also accomplish something that the dean had heard talked about for more than 30 years but that was almost never implemented. It would bring the knowledge and analytical abilities of academics to the people in understandable, jargon-free ways. Velvel raised the possibility of turning MSL's third floor into a television studio. The dean asked Sullivan to look into all this and report back.

Sullivan practically laughed out loud. She had never owned a television. In fact, she hadn't watched TV in more than 20 years. She knew nothing about television production or even what such a show might look like. However, rather than reject Velvel's idea, Sullivan listened, took notes, and hoped the dean might lose interest in a day or so.

A few days passed and the dean didn't say anything more about the television show. Obviously, she thought, he had forgotten. The next day, however, Velvel asked how research was going on the project. That's when Sullivan realized he was serious.

Sullivan checked into the costs of setting up a studio at the law school, but it was too expensive. MSL would need cameras and editing equipment, as well as a studio and production people. It could cost a million dollars or more. Renting studio time usually wasn't cheap, either, she discovered. Each taping could cost as much as $10,000.

She learned, however, that the local cable franchise company was located just two miles from the school, in Andover. She contacted Continental Cablevision (later bought by MediaOne, then AT&T, then Comcast) and discovered the company not only had a studio but a production expert, Barrett Lester. He had come up through the ranks as a producer, but then he had taken a detour and gone into management. Shortly before meeting Sullivan, however, he had gone back into producing and won several national cablevision awards. He would become regional manager of original productions for the regional cable station.

Sullivan and Lester hit it off immediately. He seemed to know instinctively what the dean wanted. Lester liked the arrangement as well, in part because the school brought in such high-caliber guests.

With Lester as director, Sullivan, Velvel, and sometimes Coyne rotated as producers and moderators. They called the series "The Massachusetts School of Law Educational Forum." For the first show, the dean moderated a panel of three guests, discussing performance-based government, on a show entitled, "Why Does Government Perform So Badly?" Despite a minimal set—just four chairs before two white columns and a folding screen—the program turned out surprisingly well, Sullivan thought.

The next topic was "The Competency of the Press." It was Sullivan's turn to moderate. Like Velvel, she invited three panelists: Lyle Denniston, Supreme Court correspondent for the *Baltimore Sun*; David Bartlett, president of the Radio-Television News Directors Association; and George Kennedy, managing editor of the *Columbia Missourian*. As taping approached,

Sullivan grew increasingly apprehensive. "This isn't for me," she thought and decided that if she had been interested in producing television shows, she would have attended Emerson College rather than law school.

By the day of the taping, Sullivan was a nervous wreck. Velvel and Coyne followed her and her guests into the television studio. From a glass control booth, they watched the taping. Sullivan hated being the center of attention. She didn't know where she was supposed to look and when.

The discussions started off well enough. Then she asked, "What are the ethics in journalism?"

Immediately, the conversation heated up. Denniston answered that there wasn't a real code of ethics. Kennedy said there should be. Bartlett interjected that restrictions on journalists could impede their creativity and news-gathering abilities. As the three guests debated fiercely, Velvel and Coyne waved at Sullivan from the control booth. Sullivan figured that they wanted her to rein in the conversation and not let it turn into a verbal brawl. Sullivan tried a different question, but her guests talked over her.

Eventually, Sullivan edged into the conversation, "What kind of sanctions do you think should be imposed on someone like Janet Cook who makes up a story about an eight-year-old heroin addict?" This only fueled the guests, and the heated debate resumed.

Once the taping had ended, Velvel and Coyne asked Sullivan if she had seen them waving. Apologetic, she replied that she had. She had tried to tone it down, but the guests were passionate, she explained.

They laughed. She had misunderstood. They were trying to tell her to keep it going. This was exactly what they wanted.

After a few shows, Lester noticed that Sullivan had overcome her nervousness and become absorbed in the mental challenges of producing weekly shows. She had boundless energy. With each new show she raised the stakes higher. She wanted to make the shows more interesting, to find better guests, to go on loca-

tion, to dig a little deeper into her subjects, and create more legitimate controversy.

"Diane really threw herself into that challenge," Lester said.

The shows grew steadily more diverse, tackling new subjects
and fascinating people. For one show, "Whether America Needs
a Third or Even Fourth Political Party," moderated by the Dean,
guests included Eugene McCarthy and John Anderson. Both had
run for president in earlier decades, and McCarthy was a genuine
hero to many because of his efforts to stop the war in Vietnam.
For other shows, Velvel, Sullivan, and Coyne invited well-known
authors, columnists, and scholars who debated topics of current
interest. Some of them included Patricia Ireland, president of
NOW; Fred Graham, chief anchor and managing editor of Court
TV; Nicholas Lemann, a writer for *The Atlantic Monthly*;
William Bratton, the former police chief of New York City;
Congressman Barney Frank; Jeff Jacoby, a *Boston Globe* colum-
nist; Professor Leonard Saxe of Brandeis and CUNY; Professor
James Robertson, a Civil War author and scholar at Virginia
Tech; John DiBaggio, the president of Tufts; Dr. Jerome Kassirer,
editor-in-chief of the *New England Journal of Medicine*;
Professor Andrew Zimbalist of Smith College; Professor Elaine
Scary of Harvard; Bill Littlefield, sports commentator for NPR;
and Jan Schlictmann, the attorney featured in the best-selling
book and movie, *A Civil Action*. There were many more.

Through the shows, Sullivan met authors, journalists, histori-
ans and even cult leaders. She and the other moderators, Coyne
and Velvel, explored subjects of social importance that included
lying in America, college sports, morality, religion in America,
higher education, sexual education in schools, media violence,
loyalty, elitism, cults, the Civil War, elder care, immigration
problems, and many others.

The shows, co-produced by Sullivan, Coyne, and Velvel, in
conjunction with AT&T Broadband, were distributed to cable stations nationwide and were available in 20 million homes. People
saw them throughout New England, in Washington, D.C., in

Washington State, in Tennessee, on Long Island, and elsewhere.

Based on the show's success, Sullivan, at Velvel's suggestion, developed a second, half-hour series, "MSL Presents: A Question of Law." This series explored legal-related topics of general interest, including hate crimes, sexual abuse of children, sexual harassment, seizure of a person's DNA, school vouchers, the role of the ACLU, legal issues in the workplace, separate but equal gyms, jury trials, tobacco disclosure laws, the disabilities act, racial profiling, grandparents' rights, the history of women in the legal profession, same-sex marriages, judicial misconduct, jury nullification, high profile attorneys, teenage curfew laws, end-of-life issues, and many other important topics.

In 2001, the dean launched a third television show, a monthly series called *Books of Our Time*. The dean conducted one-on-one interviews with authors of important and interesting books. Some of them were among the country's most well-known authors. The show included such guests as Pulitzer Prize winner Joseph Ellis, *Founding Brothers*; Louis Menand, *The Metaphysical Club* (which also won a Pulitzer); Judge Richard Posner, *Public Intellectuals: A Study of Decline*; Jill Ker Conway, *A Woman's Education*; Maureen Dezell, *Irish America*; Murray Sperber, *Beer and Circus*; Jean Edward Smith, *Grant*; Dan Oren, *Joining The Club*; and Lawrence Harrison, *Culture Matters*.

Often the guests on the various TV shows would stop at the school and have lunch with the staff and faculty. In this casual setting, these individuals would explain their views and engage in discussions with the faculty and staff. Several of the guests remarked on the quality of the faculty and the school.

The guests also seemed to think highly of the book interviews. Joseph Ellis said, "I was extremely pleased and impressed with the style and character of my interview with Dean Velvel. He permits an author to talk at length and follows the thread of a conversation in a way that combines the best interview techniques of Brian Lamb and Charlie Rose. The program deserves a large national audience."

By early 2003, MSL had produced hundreds of TV programs and won 63 TV awards. In its first year, *Books of Our Time* won a Telly Award, one of the most sought-after awards in television. Ten of MSL's other programs, most of them done by Sullivan and several by Coyne, also won Tellys. In addition, MSL received two silver Telly statuettes for the Educational Forum programs on NASA and on lobbying.

In 1997, Sullivan had earned the New England Women in Cable and Telecommunications Award for the best women's program. The topic was domestic violence. MSL later won seven Communicator Awards, mainly for Sullivan's programs. A Crystal Award was given to the school for Sullivan's Question of Law program, "You've Been Arrested: Now What?"

MSL was very proud of these awards, because its personnel were amateurs in the TV business. Yet the programs produced and moderated by this group of amateurs had won award after award in competition with television professionals.

One of the awards that meant much to Sullivan was the Gracie Award (named after Gracie Allen) that she received in 2001. Jacci Duncan, executive director of the group that bestowed the award on behalf of the Foundation of American Women in Radio and Television, remarked that Sullivan's programs "display[ed] superior quality and stellar portrayal of the changing roles and concerns of women." The award was presented at a ceremony in New York City in May 2001.

Receiving that award, Sullivan felt like "the winner," the Norman Rockwell image with which she had long identified. She had succeeded beyond all expectations. Starting from an impoverished background, initially able to afford only one college course per semester, she had become a lawyer, a law professor, and a producer of award-winning television shows seen from coast to coast. She had come a long way from the high school kid who saved pennies and nickels, hoping someday to go to college.

*****

As the dean had explained during his last appearance before the NAC, MSL and its faculty had moved beyond the ABA fight in defining its place in legal education. No longer did the MSL faculty need to look at the past with regret or mourn the battle it had lost against the ABA. Rather, they looked forward and believed the fight had made them more resilient. More important, they did not have to obey the ABA's stultifying mandates. They were free to experiment, try out new ideas, and improve legal education. Though they had lost the ABA battle, they had, in effect, won the war. Free from ABA strictures, MSL was able to grow and become a unique hybrid in legal education—a practical school for the common man, coupled with intellectual and innovative ideas—and a success in its own right.

In 1998, MSL celebrated its 10th anniversary with a party, attended by 500 faculty and alumni. Joining MSL's faculty and administration were trustees Paul Victor and Julia Fishelson and the first graduates of MSL, who had fled Commonwealth in the bleakest hour and helped start the new school. Among the latter were John and Ken Lakin, John Cascarano, and James Cropper. Other returning graduates who had signed up on the promise that the empty building that they initially saw would be filled with desks, books, and instructors who would teach them law, came that night. One was Arthur Broadhurst, who had joined the Lakin brothers' law firm and had become a Massachusetts State Representative. The MSL graduates who returned that night offered thanks to the school and its faculty for offering them legal education at a price that they could afford.

What struck Velvel, Coyne, Sullivan, Dickinson, and so many of the faculty members that night was seeing the result of the dream they all shared. The students who had been rejected from other law schools or couldn't afford them were now practicing lawyers. They didn't wear blue jeans and T-shirts, as they did when they were students, but they were now dressed in dark blue suits and were finely groomed, bearing the confidence of their accomplishments in the legal profession.

The faculty, which now consisted of 14 full-time members, realized that the school had fulfilled its mission. The school, the faculty, the dean, and the students had done what they had set out to do, and the ABA and its accreditation minions couldn't hold any of them back.

*****

In 2000, the DOJ asked the federal district court in Washington to modify the consent decree that the ABA had agreed upon in 1995. The DOJ sought to amend the decree in order to satisfy the DOE's newly made demand that the Section of Legal Education be freed of the ABA leadership's control, in order to be "separate and independent." Although control of the Section of Legal Education by the leadership had been a linchpin of the decree, the DOJ wanted to amend it so that the Council of the Section would become "the sole ultimate decision-making authority in accreditation matters." The ABA House of Delegates would act only in an advisory capacity, rather than having deci-sionmaking power. Thus, the Section, not the House, would determine when and if changes to accreditation standards were needed and whether individual schools would be accredited. In essence, the group that committed the antitrust violations, and that was still run by the same people who committed them, would be put into sole control of accreditation, just as it wanted.

MSL had given up on the DOJ by then, yet the school did not let this latest dereliction pass unnoticed. In a letter to Bruce Pearson, dated May 30, 2000, the dean wrote, "The Division should have demanded a much stronger consent decree against the ABA. Failing that, it should have brought a second case against the ABA because of continuing, serious anticompetitive actions, just as it brought a second case against Microsoft."

Velvel made plain his belief that the DOJ had given the ABA favorable treatment because Democratic politicians didn't want to anger the party's biggest contributor, the legal profession. More than that, the DOJ and the ABA had a fraternal-type of loyalty. A businessman engaged in such a broad-based conspiracy as the ABA's—particularly one that included price fixing—would be at serious risk of not just civil charges leveled by the DOJ but criminal prosecution and jail time. That's what Velvel thought. It was hard for him to believe that the ABA had barely been reprimanded.

"The job of the Antitrust Division is . . . to pry open the market to competition, lest the case be won but the cause be lost," Velvel wrote to Pearson. "That job has not been accomplished by the Division, with regard to the ABA. It has not even been more than partially attempted. The cause has been lost."

Even though the dean had given up on the DOE and had made it clear that he would not likely appear before the NAC again, he ultimately felt compelled to return in December 2000. He did so, because de los Santos and Adamany had asked him to.

Adamany was known to be a proponent of diversity. As said, he had left Wayne State University to become the eighth president of Temple University, located in the heart of Philadelphia and nationally recognized for creating opportunities for minorities and the less-privileged.

Prior to the next NAC meeting, Adamany sent Velvel a letter, dated November 15, 2000. In it, the Temple University president explained that his term on the NAC had expired, and Secretary of Education Richard Riley had replaced him. He made it clear that he did not leave the NAC by choice, and he would have gladly served another term.

Reading between the lines, Velvel knew Riley wanted to remove Adamany, a vocal opponent of the Council of the Section of Legal Education and accreditation.

In his letter, Adamany commended Velvel for his hard work and striving to be socially responsible by diversifying legal education. Adamany wrote, "As you know, I share your view that greater emphasis should be given to measures of student performance and outcomes in evaluating the accreditation standards of accrediting agencies that seek recognition from the Department of Education."

Without Admany, Velvel knew there was even less chance that the NAC would recommend revocation of the Section's status as a federally recognized accrediting body at its December meeting. This angered him. He realized that all of the facts that he and the others at MSL had compiled over the years, all of the arguments that they had presented, and all of the ABA misrepresentations that MSL had exposed, didn't mean anything. The ABA had gotten away with shafting the little guy who wanted to practice law in his community. This infuriated him.

Still, he and Coyne went to the meeting and spoke their minds, as did approximately a half dozen MSL students who spoke out about the school. Loman McClinton, Jr. was one of those students, an African-American 54-year-old Boston resident. McClinton explained his story to the NAC. He told them of growing up with every imaginable disadvantage a young boy could have. He was the son of a World War II veteran who had only a third-grade Mississippi education, and he had lived in the squalid ghettos of East St. Louis, Illinois. Public schools had written him off. So he dropped out at age 16, joined the Marines, and fought in Vietnam. Surviving two tours there, McClinton then joined the Boston Police force. He worked and studied. He made it through high school, then college, and then earned two master's degrees. Then he entered MSL. Now, he told the NAC, he's a life member of American Mensa.

"So the public school system was wrong," McClinton said. "If not for MSL, I would be facing old age possibly as a night watchman or some campus security person." He asked the NAC to acknowledge MSL and to terminate the ABA's accreditation status.

But the NAC wouldn't do that. On January 12, Secretary Richard Riley sent a letter to John Sebert (who had just replaced White as the ABA's consultant on legal education). Riley informed Sebert that the Council of the Section of Legal Education and Admissions to the Bar would be recognized as an accrediting agency for five years. It wasn't just a couple of years, as it had been in the past, but five full years.

The DOE had never responded so quickly to the Council of the Section, at least not since Velvel had been involved. The reason was obvious to the dean. In eight days, Clinton would leave the White House. Before the move, they had to tend to Democratic housecleaning chores. During this transition period, hundreds of criminals were pardoned, including billionaire Marc Rich. In terms of the Council of the Section of Legal Education and Admissions to the Bar, the Democrats knew that the Republicans weren't fans of the Section. They knew it was possible that the Republicans might revoke the Section's accreditation powers.

Velvel was tired of running full tilt toward the Council, the DOE, and the NAC, unable to get them to budge from their position. He was finished with that, he decided. He wouldn't go back. To him, the fight was in vain.

On February 6, 2001, the federal district judge granted the DOJ's motion to further weaken the prior antitrust consent decree, which was already too weak to be very effective. The motion only made it worse.

Velvel made a short list of things he hoped to accomplish in his life. Fighting the ABA in court or before a federal agency wasn't among them.

*****

It was an unseasonably cold, rainy evening on June 2, 2000, when 124 MSL students gathered at the Collins Center in Andover. Three to four years of arduous work were behind them, and they were ready to receive their degrees. Spouses, parents, children, and, in some cases, grandchildren applauded their achievement.

Associate Dean Coyne announced the students' names one by one, and they walked across the stage. The opportunities that were before them were a dramatic departure from how their lives began. They could visualize becoming practicing lawyers who examined witnesses, addressed juries, settled neighbors' disputes, wrote wills, and recovered lost wages for working people. With a lot of ambition and hard work, they could become state representatives or federal congressmen or university deans or leaders in large corporations. Anything seemed possible to them at that moment.

Addressing the students that evening was Nadine Strossen, the first woman president of the American Civil Liberties Union. "I'm especially happy to speak at this pioneering, crusading law school" she said, "because your very existence and persistence embodies the highest ideals of law, in particular opening up educational and professional opportunities to individuals who have traditionally suffered discrimination and have been excluded, and, correspondingly, facilitating access to legal services on the part of broader segments of the public. Both ideals will breathe real life into the grand words that are carved over the grand entrance of the Supreme Court, but which now state an aspiration, not a reality, namely 'Equal justice under law.'"

Strossen said that the public's perception of there being too many lawyers was "demonstrably false." She said that there weren't too many lawyers representing the poor or the middle class. There weren't too many lawyers representing the powerless or the unpopular, and there weren't too many lawyers fighting for human rights or social justice.

The problem was an old one, she said, referring to remarks made by Louis Brandeis at Harvard University in 1905. The prominent Boston lawyer and public advocate, who became a U.S. Supreme Court Justice in 1916, told law graduates that day, "We hear too much about the corporation lawyer, but nothing about the people's lawyer."

Strossen said that even though nearly a century had passed

since Brandeis had made his speech, 90 percent of all lawyers still served less than 10 percent of the population. Strossen told the graduates that her favorite work was one that brought no financial gain. It was being the people's lawyer, heading up the ACLU. "Your unique law school is dedicated to these entrenched patterns of shaking up the legal status quo," she told them. "For that, every one of you deserves a special congratulations and thanks."

*****

By spring of 2002, the tide that had held back the Massachusetts School of Law appeared to have turned. That spring, the NEAS&C returned to MSL for a regular follow-up five-year visit. Five experts in higher education were at the school for three days: Arthur Bayer, professor of economics at Babson College, Wellesley, Massachusetts; Ann Caldwell, president of Massachusetts General Hospital Health Professions, Boston; Chris Kanios, professor of law, New College of California School of Law, San Francisco; Thomas P. Massey, Dean of the College of Professional and Continuing Education, Clark University, Worcester, Massachusetts; and William J. Young, professor emeritus of Anatomy & Neurobiology, The University of Vermont, South Hero, Vermont.

In the report that followed, the inspectors wrote:

> MSL subscribes to, exemplifies, and advocates high ethical standards. This is clearly stated in its mission statement. Senior administration, faculty, students, and alumni regularly made unsolicited reference to their concern for ethics in law and in legal education, and in their belief that MSL was doing a good job in this area. In our meeting with MSL alumni, one graduate made the unsolicited statement that "MSL focuses on what's right rather than on what's legal," and that she and her fellow graduates have tried to put that

principle into practice in their own legal careers.

In addition, the NEAS&C team took a positive view of MSL's faculty, describing the law school's 14 full-time professors and 66 adjuncts as "well qualified to meet the mission of the school." The inspectors also wrote that by using practicing lawyers to give students more practical, real life experience, "the institution benefits greatly." The inspectors described the adjuncts as "a talented and dedicated corps of adjunct faculty. Most are practicing attorneys offering courses within their field of expertise." They liked MSL's writing classes, taught by non-lawyer writing specialists. The inspectors thought this "an innovative practice that responds creatively to the needs of law students and to the justified criticism of a legal profession mired in arcane legalese."

As well, the inspectors considered MSL's peer review program innovative. "This program requires all faculty, including adjuncts, to visit the classrooms of at least three other faculty each semester and to discuss their findings with the teaching colleague. The deans also regularly visit classrooms to provide support for the teaching efforts of the faculty," wrote the inspectors in their report. "Further, all faculty have their classes videotaped for viewing and critique by members of the full-time faculty during weekly lunch meetings."

Rather than creating friction, this peer review program promoted a "collegial and collaborative demeanor" among the faculty and deans. The inspectors praised the school for friendly and helpful professors, impressively dedicated to the school's mission. They wrote,

> MSL faculty can be found on campus in a variety of activities, from teaching and advising students to collaborative meetings regarding academic issues. Faculty members are consistent participants in the operation of several committees and have a genuine voice in the direction of the school. Their work ethic, both in terms of on-campus presence and actual

workload, is unique within the world of legal education.

Also in contrast to the ABA's views, the NEAS&C team agreed with MSL that the LSAT excluded many lower-income earners and second-career seekers from pursuing a legal education. "The LSAT represents the very single-minded emphasis on standardized test taking skills that dominates traditional law school admissions decisions to the exclusion of more relevant factors and alternative methods of evaluating academic capability, especially for a profession which requires, in addition to strong academic abilities, the very human qualities of maturity, compassion, wisdom, perseverance, and responsibility," wrote the inspectors. "This excessive emphasis on standardized test taking skills is largely responsible for the exclusion of large numbers of qualified applicants, many of who[m] do not have the highly developed test taking skills necessary to achieve a high score on the exam."

At the end of the NEAS&C team's report, the inspectors recommended that the NEAS&C renew MSL's accreditation for 10 years.

In a separate letter to MSL, Kanios, the law professor on the team, wrote of a kinship he felt with the small, independent school. "I think schools like ours can play some role, however small or big, in challenging the way in which legal education helps replicate the worst aspects of law practice, with its focus exclusively on winning instead of fairness and justice and the way in which lawyers participate in the polarization of society," wrote Kanios. "In short, it's great to have kindred spirits out there."

As with Kanios, MSL began to see more kindred spirits surfacing and more like-minds seeking out the school.

*****

Fourteen years after MSL had opened its doors, it had graduated 1,500 students. Though most of the alumni practiced law in Massachusetts and New Hampshire, some practiced elsewhere, such as in Florida, Texas, California, Maine, Wisconsin, Maryland, and Connecticut.

Students found many ways to use their legal education. Judy Forgays practiced real estate law in Andover, and, in 1991, she married MSL graduate James Cropper. He became general counsel for the Northern Essex Mental Health Center, a regional center serving 50,000 clients. Out of a continued fondness for MSL, he also worked part-time there as an assistant admissions officer.

Some of the students returned to MSL as professors or spoke to classes about their law practices. Others became corporate lawyers and business consultants. Arthur Broadhurst, Barry Finegold, Eugene O'Flaherty, and Brian Knuuttila became Massachusetts state representatives, and Steven Baddour became a state senator.

John Cascarano, who had held four jobs, including clam digging, to pay his tuition at MSL, had graduated in 1990, in MSL's first class, and then opened his own practice in Quincy. His friend Michael Mattson, who had grown up in the tough projects of Quincy and who had teased him for being a bookworm, watched Cascarano grow and mature. He saw the difference legal education made in his best friend's life. Not only that, Cascarano's work fascinated him.

In fact, it intrigued him so much that at age 29, Mattson realized that he wanted something more from life than just being a security guard. He realized, though, that anything that required a college education would be tough on him. He'd never done well in school. He had always struggled with writing and didn't know even some of the grammar basics, such as the difference between "its" and "it's." Raised in a dysfunctional home with an alcoholic father, Mattson was surrounded by chaos and couldn't focus on his homework. His mother did what she could, but home was a difficult place for him to learn.

Mattson had tried getting into the Quincy police and fire departments. He took the tests and did extremely well. However, the departments needed minorities to satisfy affirmative action quotas and placed him 31st on a waiting list of 500. He knew that it would be years before his name came up. Then it occurred to him that if he studied law and passed the bar, nothing could stop him. There were no quotas on lawyers. Still it would be seven years or more of college and law school. At first, this seemed like an eternity.

But in 1994, at age 29, Mattson took the plunge. He entered the University of Massachusetts in Boston. He was nervous his first day, but so was his daughter, who, on that same day, entered junior high school. Mattson knew that he had a lot to be nervous about. It had been nearly 15 years since he had taken a history class. From day one, he didn't know what the professor wanted. He failed his first two history exams. His writing was so terrible that he questioned whether he could ever succeed in a profession that relied on a good command of the English language.

A college counselor helped Mattson organize his time. This brought more structure to his studies, but it didn't help him with his writing. On his own, Mattson studied his errors. He analyzed each red pen mark and tried to figure out what he had done wrong. He was determined not to repeat his mistakes. Steadily, he improved. In fact, he did so well in English that he almost declared it as his major. Instead, he chose political science, which he decided provided a good background for law studies. By the end of his fourth college year, Mattson had a 3.4 GPA.

After college, Mattson took a Kaplan course, but he didn't do especially well on the LSATs. He received a 38 on a 50-point scale. He applied to Suffolk University, New England School of Law, and MSL. Each application cost $50 to $75. He didn't have any more money to spend.

In 1998, Mattson entered MSL. The school had served Cascarano well, so Mattson decided it would serve him well, too. Right away, he loved it. He learned things that he could apply to everyday life, be it tenant-landlord leases or wills and trusts. He taped the classes, which he listened to on the hour-long drive to school and back. Like Cascarano, he woke up early, went to the beach and dug clams at 6 a.m. He wore headphones, which enabled him to review his law school lectures. He worked as a security guard 32 hours a week, which wouldn't have been permitted at an ABA school. For Mattson, there was no other way to go to law school. He had to support his family and pay his tuition.

Mattson realized in approaching graduation on May 31, 2002, that the kid from the projects, who had little if any hope of having a decent life, had defied the odds. He followed in the footsteps of his friend John Cascarano and graduated from MSL with a juris doctorate degree. He would go back to Quincy, take the bar exam, and then practice law.

Such would be the ebb and flow of students at MSL. Alumni would recruit friends, family, and even their own children. Alumni would go back to their communities and serve as lawyers, politicians, and as an example to others. MSL's mission was fulfilled. The school brought legal education and services to the working class and to poorer neighborhoods that needed them. The school had opened up opportunities, where the ABA had closed them off. It had shown what common people could do. Its faculty and students alike—people from working-class, immigrant, and minority backgrounds, people who sometimes had been so dirt poor that they could only afford one college class at a time, like Diane Sullivan, or had to dig clams to pay their tuition, like John Cascarano and Mike Mattson—had shown what common people could do in academia, in law, in television, and in state politics when given a chance. They had shown what common people can do even though they are opposed by the powerful and wealthy. The success of these students would serve as the school's legacy.

*****

Because Velvel enjoyed military history, there would be times when he would read about the 19th century, when the Royal Navy was maintained at the strength of the world's next two most powerful navies combined. Velvel had read about a lieutenant on a British dreadnought who had posted a sign, *"Ut Veniant Omnes."* It meant, "Let them all come." That was the attitude of the Royal Navy. It could take on the world.

Velvel taped this sign to his office wall. It struck him as fitting. *Ut Veniant Omnes* could have been the motto of MSL. The very fact that the school challenged the views and arrangements of the powerful, and sought to give the excluded a chance, ensured that it would be attacked and would have to fight at every turn.

The dean was fond of pointing out that a Nobel prize-winning Belgian playwright and poet, Maurice Maeterlinck, once said that every crossroads on the path to the future is defended by a thousand men appointed to guard the past. MSL had found this true. Yet MSL had prevailed. It had survived the war, though it lost many individual battles. It had endured.

Suggested Readings

The following books provided important insights into the workings of the Supreme Court, the protests against the Vietnam War, the events in Lawrence, Kansas, during the 1960s, and the history of the ABA:

Boyd, Susan. *The ABA's First Section: Assuring a Qualified Bar*. Chicago: American Bar Association, 1991.

D'Amato, Anthony A., and O'Neil, Robert M. *The Judiciary and Vietnam*. New York: St. Martin's Press, 1972.

Friedman, Lawrence M. *A History of American Law*. New York: Simon & Schuster, 1973.

Moyers, Bill. *Listening to America*. New York: Harper & Row, 1971.

Velvel, Lawrence R. *Undeclared War and Civil Disobedience*. New York: Dunellen Publishing, 1970.

Wells, John M., and Wilhelm, Maria. *The People vs. Presidential War*. New York: Dunellen Company, Inc., 1970.

Woodward, Bob, and Armstrong, Scott. *The Brethren.* New York: Simon and Schuster, 1979.

William O. Douglas. *The Court Years, 1939-1975: The Autobiography of William O. Douglas.* New York: Random House, 1980.